Operation Dragoon

'Each of us must one day reach the end
of worldly life; let him who can win
glory before he dies; that lives on
after him, when he lifeless lies.'

Beowulf

Operation Dragoon

The Liberation of Southern France, 1944

Anthony Tucker-Jones

Pen & Sword
MILITARY

First published in Great Britain in 2009
and reprinted in this format in 2024 by
Pen & Sword Military
an imprint of
Pen & Sword Books Ltd
47 Church Street
Barnsley
South Yorkshire
S70 2AS

ISBN 9 781 03615 017 4

Typeset in Ehrhardt by Phoenix Typesetting, Auldgirth, Dumfriesshire
Printed and bound by CPI Group (UK) Ltd, Croydon, CR0 4YY

Pen & Sword Books Ltd incorporates the imprints of Pen & Sword Aviation,
Pen & Sword Maritime, Pen & Sword Military, Wharncliffe Local History,
Pen & Sword Select, Pen & Sword Military Classics, Leo Cooper, Remember
When, Seaforth Publishing and Frontline Publishing.

For a complete list of Pen & Sword titles please contact
PEN & SWORD BOOKS LIMITED
47 Church Street, Barnsley, South Yorkshire, S70 2AS, England
E-mail: enquiries@pen-and-sword.co.uk
Website: www.pen-and-sword.co.uk

Contents

Contents

Introduction

To some people, Operation Dragoon – the Allied landings in the south of France – was just a sideshow that needlessly supported the crucial D-Day landings in Normandy, which opened the long-awaited Second Front. In addition, the resulting diversion of men and equipment hampered the struggling war effort in Italy and Burma, thereby distorting the Allies' wider strategic effort. Furthermore, the liberation of Paris and the political controversy surrounding the French and American armies' expulsion of the Nazi garrison from the city, overshadowed a much bigger row over the liberation of the major Mediterranean ports of Marseilles and Toulon.

In reality this other D-Day was of considerable significance, which went far beyond its military contribution to the liberation of France, for the political ramifications were to be far-reaching and helped put at centre stage the leader of the Free French, General Charles de Gaulle. The debate about the need for Dragoon pitted not only the British Prime Minister Winston Churchill against the American Allied Supreme Commander General Dwight Eisenhower, but also de Gaulle against the pair of them. Field Marshal Bernard Montgomery branded Dragoon one of the great strategic mistakes of the war.

Indeed, it was over Operation Dragoon that ugly national self-interest finally bubbled to the surface and it was only Eisenhower's supreme diplomacy that prevented the Allies falling out amongst themselves. Publicly America was the arsenal of the free world, but behind the scenes President Franklin Roosevelt was adamant that he would do nothing to restore British or French imperial status once Nazi Germany was defeated. In particular he could not help but feel that France considered her colonial possessions more sacrosanct than the need to resist Nazi Germany. He also made a pact with Soviet leader Marshal Stalin not to meddle in the Balkans. And he promised Stalin an operation to support Overlord: and that is what Stalin got.

Dragoon was in fact the culmination of the Allies' little publicised and frankly embarrassing war against Vichy France, the repugnant pro-Nazi regime that administered the unoccupied zone in the south of metropolitan France as well as France's numerous colonial possessions. Charles de Gaulle and his Free French had such little legitimacy and political appeal that most French troops rescued from Dunkirk and elsewhere chose to be repatriated rather than join him. The upshot was that first Britain and then America had to fight a lengthy war against Vichy France's overseas interests to secure Allied positions in the Indian Ocean, the Middle East and the Mediterranean. Churchill's attack on the French fleet after the fall of France further stymied de Gaulle's appeal and his initial efforts to secure French West Africa for his cause ended in farce off Dakar.

To make matters worse, behind the scenes Churchill and Roosevelt did not hold de Gaulle in very high regard, and in light of his limited political appeal they believed that the Vichy generals were the true power brokers. One such was Admiral Jean François Darlan, who held sway in French North-West Africa, where most of the Vichy forces were deployed. In fact, Roosevelt and Eisenhower did not altogether trust de Gaulle's political intentions and had little desire to assist pro-Gaullist forces to install him in power once the Second Front was opened. Indeed, after the Allies' invasion of French North-West Africa and Darlan's subsequent assassination, de Gaulle had himself declared head of the provisional French government and began to look at the French mainland with an acquisitive eye. His first action was to call on America to rearm the shambles that was the French Army. It is notable that most French forces subsequently remained tied up in Italy; only a single division was involved in the Normandy campaign, and additional French colonial divisions were not released from Italy until Dragoon was given the go-ahead at the last minute.

Other players had a vested interest in the Second Front being opened at two points. While Roosevelt and Eisenhower were committed to honour their Tehran pledge to Stalin for an invasion in the south of France, Churchill saw it as a needless diversion of precious resources from the main event in Italy. It had been a hard slog up the Italian peninsula following the landings there in September 1943 and Churchill was determined not to relinquish his long-cherished ambition of forcing a route through Italy and Austria into the heart of Hitler's Reich. Such a move would have also helped to curb Stalin's ambitions in central and eastern Europe. Churchill's vehement opposition to Dragoon was such that he lobbied against it for a month and then threatened to resign, which could have brought down the British government. A terrible row ensued between him and Eisenhower, much to the latter's dismay.

Eisenhower's problem was that resources were so limited that Dragoon could not be conducted at the same time as Overlord, and therein ultimately lay the flaw in its strategic utility. During June and July 1944 Eisenhower, busily directing the campaign in Normandy, was caught in the middle of all these competing interests and thus dithered over his commitment to Dragoon. On 15 August 1944 Hitler, facing defeat in Normandy, signalled a general retreat from France and yet Eisenhower pressed ahead with Dragoon that very day.

Despite de Gaulle's and his generals' demands for French pre-eminence, experience dictated that American forces should conduct the initial assault in the south of France with the French Army following up in the second wave. In the event, the invasion was conducted in an exemplary fashion in the face of minimal resistance; the liberation of the major cities of Marseilles and Toulon was achieved way ahead of schedule; and Hitler's Army Group G was put to rapid flight. The situation seemed highly promising. However, subsequently there were bitter battles with the tough German rearguard as it sought to hold France's southern cities and cover the withdrawal. There was to be no repeat of the dramatic encirclement of the Falaise Pocket in Normandy.

Pushing past the mountains that border south-eastern France, the invasion force found itself held up at the strategically crucial Belfort Gap, the gateway to Germany, until the end of the year. By then the conflict had taken on a different complexion with Eisenhower's broad-front strategy and the general Allied push to and across the Rhine, Germany's last major defensive barrier. In the meantime de Gaulle was left in control of Paris and much of France, and the Allies never did break free from Italy before the war ended, leaving Stalin a free hand in eastern Europe and the Balkans.

Churchill had been right all along, although Eisenhower, great statesman that he was, ultimately had the good grace to admit that he had been wrong. This, though, never made up for the fact that Dragoon should never have taken place.

Anthony Tucker-Jones

List of Plates

A wrecked German panzer in southern France.

French troops with a captured Pak 40 anti-tank gun in liberated Toulon.

German troops withdrawing over the Rhône.

Allied armour and Free French forces pushing towards Paris.

De Gaulle and General Leclerc were adamant that French troops should take the credit for liberating Paris.

Just over a week after Dragoon, elements of Leclerc's French 2nd Armoured Division slipped into Paris on the evening of 24 August.

A French tank destroyer engages German troops on the streets of Paris.

A French woman being escorted to an uncertain fate. Throughout France retribution against those who had collaborated with the occupiers was swift and often brutal.

The retreating Army Group G, reliant on horse-drawn transport, was constantly vulnerable to Allied air attack.

A devastated column of German horse-drawn wagons and lorries outside Montélimar.

French Minister of War André Diethhelm, General de Lattre de Tassigny and Emmanuel d'Astier de la Vigerie, Minister of the Interior, reviewing French troops in Marseilles.

The Allies received a warm welcome in Paris.

General Patton, commander of the US 3rd Army.

German troops captured by the French 1st Army in Alsace.

Eisenhower in jovial mood.

The French Army was able to take the credit for liberating the key cities of Paris, Marseilles and Toulon.

Events in the Falaise area during the second half of August and the subsequent liberation of Paris made Dragoon a pointless exercise.

Chapter One

Pleasing Stalin –
the Balkans or Southern France

In August 1944, just over two months after the momentous D-Day landings in Normandy, a little-known 'other D-Day' took place in the south of France. The acrimonious argument over the validity of this operation was so extreme that it threatened to bring down the British government. General Dwight D. Eisenhower, the American Allied Supreme Commander, described the row with Britain's wartime leader as 'one of the longest sustained arguments that I had with Prime Minister [Winston] Churchill throughout the period of the war'.

Eisenhower was an experienced commander. Following Japan's attack on Pearl Harbor, he had joined the General Staff in Washington where he served until June 1942 with responsibility for war plans. After serving as deputy chief in charge of Pacific Defense, he was appointed chief of the War Plans Division. He then served as Assistant Chief of Staff in charge of the Operations Division under US Chief of Staff General George C. Marshall. In November 1942 he was also appointed Supreme Commander Allied Forces in the North African theatre of operations. In February 1943 his authority was extended across the Mediterranean to include General Montgomery's British 8th Army. After the capitulation of Axis forces in North Africa, Eisenhower remained in command of the renamed Mediterranean Theater of Operations. In December 1943 it was announced that he would be the Allied Supreme Commander in Europe.

Allied successes against the Axis forces had gathered considerable momentum following Operations Torch (the Anglo-American landings against French North-West Africa in November 1942), Husky (the capture of the Italian island of Sicily in July 1943) and Avalanche, the subsequent invasion of southern Italy (in September 1943). The proposed invasion of southern France, supported by Eisenhower and

1

President Franklin D. Roosevelt, was initially dubbed Operation Anvil and was designed to complement Operation Sledgehammer (which later became Overlord), the attack on northern France. The idea was to divide German defences in France and prevent their forces moving north to oppose the primary cross-Channel invasion that would herald the opening of the Second (or Western) Front.

While Roosevelt supported the US War Department's view that the quickest way to defeat Adolf Hitler was to invade France via the English Channel, he was under constant pressure from Congress and the public to divert greater resources to the Pacific War. At the Casablanca Conference in January 1943 General Alan Brooke, Chief of the British Imperial General Staff, touched a raw nerve when he accused Admiral Ernest J. King, Commander in Chief of the US Fleet and Chief of US Naval Operations, of favouring the war against the Japanese. The pair almost came to blows and Eisenhower reflected:

> It developed that General Brooke, Chief of Staff of the British Army, had never really liked the Overlord idea. At times during the two-day conference, he seemed to be reflecting the Prime Minister's thoughts. He came to see me privately and argued that all Allied ground troops should stay in the Mediterranean, chipping away at the periphery of the Axis Empire.

The dispute over the Pacific came about because Admiral King and General Marshall had prevailed upon the Combined Chiefs at the Conference to agree to a series of operations against the Gilbert Islands and the Japanese-mandated Marshall and Caroline Islands. Initially it was planned that operations would commence against the Marshalls, but the threat posed by the major Japanese naval and air bases at Truk persuaded the Americans to opt for the Gilberts first.

Following the Casablanca Conference it was agreed that 80,000 American troops would be shipped to Britain by the spring of 1943, in order to implement an invasion of France dubbed Operation Roundup. However, only 15,000 men had arrived by the appointed time, and while the Americans were accusing Churchill of dragging his feet over his commitment to scheduling the Second Front, they were not in a position to push the pace. Eisenhower had drawn up the plans for Roundup before assuming the mantle of Supreme Commander, and along with Sledgehammer it was never really more than wishful thinking in 1942–43.

In the event, a critical lack of landing craft meant that these plans were shelved in favour of Operation Torch in late 1942. Despite the lessons of the Dieppe Raid, this operation had to rely on securing the ports to land heavy equipment rather than bringing it ashore across the beaches.

Constructing such craft in large numbers was a major undertaking, and in 1942 landing ships and landing craft were only available as proto-types. Purpose-built landing craft did not begin to appear in the Mediterranean until mid-1943. However, once in full swing the American shipyards alone were eventually to produce over 66,000 landing vessels of all types.

What next?

Following the Torch landings, defeat of the Axis forces trapped in Tunisia was never really in doubt, although it took six months to secure North Africa. By the time of the Axis surrender there in May 1943 Churchill was preoccupied in Washington at the Trident Conference. At Casablanca no agreement had been reached over operations following the invasion of Sicily. Now Churchill wanted to invade Italy, and while Eisenhower anticipated Sicily being in Allied hands by mid-August, he was uncertain what do with the massive Allied forces in the region.

It was agreed that seven divisions (four American and three British) were to be withdrawn from the Mediterranean to the UK by early November 1943. This would leave twelve divisions in the region, plus four French divisions then being equipped and two Polish divisions in Iran, which, having escaped the clutches of Stalin, were desperate to strike a blow. It seemed ridiculous to suggest that the powerful Allied forces in North Africa and indeed in the UK should kick their heels until Roundup, which was unlikely to be mounted in the spring of 1944.

While no one questioned Eisenhower's position, in Washington General Marshall knew that he was not in a position to end operations in the Mediterranean once Sicily had been invaded. Churchill had three times the number of men, four times as many warships and was equal in the air to the Americans, so there could be no denying British dominance in the Mediterranean. Marshall tacitly gave agreement that planning should be conducted for a follow-up attack across the Straits of Messina on to the toe of mainland Italy and for an invasion of Sardinia. Churchill and Brooke were understandably pleased.

Brooke and Lieutenant-General Sir Frederick Morgan, the senior planner for the invasion of France (now dubbed Overlord), estimated that it would require an initial landing of five divisions, with a follow-up force of ten. This meant that the provision of landing craft would have to double over the next eight to ten months or Overlord would be logistically impossible. But when such requests reached Admiral Ernest King, who was preoccupied with the war against Japan, they were given little priority. King would eventually bend to General Marshall's requests, but at the time he could see no point in tying up assets in the Atlantic while the British dithered over a cross-Channel invasion. At the Trident Conference the Americans got confirmation of the proposed assault on the Japanese-held Gilbert and Marshall Islands.

When Churchill and Roosevelt attended the Quebec Conference in August 1943, Italy and France were foremost in everyone's minds. This was more than a simple conference of war leaders, though. Known as Quadrant, it was in fact a series of technical staff conferences designed to thrash out future strategy. Churchill stated:

> I emphasised that I strongly favoured Overlord in 1944, though I had not been in favour of Sledgehammer in 1942 or Roundup in 1943. The objections to the cross-Channel operation were, however, now removed. . . .
>
> As to Italy, the Chiefs of Staff proposed that there should be three phases in our future operations. First, we should drive Italy out of the war and establish airfields near Rome, and if possible farther north. I pointed out that I wanted it definitely understood that I was not committed to an advance beyond the Ancona–Pisa line [encompassing the German Trasimene and Gothic Line defences]. Second, we should seize Sardinia and Corsica, and then press hard against the Germans in the north of the peninsula to stop them joining the fight against Overlord. There was also Anvil, a projected landing in southern France in the neighbourhood of Toulon and Marseilles and an advance northwards up the Rhône valley. This was to lead to much controversy later on.

Churchill always saw Overlord as a diversion from the main agenda in the Mediterranean, where he believed the Allies should concentrate their efforts on recapturing the Dodecanese, taking Rome and bringing Turkey into the war, thereby securing the right-hand flank. He wanted Overlord delayed, although this did not tie in with Stalin's demands (he had been promised a Second Front since 1942), and Allied resources diverted from the Pacific.

This was the line Churchill took with Roosevelt at their Cairo Conference just before meeting Stalin in Tehran. The Cairo Conference (codenamed Sextant) between the British and American leaders and their senior staffs took place on 22–26 November 1943. The delegations then flew to Tehran to meet with Stalin from 28 November to 1 December, returning to Cairo to complete Sextant from 3 to 7 December.

On his arrival in Cairo Churchill thought he was going to spend the next three days lobbying for landing craft to conduct another amphibious assault in Italy, where things were not going well for the Allies. Despite the Italian surrender on 3 September 1943, Field Marshal Albert Kesselring had pulled off an audacious and daring coup and seized power. Following the Allied landings at Salerno on the 9th Kesselring had stabilised the situation. The Allied planners realised belatedly that they had lost a golden opportunity by not forcing a landing just south of Rome.

Hitler rapidly took over not only most of Italy, but also the Italian-occupied zones in Albania, the Balkans, Greece and Yugoslavia, thereby securing his potentially exposed flank. In view of Rommel's defeat at El Alamein, the subsequent Torch landings and the Germans' expulsion from North Africa and Sicily, Hitler must have been quietly pleased with himself for retrieving such a disastrous situation.

Churchill's generals saw Anvil as an unwelcome and unwanted distraction. General Harold Alexander in Italy wanted to press on northwards overland, while General Maitland Wilson, the Allied Supreme Commander in the Mediterranean, wanted to launch a sea-borne attack at the head of the Adriatic followed by a push eastwards to Zagreb, then a thrust towards Austria and the Danube. Roosevelt and the American Chiefs of Staff had to endure Churchill's and the British chiefs' determined lobbying for a commitment to this Adriatic operation.

Nevertheless the Americans were not receptive to anything that would disrupt the war in the Pacific or the opening of the Second Front. It seemed to them that Churchill always had just one more operation in mind. Also, in order not to give the impression that the British and Americans were ganging up on the Soviet Union, while in Cairo Roosevelt deliberately kept Churchill at arm's length. Conveniently, the American President's time was taken up by talks with the Chinese nationalist leader Generalissimo Chiang Kai-shek, who was also fighting the Japanese. Churchill began to fret that the campaign in Italy would be prejudiced in favour of liberating France, by the inevitable diversion of resources.

Even as late as 1943 the Americans were demonstrating a rather simplistic approach to defeating Nazi Germany, which would be epitomised by Eisenhower's broad-front strategy in the latter half of 1944. 'Our Chiefs of Staff are convinced of one thing,' Roosevelt told his son Elliot in the margins of the Tehran Conference. 'The way to kill the most Germans, with the least loss of American soldiers, is to mount one big offensive and then slam 'em with everything we've got. It makes sense to me.'

The British Prime Minister also feared for the future of Europe if Stalin became a dominant power, while in contrast Roosevelt believed in his 'Good Neighbour' policy. The Americans saw it as inevitable that once the Axis powers were defeated the Soviet Union would come to dominate Europe, and thus felt that every effort should be made to retain her friendship. Roosevelt somewhat naively believed that if he was honest and open with Stalin, then the Soviet leader would reciprocate. In addition, the US Chiefs of Staff saw no military utility in commitments in south-eastern Europe, especially the Balkans.

Stalin's Second Front
Stalin had been invited to Casablanca, but refused to attend. Roosevelt, who was keen for the Allied leaders to meet before the opening of the Second Front, put forward Cairo, Basra and Beirut as possible venues, but Stalin rejected them all. It was he who finally suggested Tehran, having been advised that the Soviet Embassy there was probably one of the most secure outside the Soviet Union. Iran had been forced into becoming an ally after British and Soviet troops invaded in 1941 to secure the country's oilfields for their war effort.

It was this meeting that established the status of the 'Big Three', though in reality Churchill was soon made to feel out of place. After his cold-shoulder treatment in Cairo, Roosevelt now further alienated Churchill by staying at the Soviet legation in his effort to cultivate Stalin's friendship.

By this stage of the war the Soviet leader was desperate for a Second Front to be opened in the west to alleviate pressure on the Red Army. The latter had taken a massive beating from Hitler's armed forces and although it had achieved some notable successes, these had been at enormous cost in manpower and resources. Secretly Stalin may have suspected that the Western Allies had lost their nerve following the disastrous Dieppe Raid the year before. Why else were the Allies pre-occupying themselves in French North Africa, Sicily and Italy? All these operations had done little or nothing to help the Red Army. To Stalin's way of thinking, only an attack on Nazi-occupied France would properly distract Hitler.

Stalin wasn't wrong. The Allies, particularly Churchill, were indeed haunted by his disastrous Dieppe Raid codenamed Operation Jubilee. Conceived as a way of testing German defences prior to reopening the Second Front, it took place on 19 August 1942. It may have provided vital lessons in amphibious warfare and combined operations, but they were gained at an appallingly high cost. In total the Canadian Army lost 906 killed, the Royal Marine Commandos lost 270 killed, wounded or captured, and the Royal Navy lost 550, as well as a destroyer and numerous landing craft. The RAF fared no better, losing 106 aircraft and 153 aircrew. In their mopping-up operations the Germans took 2,195 prisoners, in return for 591 casualties and 48 aircraft shot down. The outcome of Operation Jubilee firmly convinced the Germans that they could contain and defeat an Allied amphibious assault on French soil.

Nor had previous British amphibious attacks on Nazi-occupied Europe been a great success. Norway was a prime example, and of course the figure of Winston Churchill loomed large in that fiasco. This ill-fated operation in mid-April 1940 had been designed to prevent Hitler importing iron ore from Sweden via Narvik in Norway. The failure to secure proper integration of the three services at the executive level was primarily to blame. Certainly the British had no combined operations headquarters, resulting in the Army and the Royal Navy issuing independent and often contradictory orders during the battle.

As First Lord of the Military Co-ordination Committee Churchill had directed the Norwegian campaign in a singularly narrow manner, dominated by his personal preference for the Royal Navy. His attitude had belittled and undermined the whole process of combined operations. In the opening stages of the Norwegian campaign the Navy, more concerned with catching German battlecruisers, had immobilised the expeditionary force for five days after putting back to sea with all their equipment still on board. To make matters worse, the transport ships had been loaded economically not tactically, and there were no landing craft, no infantry support weapons and no snow gear. The Allies lacked coherent air support and as a result were severely harried by constant German air attack. The British force of 20,000 men suffered 2,060 casualties; the French committed 11,700 men and suffered 530 casualties; and the Norwegians lost 4,000 men. While the Germans lost 5,300 men, they had maintained control of Norway and the vital shipping lanes.

The French blamed the British for the disaster, and they were right to do so. Churchill and his staff had learned the fundamental lessons of integrated combined operations the hard way and at the expense of neutral Norway. Two years later Churchill launched his first major raids on occupied France, one at Bruneval to capture a radar station and another at St Nazaire to destroy the dry dock. While both were deemed a success, the latter saw 185 British troops killed and 200 captured from a raiding force of just 611 men. None of these operations boded well for Overlord, or indeed Anvil.

The subsequent successful landings in North Africa were against ill-equipped French forces that were in a state of political disarray, while those on Sicily and the Italian mainland were against an Italian Army that was largely a spent force. Striking Hitler's *Festung Europa* was an entirely different matter, even if the German forces concerned were in some cases second rate, reconstituting or recuperating.

It was clear that any future invasion of France would have to be conducted across open beaches and not against well-defended ports. In 1943 the Dieppe débâcle loomed large in everyone's minds and despite the Allies' considerable planning and preparation there was a very real fear that D-Day might go the same way.

In Tehran, Stalin was displeased to discover that a commander had not yet been nominated to direct the opening of the Second Front; he understandably interpreted this as a sign of lack of commitment on the part of the Western Allies. Churchill further aggravated him by advocating the seizure of Rome and the island of Rhodes. There followed a chilling moment when Stalin calmly discussed the execution of German officers at the end of the war; Churchill was horrified, and was equally dismayed that Roosevelt did not spring to his support.

Stalin would not yield to Churchill's proposals for an Italian assault, and the British Prime Minister found himself isolated. His plan to bring Turkey into the war was thwarted by that country's concerns about her traditional foe Bulgaria, a de facto German ally, which meant she was in no hurry to pick a fight with Hitler. This position suited Roosevelt, as it effectively prevented Churchill from renewing his call to continue operations in the eastern Mediterranean. It was self-evident that the special relationship between Britain and America was not quite so special after all, and Churchill knew that he could not always count on Roosevelt's support in the future.

'Stalin thought it would be a mistake to send part of our forces to Turkey and elsewhere, and part to southern France,' Churchill recorded at their first plenary meeting on the 28th. According to the Soviet leader:

> The best course would be to make Overlord the basic operation for 1944 and, once Rome had been captured, to send all available forces in Italy to southern France. These forces could join hands with the Overlord forces when the invasion was launched. France was the weakest spot on the German front. He did not himself expect Turkey to enter the war.

The following day Stalin called for a date for Overlord to be confirmed and insisted that it should be supported by a landing in southern France at the same time or a few months earlier. In his mind the capture of Rome and other Mediterranean operations should be viewed only as diversionary to the main event. While Roosevelt was supportive of Stalin's demands, Churchill wanted to know where the resources would be found for such an invasion, especially in terms of landing craft. To this end the Combined Chiefs in Cairo were tasked to look at this issue and make representations, and on 30 November they assessed:

(a) that we should continue to advance in Italy to the Pisa-Rimini line [German Gothic Line]. (This means that the sixty-eight LST which are due to be sent from the Mediterranean to the United Kingdom for Overlord must be kept in the Mediterranean until 15 January).

(b) that an operation shall be mounted against the south of France on as big a scale as landing craft permit. For planning purposes D-day to be the same as Overlord D-day.

(c) to recommend to the President and Prime Minister respectively that we should inform Marshal Stalin that we will launch Overlord during May, in conjunction with a supporting operation against the south of France on the largest scale that is permitted by the landing craft available at the time.

Churchill and Roosevelt were content with these recommendations and Stalin was duly informed. Foolishly the Western Allies were about to commit themselves to attacking Normandy and the French Riviera at the same time and on an impossible deadline. Churchill, Roosevelt and Stalin, as well as General Brooke, Admiral Cunningham, Air Chief Marshal Portal, General Marshall, Admiral King and General Arnold, all attended the plenary session of the Eureka Conference held in the Russian Legation on the 30th at which the proposed invasions were discussed in detail.

Churchill called for the closest cooperation among the Allies in co-ordinating their operations. He hoped that up to ten German divisions would be tied up in Italy and that the partisans in Yugoslavia would also continue to hold down German forces there. Stalin appreciated the threat to Overlord posed by German divisions transferring from the Eastern Front, so he undertook to tie down Hitler by launching a massive offensive in May. (In the event, Operation Bagration slipped to the end of June and overshadowed the success of Overlord with the sheer scale and speed of the Red Army's victory.)

Regarding Overlord itself, Churchill said 'he would like to add weight to the operation as it is now planned, especially in the initial assault'. This was a very sound recommendation, but it ultimately sowed the seeds of discord among the Western Allies over their commitment to the invasion of southern France. It was Stalin who now secured a firm undertaking from both Roosevelt and Churchill for Operation Anvil. The Three Powers declaration, issued in Tehran:

> took note that Operation Overlord would be launched during May 1944, in conjunction with an operation against southern France. The latter operation would be undertaken in as great a strength as availability of landing-craft permitted. The Conference further took note of Marshal Stalin's statement that the Soviet forces would launch an offensive at about the same time with the object of preventing the German forces from transferring from the Eastern to the Western Front.

Stalin had clearly signalled how much he valued an invasion of southern France and his opposition to any Anglo-American operations in south-eastern Europe, and he clearly anticipated that the matter was entirely closed. He may have secretly suspected that once the Second Front was opened Churchill would return to the Balkan question – why else would he ask that the attack on southern France should precede Overlord by two months. Tactically it made no sense, but Stalin had deliberately inflated its value. He knew that an invasion in both northern and southern France, coupled to their existing efforts in Italy, would ensure the Western Allies simply did not have enough resources to meddle in the Balkans.

The Soviet leader had his own grand designs for the summer of 1944 in the shape of Operation Bagration and the follow-up Lvov-Sandomierz offensive. The last thing he wanted was for matters to be complicated by the presence of Anglo-American forces in the Balkans. Ultimately he pressed for the attack on southern France because he wanted the Western Allies to be distracted from the Balkans, so that the Red Army would have a free hand to punish Hitler's eastern European Axis allies and secure Yugoslavia.

Churchill and those around him were not blind to Stalin's intentions. Brooke recalled during the meeting:

> [Stalin] approved of Roosevelt's proposal to close down operations in Italy and to transfer six divisions to invade southern France on 1 April, while the main Channel operation would take place on

1 May. I am certain he did not approve such operations for their strategic value, but because they fitted in with his future political plans. He was too good a strategist not to see the weakness in the American plan.

. . . his political and military requirements could now be best met by the greatest squandering of British and American lives in the French theatre.

While Stalin had naturally welcomed the additional operation for the Second Front in the West, it was General Marshall who subsequently ordered Eisenhower to include it in his strategic planning.

On the way back from Tehran Churchill and Roosevelt got together again in Cairo. 'In order to give Overlord the greatest chance of success,' said Churchill, 'it was thought necessary that the descent on the Riviera [Anvil] should be as strong as possible.' Roosevelt persuaded those present to agree that nothing should be done to 'hinder' Overlord or Anvil. It transpired, however, that Churchill was suffering from selective deafness on this occasion.

In Cairo, Brooke and King disagreed over Anvil. Brooke saw little point in launching such an operation with anything less than two divisions, while King argued that no firm decisions had been made at Tehran about the size of the assaulting force. Stalin advocated ten divisions. Nonetheless, it was finally agreed by the Combined Chiefs that the operation be looked at with a view to using a minimum of two divisions and that the resources for it were not to be at the expense of Overlord.

Burma loses out

Air Chief Marshal Portal made it clear that if the southern France operation were to go ahead, then other operations would inevitably suffer, notably those against the Japanese-held Andaman Islands in the Bay of Bengal. This was accepted and the Andaman assault was cancelled, although Roosevelt was reluctant to let down the Chinese Nationalists under Chiang Kai-Shek.

Stalin's promise that he would join the war against Japan once Nazi Germany was defeated was of little consolation to those British and American forces that had been fighting the Japanese in Burma and the Pacific since late 1941. Bearing in mind that Japan was also fighting China, the Soviet Union's entry into the war could have been the turning-point. In India Lieutenant-General Sir William Slim, commander of the British 14th Army, was not pleased with the outcome of the Tehran Conference:

> I had not long been back at my headquarters when events began which threatened to upset some, and then most, of the plans I had brought with me from Delhi. The seven offensive operations, scheduled for 1944, had been approved by the Combined Chiefs of Staff at the Cairo Conference at the end of November 1943. Only a week later, however, at Tehran, Marshal Stalin promised to enter the war against Japan if Anglo-American efforts were directed first to defeating Germany. Roosevelt and Churchill accepted the condition, and as part of this concentration against the main enemy, more than half the amphibious resources of South-East Asia were ordered back to Europe. As this rendered impossible the sea assault on the Andaman Islands, it was planned to use what remained for a landing behind the Japanese in Arakan. . .
>
> The practical result of all this was that the projected operations in South-East Asia in 1944 were reduced from seven to four.

Slim was far from pleased that he was forced to abandon the proposed landings in southern Burma and fall back on a costly and difficult four-pronged land invasion.

While Churchill went along with the plans for Anvil, his mind remained firmly on Italy and the Balkans. 'Reverting to the Riviera attack,' he remarked, 'I expressed the view that it should be planned on the basis of an assault force of at least two divisions. This would provide enough landing craft to do the outflanking operations in Italy, and also, if Turkey came into the war soon, to capture Rhodes.' However, the Rhodes operation was soon abandoned.

Churchill saw Anvil as a waste of effort, needlessly drawing vital troops and equipment from Italy. His staff argued that these resources would be better used maintaining the Allied effort in Italy, which would enable a decisive thrust up the Italian peninsula, through Austria and into southern Germany – and success here would render both Anvil and even Overlord unnecessary.

However, Eisenhower's generals argued that both geography and logistics were against such a plan; crossing the English Channel meant shorter lines of communication and a line of advance that was not obstructed by the troublesome Alps. Although there was also some concern that German troops in Italy might strike west at the invasion forces' eastern flank.

Roosevelt moved swiftly to head off Churchill and on 4 December 1943 Eisenhower was appointed to command Overlord. Stalin was informed of his appointment the following day, Churchill on the 6th. His Mediterranean aspirations were completely dashed. Overlord and an invasion of southern France were now to have priority, while operations in the Aegean were effectively stymied and Pisa was deemed the limit of advance in Italy. Churchill did not take all this lightly, as despite his best efforts Roosevelt and Stalin had got their way. However, as Brooke noted with some satisfaction:

> I had got the date of Overlord pushed back to 1 June so that it would not cripple the Italian campaign, and the south of France offensive turned into something more elastic which could be adjusted without affecting Italy too seriously.

While Churchill was forced to acquiesce to Overlord, he would remain stridently opposed to the concept of committing forces to southern France. He and the British Chiefs of Staff under Brooke wanted all military resources directed either to support Overlord in Normandy or to continue the fight in Italy.

Churchill had been opposed to Anvil from the start, and ultimately favoured Bordeaux not the Mediterranean. He was right that once the requirements of Anzio had delayed Anvil, the latter then made no military sense in that it would not support Overlord. Churchill believed a landing in Bordeaux would be the quickest way to take the pressure off the Allied forces in Normandy. Nonetheless, the Americans felt that his alternatives did not make sense either.

On 5 December the Combined Chiefs formalised their findings based on a two-division assault of southern France conducted to coincide approximately with Overlord. This would mean delivering 45,500 men and 7,740 vehicles. However, their assessment was that the resources available in the Mediterranean at the time of Overlord, comprising some 300 vessels, would only be able to shift some 39,000 troops (one

American division or three British brigades) and 4,520 vehicles. This left a shortfall of 6,500 men and 3,220 vehicles, which would require an extra 72 vessels to ship them, comprising 3 Combat Loaders, 12 Motor Transport Ships, 26 Landing Ship Tank (LST) and 31 Landing Craft Tank (LCT). The 26 Landing Ship Tank (LST) and 26 Landing Craft Tank (LCT) required could be made up from the spring orders originally earmarked for the Pacific. The remaining 5 LCTs could be found in the Mediterranean; although scheduled for Overlord, they were actually surplus to allocated requirements. America was supplying an additional 24 LCTs for Overlord over its original Quadrant Conference commitment, so these vessels for Anvil would not be missed. It was felt that the extra MT ships needed could be found from those already pooled in the Mediterranean under AFHQ. Similarly the special landing craft for assault support had to be drawn from those currently in the Mediterranean. This meant a greater responsibility fell on the naval forces to provide close support for the assault.

Once again the thorny issue of American requirements for the Pacific reared its ugly head. The Combined Staffs were at pains to point out that the LSTs and LCTs now earmarked for southern France represented a month's allocation for the Pacific. This diversion would impact on proposed operations in July (most notably against the Imperial Japanese Navy's main Central Pacific base at Truk) and the shortfall would have to be made up by diverting craft from the South Pacific, otherwise the operation might have to be cancelled.

If adequate shore-based fighter cover for Anvil could be provided the naval forces would need to be supplemented with up to 20 additional escorts and 2 anti-aircraft fighter direction ships. If adequate shore-based fighters could not be found, then the fleet would need up to 12 carriers with fighters, plus 6 anti-aircraft cruisers and 18 screening vessels.

Back in America after the Tehran Conference, Roosevelt shared his homespun public relations with the American people:

Within three days of intense and consistently amicable discussions, we agreed on every point concerned with the launching of a gigantic attack on Germany.

The Russian Army will continue its stern offensives on Germany's eastern front, the Allied armies in Italy and Africa will bring relentless pressure on Germany from the south, and now the encirclement will be complete as great American and British forces attack from other points of the compass. . . .

He then added, evidently believing that he had won over Stalin, even if it had been at the expense of his relationship with Churchill, that:

I may say that I 'got along fine' with Marshal Stalin. He is a man who combines a tremendous, relentless determination with a stalwart good humour. I believe he is truly representative of the heart and soul of Russia; and I believe that we are going to get along very well with him and the Russian people – very well indeed.

This was true, but only up to a point and only because Stalin was going to get exactly what he wanted: an invasion in the south of France, not in the Adriatic or Aegean.

Chapter Two

De Gaulle –
'he is a very dangerous threat to us'

After the Anglo-American invasion of French North-West Africa Roosevelt had pointedly stated: 'The future French government will be established not by any individual in metropolitan France or overseas but by the French people themselves after they have been set free by the victory of the United Nations.' Notably Overlord would involve just one French division and Dragoon only three.

As far as Roosevelt was concerned, Charles de Gaulle as leader of the Free French was not really a viable player; he had no resources or popular appeal. Free French operations against Dakar and Syria had shown that his involvement could even be counter-productive. The man was haughty and aloof, and while Churchill tried to accommodate him, Roosevelt did not. He was convinced that de Gaulle was a potential dictator who would seek to maintain the French Empire and would obstruct any American aspirations to free the North African Arab states from French colonial rule. Indeed, Roosevelt had already promised the Sultan of Morocco freedom once the war was over. De Gaulle by his own admission had only one strategy: intransigence. He had nothing to bargain with so he saw no point in bargaining. This translated into what his contemporaries saw as arrogance and rudeness.

While Churchill had officially recognised de Gaulle as leader of the Free French at the end of June 1940, this did not mean he was granted the status of head of the French government in exile. Marshal Henri-Philippe Pétain was the legal head of the French government in Vichy, and the British Foreign Office feared Churchill's backing of de Gaulle would push Pétain further into Hitler's arms. Instead of assembling the considerable resources of the French Navy and Empire to help oust Hitler, the Vichy government, already in a state of disarray, was more concerned about retaining control of its colonial possessions.

After the fall of Paris in 1940 aggressive resistance could easily have continued from France's colonial empire, but Vichy politics were such that it had no desire to side with the Allies and jeopardise its position with Hitler. Pétain and his supporters believed their role was purely to safeguard the Free Zone in southern France and protect the integrity of France's colonies in North and West Africa, the Middle East and Indo-China. This effectively meant that French interests in North Africa and the Near East posed a threat to Britain's vulnerable position in Egypt. Vichy's policy of 'wait and see' played straight into Hitler's hands, for unless he could neutralise the powerful French fleet he had no real way of threatening the French Empire. Similarly the French colonies tended to be a law unto themselves, while the colonial forces and locally raised troops operated independently of the metropolitan French Army. It could have been easy to defy Hitler but this did not happen.

The defeat of France had been swift and humiliating. The French Army had exhausted all its reserves trying to stem the relentless German tide and was not in a position to defend Paris. In a desperate attempt to slice through the German spearhead on 17 May 1940 Colonel de Gaulle with about three battalions of French tanks launched an unsuccessful counter-attack at Montcornet. It was only a matter of time before the inevitable surrender.

De Gaulle's Free French

De Gaulle fled to London and took up residence in Carlton Gardens, where he proclaimed a 'Free France'. Ironically, and perhaps appropriately, Carlton Gardens lay between Downing Street and the Vichy Consulate in Bedford Square, symbolising the uneasy position of the Free French, caught between powerful neighbours. To the west of de Gaulle's headquarters lay the *Union des Français d'Outre Mer* (UFOM), an anti-Vichy but not pro-de Gaulle organisation located in Upper Brook Street.

De Gaulle was despised by his colleagues and by virtually all the other senior French officers who had escaped from France. Churchill contemptuously dubbed him 'Joan of Arc' and President Roosevelt soon became concerned that de Gaulle would try to foist a dictatorship on a liberated France. The activities of de Gaulle's secret service organisation based in Duke Street became a source of embarrassment to the

British government as de Gaulle sought to enforce his writ over his fellow exiles.

The hollow sham of de Gaulle's popularity was exposed on 21 April 1943 when there was an attempt on his life. A Wellington bomber due to fly him to Glasgow was sabotaged at Hendon airfield. Luckily for de Gaulle the pilot detected that the elevator controls had been cut just before take-off and aborted the flight. At the time the incident was hushed up and blamed on German intelligence, but de Gaulle never flew by plane in Britain again.

When the US State Department learned that anti-Gaullist politicians in France were being betrayed to the Gestapo, an exasperated Roosevelt wrote to Churchill on 17 June 1943: 'I am absolutely convinced that he has been and is now injuring our war effort and that he is a very dangerous threat to us.' A year later Roosevelt, annoyed at being dubbed anti-de Gaulle by the newspapers, wrote to General Marshall in a rather sarcastic tone, 'I am perfectly willing to have de Gaulle made President, or Emperor, or King or anything else so long as the action comes in an untrammelled and unforced way from the French people themselves.' It was clear that he regarded de Gaulle as an undemocratic threat to France; it was after all to counter such politics that he was committing the American Army to the Second Front.

Notably, de Gaulle lacked a power base and had no viable army in exile. Between 27 May and 4 June 1940 Operation Dynamo evacuated 224,320 British and another 141,842 Allied, principally French, troops from northern France and Dunkirk. Some 30,000-40,000 French soldiers were left behind to hold the bridgehead. French morale was in disarray and France had yet to surrender on the 21st, so for most evacuated French troops there seemed little point in remaining in Britain. Indeed, many were given little choice and were ferried home via Normandy or Morocco to help stabilise the situation on the Seine, in Lower Normandy and on the Marne. Not all were keen to go as it was apparent that Paris could not hold out, but by the end of June 1940 of those rescued only 45,000 remained in Britain. After Dunkirk the authorities removed 8,000 men, mostly refugees, from French vessels in British waters and they were interned at Aintree near Liverpool to await transport to Casablanca.

The French fleet remained uncommitted and unscathed. In the waters of French North-West Africa, at Mers-el-Kebir and the naval base at Oran were 2 powerful French battleships, a light aircraft carrier, 4 cruisers, 6 heavy destroyers and various smaller vessels and submarines. Two other incomplete battleships had taken refuge at Casablanca and Dakar. There were 6 cruisers at Algiers, while moored at the naval base at Toulon were over 70 vessels. At British-controlled Alexandria there were also a French battleship and 4 cruisers. Churchill was anxious about the fate of these warships. In an ideal world they would have joined the Royal Navy and continued the war against Hitler in the Atlantic and the Mediterranean, but it was not to be. Instead the Royal Navy struck at Mers-el-Kebir with Operation Catapult on 3 July 1940. Both sides were dismayed at what had happened, but there was no going back. The French suffered 1,299 dead and 350 wounded. At the same time all those French warships in British harbours were taken over by armed boarding parties.

The outraged Vichy government under Marshal Pétain closed ranks, determined never to cooperate with either Churchill or Charles de Gaulle. Churchill knew the Anglo-French alliance was completely in tatters when the bulk of the remaining French troops evacuated to Britain chose to be repatriated rather than join the Free French. This must have been a particular insult to the Royal Navy, whose crews had shed so much blood saving them.

No French sailors wanted to join de Gaulle's Free French forces either and at the end of July some 1,100 of them sailed from Southampton on the French passenger ship *Meknes* bound for unoccupied France. A German torpedo-boat sank the *Meknes* with the loss of 400 lives and Churchill was widely blamed for the disaster. In total, some 30,000 sailors and soldiers had chosen repatriation by the end of the year. This mass exodus showed just how unpopular de Gaulle was.

Those who did rally to de Gaulle were pitifully few in number; by August 1940 he had at most 3,000 men gathered at Aldershot. By the following November the Free French Navy numbered just 4,126. Much to the embarrassment of de Gaulle, the Czech, Polish and Norwegian exiled forces could muster almost as many men as him. Also in Britain at this time were 2,720 French wounded, plus 7,547 men from the French Navy and merchant navy who were rounded up and placed in makeshift camps in the north and midlands. Even volunteers of foreign extraction coming to Britain to fight for the Free French were given a very cold reception by the British authorities. Chilean pilot Margot

Duhalde arrived in May 1941 with twelve of her countrymen and was immediately arrested. 'Scotland Yard was waiting for us,' she recalled. Ironically the Free French, who had no use for women pilots, eventually handed her over to the British Air Transport Auxiliary.

Similarly, when the French colonies of Lebanon and Syria were placed under Free French command in July 1941, the bulk of the garrison forces there chose to be repatriated rather than join them. Out of the 37,736 men offered this choice, just 5,668 joined de Gaulle and of those only 1,046 were native Frenchmen, the rest being mainly Germans or Russians from the Foreign Legion, North Africans or Senegalese.

Churchill was much more supportive of the idea of reinstating France's status, even if it meant supporting de Gaulle, and in late 1941 he wrote to Roosevelt:

> Now is the time to offer to Vichy and to French North Africa a blessing or a cursing. A blessing will consist in a promise by the United States and Great Britain to re-establish France as a Great Power with her territories undiminished.
>
> Our relations with General de Gaulle and the Free French movement will require to be reviewed. Hitherto the United States have entered into no undertakings similar to those comprised in my correspondence with him. Through no particular fault of his own movement [he] has created new antagonism in French minds. Any action which the United States may now feel able to take in regard to him should have the effect, *inter alia*, of redefining our obligations to him and France so as to make these obligations more closely dependent upon the eventual effort by him and the French nation to rehabilitate themselves.

In turn de Gaulle felt Churchill had sold out in the name of maintaining the Anglo-American alliance, remarking:

> Churchill had made for himself a rule to do nothing important except in agreement with Roosevelt. Though he felt, more than any other Englishman, the awkwardness of Washington's methods, though he found it hard to bear the conditions of subordination in which United States aid placed the British Empire,

and though he bitterly resented the tone of supremacy which the President adopted towards him, Churchill had decided, once [and] for all, to bow to the imperious necessity of the American alliance.

By 1942 the Allies hoped that General Henri Giraud, who had escaped imprisonment by the Germans, supported by Generals Charles Emmanuel Mast in Algeria and Emile Béthouart in Morocco, would rise up against Vichy. Even so, in September Eisenhower warned his military planners about the risk of the French Army resisting the proposed landings in North-West Africa. 'In the region now are some fourteen French divisions rather poorly equipped but presumably with a fair degree of training and with the benefit of professional leadership,' he cautioned. 'If this Army should act as a unit in contesting the invasion, it could, in view of the slowness with which Allied forces can be accumulated at the two main ports, so delay and hamper operations that the real object of the expedition could not be achieved, namely seizing control of the north shore of Africa before it can be substantially reinforced by the Axis.'

Punishing Pétain's Vichy

In late October 1940 Hitler had tried to pressure Pétain into securing French North-West Africa against Britain. Still smarting from the attack on Mers-el-Kebir, he agreed that within the limits of its ability the French government would support Axis efforts to defeat Britain. In return Hitler agreed to compensate France with territory from the British Empire. When news of this meeting leaked out, President Roosevelt sent Pétain a message warning him of the dire consequences of betraying Britain.

French-administered Algeria, Morocco and Tunisia were now proving a severe problem for the British attempting to contain initially Italian and then joint Italian-German attacks on British-controlled Egypt. Once France was out of the war, Italy was able to act with impunity against British interests in North Africa, secure in the knowledge that there was no threat to Libya's western border from French Tunisia. The Allies' plan to trap the Axis forces fighting in North Africa required the cooperation of French North-West Africa. The problem was that Pétain, supported by Pierre Laval and Admiral Jean

François Darlan, commanded far greater respect than the upstart Charles de Gaulle's Free French.

Initially Britain had tried to get General Maxime Weygand, the French commander in the region, to break with Vichy, but to no avail. Even if he had been sympathetic to the Allies it would have been futile as he was forced out in November 1941 after Hitler's threat to occupy the whole of France. The following April the pro-German Pierre Laval replaced Admiral Darlan as the political power behind the throne in Vichy. To further complicate matters, Algeria was administered as a province of France ruled directly by Vichy, whereas Morocco remained a protectorate and the French Resident General, General Nogues, could only 'guide' the Sultan.

In late October 1942, at a secret conference on the Algerian coast with General Mark Clark, the Deputy Allied Supreme Commander, General Charles Emmanuel Mast, French Commander-in-Chief in Algiers, guaranteed there would be little resistance from the French military and air force in the event of an invasion, although it was thought that the resentful French Navy, perhaps understandably, would resist the landings. To try to avoid antagonising the French any further, it was decided that Operation Torch would be a largely American affair. However, there were insufficient American forces for the attack on Algiers, so they had to be supported by British troops. General Eisenhower hoped the French would not fight but noted: 'However, there was nothing in the political history of the years 1940–42 to indicate that this would occur; it was a hope rather than an expectation. Consequently we had to be prepared to fight against forces which in all numbered 200,000.' There were actually some 55,000 ground troops in Morocco, 50,000 in Algeria and 15,000 in Tunisia, equipped with 250 armoured vehicles and up to 500 aircraft.

Early on 8 November 1942 Pétain was informed that Britain and America had invaded French North-West Africa. He faced a difficult choice: to fight and defend that which he had sought to preserve, or to go along with the Allies' demands. Pétain made his decision and immediately broke off diplomatic relations with America, warning the US chargé d'affaires that his forces would resist the Anglo-American invasion.

The assault forces only had small Landing Craft Personnel (Ramp), Landing Craft Vehicle and Landing Craft Mechanised, the latter two types able to carry only a single lorry or tank respectively. The key vessel for getting tanks ashore, the Landing Ship Tank or LST, capable of carrying up to 60 tanks/vehicles or 300 troops, was not commissioned until December 1942.

The main assault went in at Oran, in addition to which three task forces landed on either side of the city. Despite stiff resistance, American armoured units had penetrated the port by 1000 hours and at noon the French garrison surrendered. Unknown to the Allies, Admiral Darlan was in Algiers at the time visiting his ill son. This completely compromised General Alphonse Juin, the French military commander in Algiers, who had planned to act for the Allies. The eastern advance on Algiers itself was brought to a temporary halt by the threat of attack by just three French tanks. Similarly, during the landings at Casablanca French tank and infantry columns approaching from Rabat had to be driven off by aircraft from the American battleship USS *Texas*. The French also resisted the landings at the Atlantic port of Safi in Morocco.

Darlan ordered a ceasefire two days later, only to have it overruled by Pétain. But continued resistance was futile and Darlan reached a settlement with the Allies on the 13th, under the terms of which the French colonies would be treated as friendly sovereign territory rather than occupied territory. Had the French cooperated, the Allies could have pushed into Tunisia within two days of the landings in Algeria. Instead, the Germans had time to strike eastwards from Tunis, successfully safeguarding their panzers' passage from Libya into Tunisia. Under the Franco-Italian armistice, Mussolini had imposed a 50-mile demilitarised zone between Libya and Tunisia but this now counted for nothing as German and Italian tanks were soon crossing it to secure their exposed western flank.

The Allies' inability to extend the landings and push eastwards into Tunisia was to prove a major failing of Operation Torch. In the port of Tunis Admiral Jean Pierre Esteva, Resident General in Tunisia, though loyal to Darlan and Vichy, was privately sympathetic to the Allies. Nevertheless, he simply did not have the resources with which to obstruct the Germans who began to arrive in force by air on 9 November. At least a quarter of the French garrison remained loyal to Vichy and did nothing to impede the German invasion. At Bizerte some Vichy French units even joined the Germans. Luckily the rest of the garrison in Tunisia chose to observe the ceasefire and support the

Allies. The French ground forces commander, General George Barre, withdrew with about five battalions into the mountains west of Tunis and moved towards the Allies in Algiers, while other French troops moved into the Grande Dorsale range of mountains.

General Juin's 30,000-strong *Detachement d'Armée Française* (DAF), consisting of Barre's weak division, a division raised in the Constantine area and some Saharan units, was assigned to cover the two Dorsale ranges. Its job was to prevent the Germans penetrating the Tebessa area of Algeria and to protect the right flank of the British in the forthcoming Tunisian campaign. This effectively marked the end of the war between the Allies and France.

In the four days of fighting, American forces suffered 1,434 casualties, including 556 killed, 837 wounded and 41 missing. The British sustained 300 casualties, while the French lost 700 dead, 1,400 wounded and 400 missing. Privately the Americans were pleased that Vichy had chosen to fight, as it gave them the opportunity to blood their inexperienced army before it had to contend with the battle-hardened Wehrmacht. The invasion also provided a vital testing-ground for the subsequent amphibious assaults on Sicily and Normandy. It also proved to Roosevelt that the Vichy French were largely untrustworthy as they, along with the Free French, were split by so many factions they seemed unable to speak with one voice.

De Gaulle's New Army

Churchill publicly declared his faith in de Gaulle at Mansion House in London on 10 November 1942 and tried to reassure Vichy France of Britain's intentions towards her vanquished ally:

> While there are men like General de Gaulle and all those who follow him – and they are legion throughout France – and men like General Giraud, that gallant warrior whom no prison can hold, while there are men like those to stand forward in the name and in the cause of France, my confidence in the future is clear.
>
> For ourselves we have no wish but to see France free and strong, with her empire gathered around her and with Alsace-Lorraine restored. We covet no French possession; we have no acquisitive appetites or ambitions in North Africa or any other part of the world.

De Gaulle now had a golden opportunity to establish a power base and an army. Following Operation Torch he moved his headquarters to Algiers and appointed General Pierre Koenig as head of the French military mission in London. Crucially there were still some 100,000 French troops in Morocco and Tunisia, and their presence would help him consolidate his position.

Hitler's response to the Allied landings in French North-West Africa was swift and predictable: the Wehrmacht and SS rolled into the Free Zone in the south of France on 11 November 1942. Despite Hitler's assurances to Pétain about the safety of the French Navy, on the 27th German troops attacked and overwhelmed the naval base at Toulon. The final defeat of the fleet was a blow to French national pride, as was the loss of Toulon itself. The port held a special place in the hearts of all Frenchmen, for it was where Napoleon Bonaparte had saved the French Revolution from counter-revolutionary forces in 1793 and set himself on the path to dominance in Europe.

French sailors held the Germans off long enough for 75 warships and submarines to be scuttled at their moorings. Although this meant that these warships were denied to the Axis Powers, who had hoped to use them in the Mediterranean, equally they were lost to the Allies. Just three French submarines escaped to join the Free French at Algiers. The subjugation of the whole of metropolitan France was complete. The Allies were now presented with a dilemma: should they attack Sicily, mainland Italy or the south of France.

Admiral Darlan was assassinated on 24 December 1942 and General Henri Giraud succeeded him as the civil and military chief of French North-West Africa. He soon upset the Allies by ordering the arrest of a number of Frenchmen who had aided Operation Torch. Giraud met Roosevelt, Churchill and de Gaulle at Casablanca in January 1943. During the meeting it was agreed that Giraud and de Gaulle would become co-presidents of the French Committee of National Liberation (FCNL), but when de Gaulle arrived in Algeria on 30 May he soon used his superior political skills to become overall leader of the organisation. Rather grudgingly, Churchill recognised the FCNL on 27 August 1943.

After the Allies' invasion of French North-West Africa the French Army was in such a state of disarray that it was unable to take part in the invasions of Sicily and Italy. Its most desperate need was for weapons.

These were slow in arriving, not least because in America, the armoury of the Free World, Eisenhower regarded the French forces as just one of the many exiled European armies competing for resources; in addition, many Americans were not convinced of the fighting value of French troops. However, Eisenhower's Naval Aide, Captain Harry C. Butcher of the US Naval Reserve, was only too conscious of his boss's role in rearming the French Army and its value to the coming invasion of southern France. He commented:

> Ike [Eisenhower] had played a considerable part in the effort of the US to equip the rebuilt French Army. He feels we have in it a very considerable investment, and the French troops, plus the Americans and British, must be used to obtain a final decision against Germany. Therefore, a gateway for them into France must be obtained or all our French investment will have been wasted. Unless we have a southern France invasion, a great number of American and other forces would be locked in the Mediterranean.

At the French Rearmament Ceremony, staged in Algiers on 8 May 1943, Eisenhower himself said, 'Today, General Giraud, through you, as one of the consistent and implacable foes of Hitlerism, and the leader of the French forces in North Africa, I am happy to transfer these implements of war to Frenchmen inspired by that purpose.' He then read out a stirring cable from Roosevelt, which set Allied sights firmly on the liberation of Paris and the establishment of French democracy:

> French valour and French patriotism now have a trenchant sword with which to help strike from France the shackles of oppression. The victorious Jeanne d'Arc carried her battle standard into the coronation cathedral. Now that the only Axis soldiers left on African soil will soon be in graves or in prison camps, let us set our hearts and minds on complete victory, so that we may march, with this equipment, up the Champs Elysee to the Arc de Triomphe, where lies the Unknown Soldier, symbol of French heroism. There we will render a salute to the Tricolour, once again floating proudly, peacefully and forever over a freed French people, who will re-establish their own government in accordance with their own conceptions of right, liberty and justice.

General Giraud wanted to reorganise the French Army into 13 divisions, but shipping requirements meant that the Americans at the Casablanca Conference in January 1943 could only commit to supplying 11. The first convoy arrived in North Africa on 14 April and by July 75,000 French troops had been equipped with American weapons, uniforms and vehicles. In the meantime de Gaulle's two Free French divisions had been poaching recruits and were redeployed to Tripolitania (Libya).

Giraud, though, was obliged to factor de Gaulle's units into his plans, and this plus a shortage of support personnel required him to disband five divisions, and therefore he ended up with just eight (including three armoured) available to take part in the liberation of Europe. Two of these, the 1st Motorised and 2nd Armoured, remained staunchly Gaullist units, while four others were composed almost entirely of colonial soldiers.

The French I Corps was reconstituted on 16 August 1943 at Ain-Taya in Algeria under Lieutenant-General Martin. It consisted of the 4th Moroccan Mountain Division (4e DMM), the 1st Regiment of Moroccan *Tirailleurs* (1er RTM), the 4th Regiment of Moroccan Spahis (4e RSM), with light tanks, the 2nd Group of Moroccan Tabors (2e GTM), the *Commandos de Choc* battalion and the 3rd Battalion, and the 69th Mountain Artillery Regiment (69e RAM). These key French combat units were re-equipped with American-supplied uniforms and weapons as part of the rearmament of the French Army of Africa. It would not be long before the corps was blooded in liberating French territory.

By early September the German 90th Panzergrenadier Division and the *Reichsführer-SS* assault infantry brigade were evacuating Sardinia and transiting via southern Corsica. In response, the French launched Operation *Vésuve*, landing elements of I Corps at Ajaccio on the 13th, just three days after being informed that the Italian troops on the island were willing to fight for the Allies. Aiming to cut off the withdrawing German troops, I Corps linked up with Corsican partisans who also wanted their occupiers gone.

When the German forces under General von Senger und Etterlin began disarming the Italians, General Magli ordered them to consider the Germans as an enemies. From that point Italian units on the island cooperated with the French forces. Unfortunately though, SS troops captured 2,000 men on the 13th after surprising the Italian *Friuli* Division in the northern port of Bastia, and secured the port from which they could evacuate. Although supported by the Royal Navy, the French were unable to land swiftly enough to prevent the bulk of the Germans from reaching their exit ports on the east coast.

The final battle with the German rearguard took place around Bastia and the island was secured by 4 October. The Germans suffered 700 casualties and lost 350 taken prisoner, but most of their forces escaped. The Italians lost 800 men, mostly from the *Friuli* Division, while French losses were modest, with 75 killed, 12 missing and 239 wounded. The French I Corps remained on Corsica until May 1944 conducting training exercises. On 18 April that year it was subordinated to General de Lattre's Armée B (Army B).

By mid-October 1943 Hitler had reinforced his forces in Italy with 27,000 troops who had escaped from Corsica and Sardinia. In the meantime Field Marshal Albert Kesselring had managed to keep the Allies at bay and disarm the Italian Army. He then brought the invaders to a halt 160 km from Rome. Eight months were to pass before the Allies reached the Italian capital, and then it would take another eight months before they managed to break out into the plains of northern Italy.

During the Corsican operation de Gaulle and other Allied leaders criticised Giraud for arming the communist-dominated *Front National* resistance group. Giraud was also implicated in the Pecheu affair; M. Pecheu was the Vichy Interior Minister whom Giraud had permitted to come to Algiers, where he was charged with complicity in the execution of French workers by Germans. Pecheu himself was shot and the French Committee of National Liberation decided in April 1944 that Giraud should stand down as commander in chief and he was put on the retired list. His enemies tried to assassinate him in Algeria on 28 August but he survived. By November 1943 de Gaulle was in complete control of the FCNL, which in turn controlled most of France's colonial possessions and more importantly the French troops now being equipped by America. During the Italian campaign of 1943 and 1944 some 100,000 French troops took part in the fighting against the German Winter Line and the Gustav Line. In the meantime frantic re-equipping went on in French North Africa, and by the time of the Normandy invasion Free French forces totalled over 400,000 men under arms.

General de Lattre

In the autumn of 1943 General de Gaulle hinted to General Philippe Leclerc de Hauteclocque, commander of the Free French 2nd Armoured Division, that the Allies might employ his division for the Overlord operation. Leclerc was a staunch Gaullist and his men were veterans of the fighting in Libya and Tunisia. In the summer of that year his force had become known as the *2e Division Blindee* and was fully equipped along the lines of an American armoured division, with Sherman medium and Honey light tanks, armoured cars, self-propelled guns and towed artillery. Its organisation included two powerful tank regiments, the *501e Chars de Combat* and the *1er Regiment de Marche de Spahis Marocains.*

Understandably, Leclerc began to press for transport to Britain, causing a row with General de Lattre de Tassigny, who wanted the 2nd Armoured Division as part of his Army B (1st Army), which was earmarked for the invasion of southern France. When Leclerc's force was finally shipped to Britain in April 1944, all the black colonial troops were returned to France's African possessions, on the grounds that they would be unable to cope in Europe. The remainder found themselves in Yorkshire, rapidly converting from bush and desert warfare to an armoured role more suitable for the fighting to come in Europe. As if to drive home the division's destination, all the tanks and vehicles had a map of France painted on them. Leclerc and his men hoped to fight alongside the British in the opening assault, but instead the division was attached to General George Patton's US 3rd Army, which was allocated the break-out role.

By early 1944 the French Army had sent to Italy under General Juin an expeditionary corps of four divisions, consisting of the 1st Motorised, 2nd Moroccan and 3rd Algerian Infantry Division, and the 4th Moroccan Mountain Division. The 2nd Moroccan Infantry Division had been formed on 1 May 1943 and committed in Italy at the end of November 1943; the following month it was followed by the 3rd Algerian Infantry Division, also created on 1 May 1943 after the conversion of the Constantine temporary division. The 4th Moroccan Mountain Division had come into being on 1 June 1943, after being raised from the 3rd Moroccan Motorised Division, but was not committed to Italy until February 1944. Lastly the 1st Free French Division formed on 1 February 1943 was converted to the 1st

Motorised Infantry Division on 24 August 1943 and sent to Italy in April the following year.

As commander of Vichy forces in French North Africa, Juin had fallen out with de Lattre over how best to defend Tunisia from Axis incursions should the British win in Libya. De Lattre had wanted to conduct a forward defence, but Juin knew that this could leave Algeria vulnerable. He also knew that to bring forward reinforcements from Morocco and Algeria would violate the armistice with Hitler. Their best hope lay in holding the hills to maintain a foothold and screen Algeria. In January 1942 de Lattre was sacked and posted to Vichy France.

De Lattre was clearly not a Gaullist, having commanded the Montpellier region under the Vichy regime, but he was arrested by the Vichy authorities in late 1942 for planning to oppose the German take-over of the unoccupied zone. He was sentenced to ten years' imprisonment but managed to escape to Britain in September 1943. De Lattre now faced two problems: even before 1940 he had not seen eye to eye with de Gaulle, whom he now had to support, and secondly, what could he usefully do? His greatest desire was for a field command and he was soon lobbying the British, Americans and Free French to create a French Army in North Africa. After a short stay in hospital for a damaged lung, he flew to Algiers to see de Gaulle and Giraud. The latter was an old ally and got him appointed as commander of the French 2nd Army, which encompassed all the French forces in North Africa. He would have to wait until April 1944 before he was officially informed that his force, designated Army B, would be committed to Anvil. In the meantime he faced the headache of forging ardent Gaullists, colonial forces, former Vichy supporters, escapees and other disparate units into a single coherent command capable of combat operations. His efforts were further complicated by the fact that the best units were either now with Juin fighting in Italy or already earmarked for Normandy. In addition, de Lattre needed weapons and equipment, not only for his assault force but also for eager recruits once they were back on French soil.

De Lattre had the backing of de Gaulle, as neither was happy at the idea of a French Army within the American command structure and reliant on American logistic support. Both felt Roosevelt and Eisenhower did not fully appreciate that a revitalised French Army could be charged with liberating its homeland. They in turn were insensitive to

Roosevelt and Eisenhower's concerns over the future of the French Empire and whether de Gaulle was the right man for the top job.

De Lattre, though, was not easily dissuaded and the Americans eventually agreed to supply weapons and equipment for five infantry and three armoured divisions. This was not considered quite so generous when it became apparent that it included Juin's four divisions already in Italy and Leclerc's armoured division. Under these circumstances friction was inevitable. One can only feel sorry for Eisenhower, even while admiring his stamina, as he was caught between the competing demands of Churchill and de Gaulle. It is astonishing that the alliance managed to survive these strains; that it did is testament to Eisenhower's quite remarkable management skills. A lesser statesman could have greatly exacerbated the situation.

De Lattre now began to cast an envious eye on Juin's corps, advocating that it should be brought back from Italy and placed under him. In this he was supported by General de Gaulle and the Allied command, and Juin's forces duly joined him in July, giving him a total of seven divisions. De Lattre showed great diplomacy in assimilating the four divisions who were devoted to Juin, tactfully keeping General Marcel-Maurice Carpentier, Juin's Chief of Staff, and all the existing divisional commanders.

In February 1944 de Gaulle created the French Forces of the Interior (FFI) under General Koenig in an effort to unite all the various resistance groups. In the run-up to Overlord and D-Day Britain and America were loath to discuss their plans with Koenig, for information sent to Algiers would end up in Paris, where the Resistance movement was so heavily infiltrated by the Germans it would inevitably reach Hitler.

The FCNL now became the provisional government of the French Republic, although cynics smiled at the word 'provisional'. De Gaulle now considered himself head of the French government, though neither America nor Britain recognised him as such. At the end of the month he returned to London, where he disassociated himself once more from the Allied cause by refusing to broadcast a message to his fellow countrymen on D-Day.

Chapter Three

Churchill and Monty take on Ike

In late December 1943 General Bernard Montgomery bade an emotional farewell to the officers and men of his beloved 8th Army at Vasto Opera House in Italy. Major-General Francis de Guingand, Monty's Chief of Staff, who was to accompany him, recalled the occasion:

> My Chief was very quiet and I could see that this was going to be the most difficult operation he had yet attempted. We arrived inside and he said, 'Freddie, show me where to go.' I led him to the stairs leading up to the stage. He mounted at once, and to a hushed audience commenced his address to the officers of the Army which he loved so well.

Montgomery's place in the history books was already secured after his actions in North Africa and Sicily, but now he was going on to bigger and better things, having been appointed to command the 21st Army Group that was to assault northern France. He flew out from Italy on 31 December, and his arrival would sow the seeds of British opposition to Operation Anvil, the proposed invasion of southern France. Freddie de Guingand noted their progress:

> Our course allowed us a glimpse of Etna and then nothing until the North African shore. We landed to refuel at Algiers, taking off immediately for Marrakech, where we arrived about six in the evening. Here we changed aircraft. Montgomery went off to spend the night with Winston Churchill, who was convalescing there, . . .

It may have been imprudent of Churchill to show Montgomery the Overlord plans before he was fully briefed by the planning staffs in

London. Indeed, even before Monty had arrived in Morocco General Sir Hastings Ismay, the Prime Minister's Military Secretary, received a cable from Marrakech saying Churchill 'is full out on Overlord and Anvil but suspects Eisenhower and Montgomery will demand considerably heavier assaults in the full moon period'. Understandably Ismay was not happy and signalled back:

It is most undesirable that Monty should be given an opportunity of criticising the plan before he has discussed it with the people who prepared it. They alone can explain the reasons which have led to the adoption of the plan in its present form. We are sure it would be much better for Monty to reserve judgement until he comes home . . .

Nonetheless, Montgomery spent the evening in Marrakech preparing written comments for the Prime Minister. The following day he remarked, 'Today, 1 January 1944, is the first time I have seen the Appreciation and proposed plan or considered the problem in this way.' This was not entirely true; Eisenhower and General Walter Bedell Smith had discussed the Overlord plans in some detail with him in Algiers just days earlier.

Montgomery claimed that Churchill was pleased with his work: 'He said he had always known there was something wrong in the proposed plan, but that the Chiefs of Staff had agreed with it and that left him powerless. Now a battlefield commander had analysed it for him and had given him the information he needed he was grateful.' Monty obviously appreciated that he was stirring things up and added:

I asked for my paper back, saying it was written entirely without inter-service discussion and I did not want to start my new job by troubles with the planners in London. But he kept it, promising to use it himself only as background information. I had the subsequent impression that background was liable to intrude into the foreground.

Montgomery did not like the proposed plan and insisted to Churchill that Overlord needed greater initial punch. He also argued that it would take ninety days for a force landed in the south of France to have any influence on the Normandy operation. The implication was that Anvil would be a waste of time and resources.

In truth, Eisenhower had already expressed misgivings about the size of the Overlord assault force, having seen the plans in late October. After the war Eisenhower stated that he and his Chief of Staff General Bedell Smith 'decided, off the cuff, that a five-division attack was far more desirable'. In contrast, Monty claimed that Eisenhower told him in Algiers that 'he had only a sketchy idea of the plan and that it did not look too good'. It is clear, though, that Monty did not deserve all the credit for the changes made to the plan.

Once in England, de Guingand was to find himself in accord with his boss – Overlord must be beefed up:

> It had been arranged that Bedell Smith, Eisenhower's Chief of Staff [Ike was in America], and I should discuss the existing plan together, and give Montgomery our views on his arrival from his visit to Churchill in Marrakech. The existing plan which we found was briefly as follows. An assault by three divisions and tanks between Grandcamp and Caen. Behind these two follow-up divisions, and behind them two more divisions which would be afloat in ships on 'D' day. Given exceptionally good weather conditions it was calculated that we should have nine divisions ashore by the end of the sixth day. . . .
>
> Bedell Smith's and my reactions were, I suppose, similar to those of any other trained soldier. We wanted a greater weight of assault, a quicker build-up, a larger airlift, and we thought the area of assault too restricted.

Indeed, by January 1944 commitment to Anvil was beginning to look a bit shaky, because of its perceived lack of utility to Overlord. For the next seven months Eisenhower would have to endure unrelenting pressure from Churchill and Montgomery, who were both intent on stripping away resources from Anvil, diverting the operation elsewhere or cancelling it altogether. Eisenhower was soon to rue the day that the Western Allies had committed themselves to a diversionary attack in support of Overlord.

Monty sent Ike a cable on 10 January 1944 telling him that he wanted to expand Overlord to a five-division assault, stating that this could easily be done if Anvil were to be cancelled. Montgomery argued strongly that Overlord must be enlarged in scope and requested an immediate decision:

> This can be done if Anvil is reduced to a threat and the assault craft thus released are made available for Overlord. . . . The really important point is to get a decision now, at once. Provided we can get what I recommend then I consider Overlord has every chance of a quick success . . . Time is very short. Will you hurl yourself into the content and get us what we want.

Montgomery had put Eisenhower on the spot. He was clearly saying that if Ike did not give Overlord total priority over Anvil, then this would greatly hamper any chance of the Normandy invasion achieving 'a quick success'. To Eisenhower and the US Chiefs of Staff, Anvil was a logical diversionary operation to keep German forces away from northern France. Now here was Montgomery, an enormously experienced and astute battle commander, saying that such an operation would negatively impact on the operational success of Normandy.

Inevitably, the question of resources remained a vexed subject. To extend Overlord meant more landing craft. South-East Asia had already been stripped of its landing craft, to the detriment of operations against the Japanese, while in the Mediterranean there were just sufficient craft to lift the two divisions assigned to Anvil. Churchill noted:

> Having recently returned from the Mediterranean, he [Eisenhower] knew all about Anvil, and now as Supreme Commander of Overlord he could best judge the needs of both. It was agreed to take the ships from one division from Anvil and to use them for Overlord. The ships for a second division could be found by postponing Overlord till the June moon period. The output of new landing craft in that month would fill the gap.

Marshall favours Anvil

Only too aware that the US Chief of Staff General Marshall favoured Anvil, Eisenhower rejected Montgomery's suggestion:

We must remember that the Russians had been led to expect that the operation would take place. . . . We had to make recommendations to the Combined Chiefs of Staff not later than 1 February as to the future of Anvil . . . We must consider whether we could not manage a successful Overlord without damaging Anvil.

He added they must not lose sight of the advantages to Overlord which Anvil would bring, and stressed that it was an important diversion, adding, 'Furthermore, there are certain strong considerations not purely military which have been brought to my attention here and must be weighed.'

Marshall's well-founded concern was that the Germans would undoubtedly take desperate measures to crush Overlord; this they could achieve by pinning down the Allies in Italy and then creating a large reserve by drawing spare divisions from the Balkans, Italy and southern France for operations in western France against any beachhead.

In Italy the Allies launched their offensive in the south on 12 January 1944, with Juin's French Expeditionary Corps assaulting Cassino and the British X Corps attempting to exploit previous gains on the Garigliano river. Both assaults failed to break through the German Gustav Line, although some limited progress was made. A week later the US II Corps attacked from the centre of General Mark Clark's US 5th Army, attempting to cross the Rapido river, but after just two days the Americans were forced to call a halt. The assault on the Gustav Line, the lynch-pin of the Allied plan, had bogged down. The lack of success at Cassino indicated there would be no progress towards Rome during March.

General Sir Harold Alexander, the Allied commander in Italy, was in the process of strengthening his twenty-one divisions by another seven. Nevertheless the Germans had twenty-four divisions in Italy, nineteen of which were committed to the fighting in the south. Alexander had stated that just six to eight German divisions would be sufficient to delay his advance on the Pisa-Rimini Line. This meant that if the Germans conducted a series of fighting withdrawals to or beyond the Apennines, then they could free up ten to fifteen divisions for combat in France, not to mention those already stationed in southern France.

Marshall signalled Eisenhower on the 16th, spelling out his concerns:

The news from the Italian Front indicates that there is no probability of a decisive tactical change in the situation from that which existed at the time you met with the British Chiefs of Staff to represent the US Chiefs of Staff in the Overlord–Anvil matter. . . .

We know from Magic [intelligence intercepts] that the Germans are fearful of a landing in the northern Adriatic or on the coast of southern France. However, if they once become aware of the fact that the facilities for such a landing are not available they could rearrange their forces to your great disadvantage. . . .

We are about to open discussions with the British Chiefs of Staff concerning Anvil and they have requested [General] Wilson to let them have his estimate on the Mediterranean by 18 March. . . .

Marshall then added a get-out-of-jail clause, saying he would support Ike's decision (regardless of the fact that he and most of the US Chiefs of Staff were firmly in favour of Anvil and that Eisenhower was answerable to him and Roosevelt):

It is my intention, with which [General] Arnold [Commander USAAF] agrees, that we will support your desire regarding the Anvil decision, whatever it may be. So the foregoing statement of my views is not to be accepted by you as pressure from me to have matters arranged other than the way you would wish to see them set up.

Ultimately this woolly statement was of no help whatsoever in guiding Eisenhower as he wrestled with the tricky questions of the size, shape and location of Operation Anvil. If anything, the US Chiefs of Staff had done him a great disservice, because deep down he knew that Marshall was very pro-Anvil.

Shortly after his arrival in London, Eisenhower brought all the players together to debate the issue. He commenced his historic role as Allied Supreme Commander on 20 January 1944 at Norfolk House. The following day he attended his first meeting with Montgomery, his appointed Commander in Chief of Overlord's assault forces. Monty was only too well aware that while Ike supported the strengthening of Overlord, he did not believe that Anvil should be abandoned. In light of the friction that had already passed between the two it was a momentous meeting. Monty argued fervently that a wider invasion front would confuse and hamper the commitment of German reserves against Overlord. Eisenhower in contrast was clearly of the view that Anvil should not be impoverished for the sake of strengthening Overlord. This set the stage for the inevitable showdown between the Supreme Commander and the British Prime Minister.

In Italy in the meantime the US VI Corps set sail from Naples on 21 January, its destination Anzio. Operation Shingle, the landings at Anzio, took place the following day. These were intended to help turn the German Gustav Line, but the hoped-for early thrust inland to cut off the German defences did not occur and the invasion forces were hemmed in by elements of the 26th and Hermann Goering Panzer Divisions, as well as the 3rd and 16th SS Panzergrenadier Divisions supported by about 220 panzers. In two weeks of fighting the Anglo-American forces suffered almost 7,000 casualties.

Lieutenant-General Mark Clark estimated it would take three weeks for his US 5th Army to link up with the Anzio beachhead. By that stage there would be 130,000 men in the bridgehead, 90,000 of them American. Due to the lack of progress Lieutenant-General Lucian Truscott replaced General Lucas as the commander at Anzio. Of course, as long as the forces at Anzio remained bottled up, they were tying up valuable shipping which was keeping them resupplied.

Four major offensives took place between January and May 1944 before the Gustav Line was eventually broken by a combined assault of the US 5th Army and the British 8th Army (involving British, US, French, Polish and Canadian Corps) concentrated along a 20-mile front between Monte Cassino and the western coast. The forces at Anzio did not break out of their bridgehead until late May. Even then the opportunity to cut off and destroy a large part of the German 10th Army was lost when the Anzio forces changed their direction of attack to move parallel with the coast to capture Rome.

Just a deception

On 23 January Eisenhower spelt out his thinking on the utility of Anvil in a signal to Marshall; he claimed he saw it more as an actual operation than a deception dependent on resources. He also showed that he endorsed Montgomery's thinking over Overlord:

I regard Anvil as an important contribution to Overlord as I feel that an assault will contain more enemy forces in southern France than a threat. The forces of both the US and French are in any case available; and the actual landing of these forces will increase the cooperation from resistance elements in France.

Overlord and Anvil must be viewed as one whole. If sufficient forces could be made available the ideal would be a five-divisional Overlord and a three-divisional Anvil or, at worst, a two-divisional Anvil. If insufficient forces are available for this, however, I am driven to the conclusion that we should adopt a five-divisional Overlord and a one-divisional Anvil, the latter being maintained as a threat until enemy weakness justifies its active employment. This solution should be adopted only as a last resort and after all other means and alternatives have failed to provide the necessary strength by the end of May for a five-divisional Overlord and two-divisional Anvil.

In truth it is likely that Eisenhower's decision was influenced by the Skyscraper plan, which proposed a cross-Channel attack in the spring of 1943 employing an assault force of 4 divisions, with a follow up of 6 divisions, supported by 4 airborne divisions. He may have also drawn on Operation Harlequin (part of the Cockade plan to prevent German divisions in the west being redeployed to the Eastern Front) that proposed a feint towards the Pas-de-Calais, but the lack of landing craft led to it being cancelled.

The British Chiefs of Staff, backing Montgomery, were also of the view that Overlord should be five divisions strong, whatever the cost to Anvil, and that the latter should be of one or two divisional strength. Rightly, the US Chiefs of Staff saw Eisenhower's threat in lieu of an attack as a waste of time and insisted that it should be nothing short of two divisions. 'On this telegram,' Churchill later noted, 'I minuted "Apparently the two-division lift for Anvil is given priority over Overlord. This is directly counter to the views of Generals Eisenhower and Montgomery".'

Shortly afterwards the British Chiefs of Staff, in consultation with Churchill, sent the Americans a lengthy telegram, the gist of which was that Overlord was paramount. It was clear by this stage that Churchill was firmly, if not vehemently, against Anvil. He pointed out that:

They [the British Chiefs of Staff] questioned the wisdom of under-taking Anvil at all, in view of the way things were going in Italy, and pointed out that when Anvil first found favour at Tehran we expected that the Germans would withdraw to a line north of Rome. But now it was clear beyond all doubt that the Germans intended to resist our advance in Italy to the utmost. They also pointed out that the distance between the south of France and the beaches of Normandy was nearly 500 miles, and that a diversion could be created from Italy or some other point just as well as through the Rhône valley. Anvil in fact was too far away to help Overlord.

Whatever transpired, it was clear that Anvil could not be conducted in parallel with Overlord as originally envisaged. On 24 January Brooke recorded in his diary:

Had a long Chiefs of Staff meeting at which Eisenhower turned up to discuss his paper proposing increase of cross-Channel operations at expense of South France operations. I entirely agree with the proposal, but it is certainly not his idea and is one of Monty's. Eisenhower has got absolutely no strategical outlook. He makes up, however, by the way he works for good cooperation between allies.

On 1 February 1944 the Combined Chiefs of Staff approved the proposals for a revised Overlord assault, to take place no later than 31 May, deploying five divisions and two airborne divisions. They promised extra landing craft but noted the US Chiefs' insistence on a two-division assault in southern France soon after.

The revised plan for Overlord using five divisions had major implications for the amphibious forces required to lift and protect such a force. It was assessed by Eisenhower's headquarters that they would need an additional 47 Landing Ship Tank, 7 Landing Ship Infantry, 144 Landing Craft Tank and 72 Landing Craft Infantry to transport the troops and their armour. To safeguard this greatly enlarged task force the escorts would have to be enhanced by 24 destroyers and 28 motor launches supported by 4 flotillas of minesweepers. A bigger invasion front also meant a larger bombardment group requiring an extra 2 battleships, 5 cruisers and 12 destroyers.

Such resources would have to be found elsewhere and these requirements were clearly a threat to other amphibious operations. Also they
had to be in place six weeks before D-Day. The Joint Chiefs of Staff
were quick to question how Eisenhower's staff had come up with these
figures and reminded him that 92 LCTs and 25 LCI(L) were currently
out of service. They also questioned the British shipyards' ability to
churn out 96 LCTs a month. Eisenhower's somewhat terse response
was that almost all LSIs, LSTs, LCIs and LCTs were serviceable and
these had been taken into account. He also demanded that a firm
commitment be given over the provision of the additional resources
needed for Overlord.

The reception of the Anzio landings had shown how the Germans
intended to behave; having deployed their reserves, it was clear they
intended to keep as many Allied divisions tied down there as possible.
'This campaign', General 'Pug' Ismay, Churchill's Military Secretary,
wrote to his boss on 4 February, 'will provide in full measure the diversion to Overlord which it had been intended to create by Anvil. Thus it
looks as though Alexander will require a proportion of the French
troops and American divisions allocated to Anvil.'

Certainly Operation Shingle was likely to provide important lessons
for the opening of the Second Front, and understandably the Allied
Chiefs of Staff kept a close watch on developing events. On 8 February
Churchill asked Admiral Cunningham for the LST shipment rates for
military vehicles over the last two weeks. He was not encouraged by an
alarming disparity in the figures, remarking:

> I had hoped that we were hurling a wild cat on to the shore, but
> all we had got was a stranded whale. The spectacle of 18,000 vehi-
> cles accumulated ashore by the fourteenth day for only 70,000
> men, or less than four men to a vehicle, including drivers and
> attendants, though they did not move more than twelve to four-
> teen miles, was astonishing. We were apparently still stronger
> than the Germans in fighting power. The ease with which they
> moved their pieces about the board and the rapidity with which
> they adjusted the perilous gaps they had to make on their
> southern front was most impressive. It all seemed to give us
> adverse data for Overlord.

Just eight days later the Germans threw over four divisions at the Anzio beachhead. Fortunately the US VI Corps weathered the storm.

The British assessment was that once Overlord was under way, there would only be enough landing craft in the Mediterranean to shift a single division. Even if they managed two, this would hardly constitute the strategic pincer movement that Eisenhower and Stalin envisaged. In early February Churchill was proposing to land two armoured divisions in Bordeaux twenty days after the cross-Channel operation. The British Chiefs of Staff were not keen on this and Brooke recalled, 'I think we have ridden him off this for the present.'

On returning to London on 17 February after visiting his troops, Monty found that things were drifting the other way:

> During my absence on tour the question of the craft and shipping necessary for Overlord made little headway. Actually matters got worse as two delegates were sent over from Washington with a plan for cutting down our demands and giving more craft to Anvil. Their proposals were put to me and I refused to accept.

Eisenhower, whose ultimate role was to become a first class diplomatic adjudicator, proposed on behalf of the Washington planners that 30 LCIs and 7 LSTs be assigned to Anvil. Montgomery was having none of it and immediately sent Eisenhower a terse message. He complained that the initial success must be guaranteed as well as the subsequent build-up once ashore.

Montgomery felt that Eisenhower's proposals did nothing short of endangering Overlord's success by compromising tactical flexibility. He made it perfectly clear that he would not budge on this issue: 'From an Army point of view the proposals put forward to me are not acceptable. I recommend, definitely, that the proposals be turned down, and that the craft and shipping essential for Overlord be made available.'

The following day Eisenhower urged Montgomery to compromise, and perhaps surprisingly Monty, who had got his way with all other issues with the new Overlord plan, acquiesced. When Montgomery dined with Brooke on 18 February, the latter was dismayed to learn that Overlord was to be compromised in favour of Anvil, especially in light of the parlous situation in Italy. Alexander was already secretly pressing to have Lieutenant-General Truscott, the American commander at

Anzio, replaced by someone like Patton. Brooke had lost his temper
with Churchill, who was all for placing Alexander in charge of the
bridgehead and having Wilson assume general command in Italy.
Brooke had prevailed on the Prime Minister not to intervene and to
leave it to the commanders on the ground, but Montgomery's news was
the final straw.

Eisenhower hosted a Chiefs of Staff meeting on the 19th to discuss
the desirability of Anvil coinciding with Overlord. Brooke noted with
disbelief in his diary:

> Luckily I had discovered last night from Monty that he and
> [Admiral] Bertie Ramsay had agreed to curtail the cross-Channel
> operation to provide for a south of France operation. They should
> have realised that the situation in Italy now made such an
> operation impossible. They had agreed to please Eisenhower, who
> was pressing for it to please Marshall!

Going in to fight Monty's corner Brooke added:

> I had a little difficulty with Eisenhower, but not much, to make
> him see sense, as all he required was a little pressure to go back to
> the plans he really liked best now that he had at least shown some
> attempt to support Marshall's idea. I think the matter is now all
> right.

Captain Harry Butcher, Eisenhower's Naval Aide, witnessed the difficult position his boss was placed in:

> Ike, representing the US Chiefs of Staff, went into the 'ifs and
> ands' of Overlord and Anvil to the British Chiefs of Staff this
> morning. The fact that he represents the US Chiefs of Staff in
> dealing with the British Chiefs throws a tremendous weight on his
> shoulders. It makes him the recipient of all the arguments and
> pressures which the British, particularly the Prime Minister, may
> wish to advance for or against any particular project involving the
> US Joint Chiefs and affecting the European Theatre. The
> Supreme Commander has wrestled continually to keep Anvil
> alive; by today it had a bad sinking spell.

Butcher went on to observe that this was all the work of Montgomery:

> Monty thinks Anvil should be abandoned. He would rather have
> plenty of landing craft for the cross-Channel operation. He prefers
> a strong Overlord. He has lunched with the Prime Minister at
> Chequers and strongly advocates to Ike that the Combined Chiefs
> be advised that it is better to have two really major campaigns, one
> in Italy and one in Overlord.

Fully appraised of Brooke's views, Montgomery sought a briefing on
Italy from his friend Major-General Frank Simpson, Director of
Military Operations at the War Office. 'I am told by the Operations
Directorate at the War Office that the divisions in Italy have had a lot of
casualties, are tired, and generally are not too well situated for getting
on to Rome and beyond,' he wrote to Eisenhower. 'They require re-
grouping, resting, and so on. Also the battle has to be continued so as to
keep drawing German divisions down that way – all of which is very
good.'

Monty now went on to show his hand, effectively abandoning his
previous agreement with Eisenhower:

> Under these circumstances, I do not see how the withdrawal of
> divisions from Italy for Anvil is possible. If this is the case I hope
> that we shall get the full number of craft that we would really like
> for Overlord, there is no point in cutting ourselves down and
> accepting a compromise solution for Overlord, if Anvil can never
> come off; it would be better to have a really good Overlord, with a
> good choice of craft, a good reserve of craft, a good margin all
> round, and so on. I suggest that this aspect should be cleared up.

But Eisenhower, with a million and one things to think of with the planning of Overlord, was not quick to reply. Having been prepped by
Brooke, Montgomery then dined with Churchill on the 20th and the
following day called on Eisenhower to cancel Anvil once and for all:

> As a result of what he told me about the situation in Italy it is my
> definite opinion that all resources in the Mediterranean theatre
> should be put into the campaign in Italy. I further consider that we

should now make a definite decision to cancel Anvil; this will enable the commanders in the Mediterranean theatre to devote their whole attention to fighting the Germans in Italy – at present they have to keep Anvil in their minds, and plan for it, and this must detract from the success of the present battle in Italy.

If para 2 above is agreed, then all the craft now being kept for Anvil can be released at once for Overlord. The effect of this on Overlord will be tremendous.

To sum up: I recommend very strongly that we now throw the whole weight of our opinion into the scales against Anvil. Let us have two really good campaigns – one in Italy and one on Overlord.

To General Sir Henry Maitland Wilson, the British theatre commander in the Mediterranean, the American preoccupation with France's southern ports seemed to imply a strategy aimed at defeating Germany during the first half of 1945 at the cost of an opportunity of defeating her before the end of 1944.

Interestingly, as demonstrated in his war directives, Hitler saw the Italian front as the key, since holding on in Italy helped reduce Allied air attacks on his factories in central Europe and protected the vital raw materials of the Balkans. In contrast, southern France had no strategic value to him whatsoever. A withdrawal from there would surrender nothing of military or economic value and would not give the Allies access to airbases that were any nearer his war industries than they already possessed. His U-boat bases on the Bay of Biscay were no longer of any great utility and the disruption of the French railways had already curtailed what raw materials he obtained from France and Spain. The Battle of the Atlantic was all but won by the Allies, having climaxed during March–May 1943 with heavy U-boat losses. Subsequent German efforts launched in September 1943 to wrest back the initiative in the Atlantic failed to halt Operation Bolero, the Allies' huge build-up in Britain for Overlord, and resulted in further heavy losses. In terms of providing Hitler's first line of defence and preventing the opening of the Second Front, the failure of the U-boats to strangle the flow of troops and supplies from North America to Britain was a very significant blow to his war effort. By the end of the war the German Navy had sunk 3,500 merchant vessels and 175 warships with the loss of over 30,000 lives, at a cost of 783 U-boats and 28,000 crew.

After all the horse-trading over LST allocations for the Pacific in mid-February 1944 the Americans were able to remove Truk Island from their invasion list. Air power proved to be the key, not LSTs. At the beginning of February the Americans had secured Kwajalein Atoll. Admiral Chester Nimitz then eyed Eniwetok Atoll, which would complete the liberation of the Marshall Islands. As the Kwajalein operation had not required the 5th Amphibious Forces reserves, these were now available for Operation Catchpole.

First, though, Task Force 58, consisting of fleet carriers, battleships and cruisers, launched a devastating air attack on Truk. The Japanese lost 2 light cruisers, 4 destroyers, 2 submarines, 5 auxiliaries, 24 merchantmen and 250 aircraft, most of the latter caught on the ground. Never again would the Japanese use Truk as a major operating base. The carriers returned in April to finish their work, while Eniwetok was captured by 21 February.

Top-level meetings
Under pressure from Marshall, Brooke, Montgomery and Churchill, Eisenhower must surely have wished that Roosevelt had never raised the prospect of Anvil with Stalin. He had little choice but to convene another top-level conference about Anvil on 26 February, attended by Montgomery, Bedell Smith, Leigh-Mallory, Freddy de Guingand and Admiral Ramsay. The latter understandably needed an immediate decision, otherwise his finely laid naval plans for Overlord would become useless if Anvil was cancelled and its landing craft were suddenly to become available. In effect, with these additional craft the landing schedules for the follow-up troops could be brought forward by 24 hours, a factor that could be critical to the success of Overlord if the Germans launched swift and powerful counter-attacks. Montgomery made it clear he would only countenance leaving enough craft in the Mediterranean to lift one division.

Eisenhower was minded to call it a day, give in and abandon Anvil, but instead he dithered, as Harry Butcher noted:

Following Ike's representations to the British Chiefs of Staff as to the need for continued planning for Anvil, conclusions now have been agreed by the Combined Chiefs of Staff and approved by the President and the Prime Minister.

The Italian Fronts are to be given overriding priority of all the existing and future operations in the Mediterranean, but Anvil is to be planned with the hope of launching it shortly after Overlord. Another appraisal will be made 20 March.

As this action largely meets Ike's wishes, he is satisfied. He does not want to abandon Anvil unless absolutely necessary, despite the position previously taken by the British Chiefs of Staff, who favoured its abandonment in harmony with the views expressed by General Montgomery.

Montgomery and Ramsay were aghast, for all Eisenhower had done was put off for yet another month any firm decision on Anvil. As a personal concession to Monty, Eisenhower did offer to send a telegram to Marshall stating that in his opinion Anvil was impossible, but Bedell Smith put a stop to this for fear that it would look as though Eisenhower was pre-empting the 20 March feasibility assessment.

Smarting at this reversal, Monty tried to put a brave face on the situation, acknowledging that Eisenhower was caught between two masters. He recorded in his diary:

This is, at last, a firm statement. There has been a great deal of passing the ball backwards and forwards between London and Washington. Eisenhower has had great pressure from Washington, where opinion is very much in favour of Anvil. . . .

So it is very necessary that we should all try to save Eisenhower from reproaches from Washington, and save his face when he wants to come down hard on the side of what we want to do.

Ike was given just two days' respite from the matter while Montgomery went on an inspection tour of Canadian Army units and the London docks. In the afternoon of 28 February Monty turned up at Eisenhower's headquarters and urged him to cancel Anvil now rather than wait three weeks. To add to Eisenhower's woes, Alexander was now being difficult and refusing to release thirteen LSTs for Overlord, which he said he needed to supply the Anzio beachhead.

In fact, it was not until 20 March that Eisenhower officially came down in favour of cancelling Anvil, three months after Monty had first pleaded with him to favour Overlord over Anvil. It was agreed that a directive be prepared for General Wilson:

> A draft directive to the Supreme Allied Commander, Mediterranean, based on the assumption that the Anvil assault is impossible of execution was discussed.
>
> The Supreme Commander directed that the draft directive be changed in respect to the method for assisting Overlord to provide for maintenance of the highest possible tempo of offensive action, including the mounting of a positive threat against the South of France and the [Italian] Ligurian coast and provision for taking immediate advantage of Rankin conditions should they occur.

Rankin was a three point contingency plan for bringing the invasion of France forward should Germany suffer an economic/military collapse, or if the Germans either withdrew their troops from the occupied territories or surrendered during 1943/4. Implementing Rankin in 1943 would have been largely impossible, especially once the Allies had committed their amphibious resources to the invasions of Sicily and Italy. However, even by November 1943 the British Chiefs of Staff were still referring to Rankin, in the vain hope that the inevitable casualties incurred by Overlord could be avoided.

It was envisaged that Operation Rankin A could be launched against the Cotentin peninsula in January 1944 or the Normandy coast in April 1944, and would be supported by supplementary landings in the Pas-de-Calais and or in the south of France. By this stage it would have meant moving Overlord forward using all available resources. While the existence of Rankin was strategically prudent it was yet another factor impinging on the planning staffs' decisions over implementing Overlord and Anvil. Eisenhower's reference to it was largely wishful thinking.

On the afternoon of the 21st Eisenhower drafted a Top Secret personal message for Marshall, in which he cast doubt on Anvil:

> I will be asked to meet with the British Chiefs of Staff tomorrow on the final question of Anvil. I have been giving constant thought

to this subject together with the staff and several commanders during the past month. While I have no recent appreciation from General Wilson, yet I intend to present the following based on our own careful study and earnest conviction. . . .

2. It is now the firm opinion of the Supreme Commander that Anvil, as originally visualised, is no longer a possibility, either from the standpoint of time in which to make the necessary preparations, or in probable availability of fresh and effective troops at the required date. . . .

He went on to point out that the landing ships allocated to Overlord were barely sufficient, even assuming they arrived on time, serviceability rates were maintained and that none were lost to enemy action. There was simply no margin and the operation was in fact short of the minimum number of LSTs by four vessels. He continued:

4. The fact has been constantly realised, and the Supreme Commander has been willing to accept the situation only so long as he felt reasonably sure of a strong and simultaneous Anvil. With the cancellation of a simultaneous Anvil he considers it essential to strengthen Overlord and also to increase flexibility of the build-up during the critical days. . . .

5. The Supreme Commander, accordingly, is of the opinion that all serviceable landing ships and craft presently allocated to the Mediterranean and above those necessary to furnish ship-to-shore lift for one division should be reallocated to Overlord.

In an effort to placate Marshall, Eisenhower added:

6. Although convinced that Anvil as at present conceived is no longer possible, the Supreme Commander feels that the abandonment of this project must not lessen our intention of operating offensively in the Mediterranean, initially in Italy and extending from there into France as rapidly as we can. He believes that the forces in the Mediterranean must constantly look for every expedient, including threat and feint, to contain the maximum possible enemy forces in that region.

However, there could be no hiding the blow that Churchill and Montgomery had been so vigorously lobbying for:

7. The Supreme Commander accordingly recommends:
   a. That the decision be made to abandon Anvil in its present conception of a two-division assault building up to ten divisions, and that a directive for operations in lieu thereof, similar to the attached, be transmitted to the Supreme Allied Commander in the Mediterranean Theatre.
   b. That there be withdrawn from the Mediterranean the following craft and ships for reallocation to Operation Overlord: twenty-six LCT, forty LCI(L), one LSH (the Bulolo), one LSE, one LSD. The above ships and craft to arrive in the UK by 30 April.

Marshall did not take what was going on in London lightly. Eisenhower called another Chiefs meeting on 27 March, involving Brooke, Cunningham, Ismay, Portal, Ramsay and Bedell Smith, to discuss the US Chiefs' proposals for operations in the Mediterranean. Before them was a new target date for Anvil set for 10 July.

The US Chiefs were so concerned about keeping Anvil alive they were prepared to withdraw landing craft from the Pacific. Eisenhower as usual sought to please everyone, though he emphasised that to his way of thinking a two-divisional assault in July 'would contribute substantially to the success of Overlord'.

Bedell Smith tried to act as peacekeeper, reminding everyone that Anvil was not the Second Front in itself but was intended as a diversionary operation in support of Overlord. He also pointed out that the French should take responsibility for this operation under the command of General Giraud. Lieutenant-Commander J.E. Reid, the meeting secretary, recorded Bedell Smith's thinking:

If we accept the proposed allocation of additional landing craft, it would be possible to launch a two-divisional assault with French troops. He estimated that there are sufficient French divisions in the Mediterranean to continue the follow-up until the middle of August, by which time Overlord should be firmly established. An American division could be added to lend support. The net result would be that by taking full advantage of utilising all available French forces for the Anvil operation, it would be possible to achieve an effective diversionary assistance to Overlord and at the same time other forces available for the Mediterranean could be employed to maintain a strong position in Italy.

This in principle was a good idea; nonetheless everyone knew that the French Army was not in a position to be able to spearhead a seaborne assault. It simply did not have the experience or indeed the equipment, regardless of what de Gaulle or de Lattre might say about French honour.

Understandably, the British were not happy. Brooke 'was not prepared to accept firm commitments at this time regarding the precise location of a diversionary attack to be made four months hence'. Reid's minutes also recorded Brooke's displeasure over what he saw as the Americans prioritising the Pacific campaign over Europe:

Sir Alan Brooke then drew attention to the point that if our basic strategy, which was to defeat Germany first, had been adhered to, the landing craft required for Anvil would now be available and they would not be in the Pacific, as was the case. He considered that the failure to adhere strictly to the basic strategy had already resulted in a setback of approximately six months in the defeat of Germany. Furthermore, he said the lack of sufficient landing craft and other resources in the Mediterranean resulted in our failure to take full advantage of the fall of Italy.

This conveniently overlooked the fact that the Allies had become embroiled on the Italian mainland in the first place at the behest of the British and Churchill's indirect strategy. Brooke agreed that the key objective in the Mediterranean was to draw as many German troops away from Overlord as possible, and he felt that the capture of Rome would best achieve this. He added that launching Anvil would need at least ten divisions and that stripping the Mediterranean could only leave the Allies on the defensive both there and, inevitably, in the south of France.

Air Chief Marshal Sir Charles Portal supported Brooke, feeling they should not commit themselves to the US Chiefs' proposals. He advised that by 10 July opportunities might have arisen that would allow the deployment of their forces to far greater advantage than envisaged by Anvil. Eisenhower defended Marshall's corner, replying that he had been 'pleading' for the past two years to give the war effort against Germany priority. In addition, he pointed out that it was Marshall who had secured Pacific resources for use in the Mediterranean. Also Roosevelt could not ignore public opinion nor indeed Congress, where there was a groundswell of opinion for an all-out offensive in the Pacific.

Eisenhower was not convinced that an offensive to capture Rome was a good Anvil substitute in terms of containing German forces. He sought to find a reply that would be acceptable to both the British and the US Chiefs of Staff. It was clear to him that the main concern of the US Chiefs was to gain assurances that preparations for Anvil would continue, though they were not so interested in exactly where the diversion was to be directed. Essentially he was still dragging his feet by suggesting that nothing should be allowed to harm General Wilson's ability to contain the maximum German forces in Italy; they would get the sea lift in place by 10 July, but the point of attack could be settled later. Ultimately the decision would rest with the Combined Chiefs of Staff.

During the meeting the British still pressed for Italy to be given priority:

> Sir Andrew Cunningham inquired as to whether or not it would be in harmony with the US Chiefs of Staff's proposals, if the Supreme Commander, at a later date, should recommend that the capture of Rome was the best means of containing the maximum number of German forces. He wondered whether or not that would constitute the breaking of our engagements.

General Smith did not help matters by stating he thought the US Joint Chiefs of Staff would consider it a breach of commitment if an attack were made south of Pisa, but that an attack to the north might not be considered as such.

To further irritate Marshall, the following day the British Chiefs of Staff signalled him to highlight how the difficulties in Italy were presenting problems in timetabling Anvil, or indeed committing to it at all. Marshall felt General Alexander was dragging his heels and disagreed with his assessment that an operation to link the front and the bridgehead could not be mounted until 14 May. To Marshall's way of thinking Alexander was looking to hold on to his resources for subsequent operations. As far as he was concerned, General Wilson must be ordered to commence preparations for Anvil.

Nor did Eisenhower's 'carefully worded answer to the US Joint Chiefs of Staff's proposals' have the desired effect. General Marshall would have nothing less than a firm commitment to Anvil: 'We cannot accept a diversion of landing craft from the Pacific operations unless it is the firm intention of the Combined Chiefs of Staff now to mount Anvil on a two-division basis, target date, 10 July, in time to support Overlord.'

As far as Marshall was concerned, if the British Chiefs of Staff got their way and postponed the order to General Wilson to get the ball rolling, then the initiative would pass to the Germans. Quite rightly, he would not provide the resources if a firm plan did not exist and everyone had signed up to it. Marshall concluded:

> Our view is that there should be no delay in providing the Allied
> Commander-in-Chief, Mediterranean, with a firm directive. . . .
> In this directive, the three US fighter groups remain in the
> Mediterranean and we have allowed for the British Chiefs of Staff
> to make adjustments in the matter of total LSTs withdrawn from
> the Mediterranean to support Overlord.

Matters came to a head in early April and the Americans for the first time offered to transfer assault craft from the Pacific, promising to place 26 tank landing ships and 40 landing craft at Wilson's disposal if the British would commit themselves to Anvil. The British reluctantly agreed to 10 July, though insisted that the Combined Chiefs of Staff be allowed to veto the operation if the situation changed in Italy.

Brooke recorded the seemingly unending wrangling:

> 17 April. Arrived back early in the office to find myself swamped
> with telegrams. After COS lunch with PM at 10 Downing Street;
> Eisenhower, Bedell Smith and Alexander were there. The conver-
> sation at once again turned to the Mediterranean strategy and to
> the American Chiefs of Staff's failure to agree with us as to the

necessity to press on with operations in Italy without impairing the prospect by preparations for an operation against southern France. Eisenhower produced all the arguments we heard the other day . . .

The Combined Chiefs of Staff finally issued their directive to General Wilson two days later. The objective of Anvil was 'to give the greatest possible assistance to Overlord by destroying or containing the maximum number of German formations in the Mediterranean'. General Brooke recorded on a sour note:

19 April. At last all our troubles about Anvil are over. We have got the Americans to agree, but have lost the additional landing craft they were prepared to provide. History will never forgive them for bargaining equipment against strategy and for trying to blackmail us into agreeing with them by holding the pistol of withdrawing craft at our heads . . .

Chapter Four

Ike says 'No' to Churchill

In Italy on the night of 11/12 May 1944 the US 5th and British 8th Armies launched their long-awaited spring offensive against the German defences known as the Gustav Line along the Sangro river. Thwarted in their repeated attempts to break through at Cassino in February, March and April, the Allies were relieved when the Germans abandoned Monte Cassino after a week of heavy fighting by Polish forces, and the French Expeditionary Corps and US II Corps succeeded in breaking the Gustav Line by the 15th.

The French took credit for Operation Diadem as this was an opportunity for their military honour to be restored. The French Expeditionary Corps started to arrive in Italy in November 1943 and by May 1944 was fully up to strength. The French colonial troops were quite distinctive, particularly the Moroccan *goumiers* in their striped *djellebah* that formed part of their uniform and American M1917A pattern helmets. The *goumiers* were originally irregular forces, nominally raised to serve the Moroccan Sultan, but now serving with the French as regular soldiers. The Algerians tended to be kitted out with a mixture of French and American uniforms.

The Moroccans first really made their presence felt in Italy, when General André Dody's division tipped the balance during Operation Raincoat in mid-December 1943. His men helped push the Germans back to the Gustav Line, but overall the offensive failed to put the Allies in a strong position to support the forthcoming Anzio landings.

Diadem was launched in May 1944 and de Gaulle arrived to lend General Juin his support. While the US 5th Army suggested advancing along the Ausente valley, it was Juin who proposed attacking through the mountains while making no attempt to outflank Aurunci. To do this it was necessary to break out of the Gargliano bridgehead so the French

56

could take Monte Majo and the Ausonia defile. General Clark, impressed by Juin's boldness, agreed.

The 2nd Moroccan Infantry Division under General Dody was given the task of taking Majo and its three spurs. On the right was Brosset's 1st Free French Division and on the left de Monsabert's 3rd Algerian Infantry Division, which was tasked with securing Castleforte to open up the Ausente. Afterwards the Mountain Corps comprising General Savez's 4th Moroccan Mountain Division and General Guillame's Group of Moroccan Tabors could then push to the Aurunci massif.

On 13 May, in the face of stiff German resistance, the Moroccans succeeded in breaching the Gustav Line at Monte Majo, one of its deepest (though most weakly defended) points. Ausonia was captured two days later. The fall of Majo unhinged the XIV Panzer Corps' left wing, greatly contributing to the Allies' success.

Then II Corps pushed north towards Terracina, which fell on 23–24 May, and on towards the Anzio beachhead against rapidly crumbling resistance as the Germans began withdrawing north-east towards Rome. On the 23rd the US VI Corps broke out from Anzio and two days later linked up with the II Corps troops. In a surprising move, considering how they normally treated occupied cities, the Germans declared Rome an open city and US forces took possession of it on 4 June.

In the Vatican at the time was 15-year-old Haroldino Tittmann, who recorded in his diary:

> Today we did nothing except watch the Germans retreat. I got the best view of all, as I had gone into the nuns' garden, which over-looks the road on which the Germans were retreating . . . They were extensively using horses to draw carriages, wagons and every kind of contraption you could think of. Some were even on bi-cycles. They had stolen all Rome's horse-drawn cabs. They also used horses to pull their artillery. One felt rather sorry for them; they looked so young. . . . They looked terribly depressed.

President Roosevelt remarked on the success of this joint effort in Italy and proclaimed:

> It is also significant that Rome has been liberated by the armed forces of many nations. The American and British armies – who

bore the chief burdens of battle – found at their sides our own North American neighbours, the gallant Canadians. The fighting New Zealanders from the far South Pacific, the courageous French and the French Moroccans, the South Africans, the Poles and the east Indians – all of them fought with us on the bloody approaches to the city of Rome. . . .

Our victory comes at an excellent time, while our Allied forces are poised for another strike at western Europe – and while the armies of other Nazi soldiers nervously await our assault. And in the meantime our gallant Russian allies continue to make their power felt more and more.

A slightly sour note crept in as he added his thanks to those who would also be key players in the coming invasion of southern France:

No great effort like this can be a hundred per cent perfect, but the batting average is very, very high.

And so I extend the congratulations and thanks tonight of the American people to General Alexander, who has been in command of the whole of the Italian operation; to our General Clark and General Leese of the 5th and 8th Armies; to General Wilson, the Supreme Allied Commander of the Mediterranean theatre, [and] General Devers his American deputy; to [Lieutenant-] General Eaker; to Admirals Cunningham and Hewitt, and to all their brave officers and men.

However, the gloss of this victory was soon to be tarnished, as General Clark pleaded with Marshall when he came to the Italian capital that month for an invasion of the Balkans. As ever, Marshall was inflexible on the matter and Clark despairingly recorded in his diary: 'The Boche is defeated, disorganised and demoralised. Now is the time to exploit our success. Yet, in the middle of this success, I lose two corps head-quarters and seven divisions. It just doesn't make sense.'

Riviera or Po Valley
Operation Overlord, the long-anticipated invasion of Nazi-occupied northern France, commenced just two days after the fall of Rome. In total, 236 LSTs were committed to Overlord, along with 768 Landing

Craft Tank and 48 Landing Craft Tank (armoured). To bring ashore the thousands of motor vehicles there were 839 Landing Craft Vehicles and Personnel, 128 Landing Craft Mechanised (1) and 358 Landing Craft Mechanised (3). There were also 228 Landing Barge Vehicles (2) to support the landing operations.

By the end of D-Day, 6 June 1944, about 150,000 men had been put ashore and the Allies had occupied a front of some 50 km. Churchill broke the news to the House of Commons:

> I have also to announce to the House that during the night and the early hours of this morning the first of the series of landings in force upon the European continent has taken place. In this case the liberating assault fell on France. An immense armada of upwards of 4,000 ships, together with several thousand smaller craft, crossed the Channel.

He then added with a flourish, 'I cannot, of course, commit myself to any particular details.'

Roosevelt's intention was that France, once liberated, would be run by an American military administration, which was the last thing de Gaulle wanted. On returning to Britain just before D-Day, he became embroiled in bitter arguments with both Churchill and Eisenhower. At one point Churchill was on the verge of sending him back to Algiers, and by the time Overlord began no agreement had been reached over how the newly liberated territory in France was to be governed or by whom. De Gaulle finally came ashore in Normandy on 14 June, and once at Bayeux he ensured that the American military administration was stillborn. His FFI supporters moved quickly to take power in order to pre-empt the socialist and communist-dominated resistance groups.

General Wilson was ordered to continue his Italian offensive on 14 June as far as the Pisa-Rimini Line (known as the Gothic Line) and after that to prepare for a diversion of resources against southern or western France or the head of the Adriatic. Wilson met Generals Marshall and Arnold in Italy on the 17th and suggested that Alexander be given the resources to get through the Pisa-Rimini Line and on into the Po valley. Then, supported by an amphibious assault against the Istrian peninsula, he could exploit the Ljubljana Gap and push into the Hungarian plains beyond. Hitler would thus be forced to withdraw substantial troops

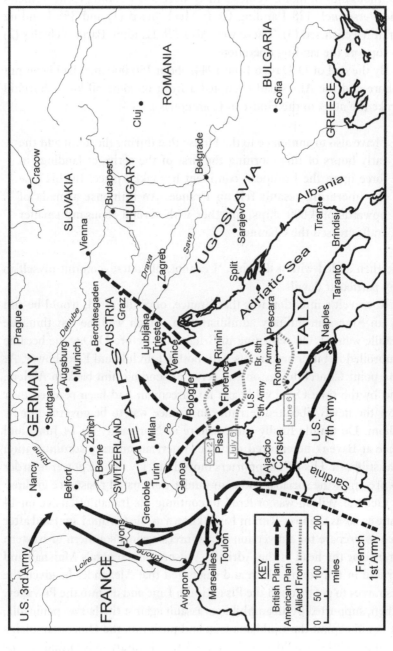

Competing British and American plans for the southern assault on Nazi Germany. (*Dennis Andrews*)

from France if Alexander's force threatened the Upper Danube and the strategic heart of Europe. Wilson argued that while the support this would give to Eisenhower would certainly be less direct, it would be more effective than Anvil.

Marshall responded that Eisenhower wanted Anvil because 'the need for an additional major port was more pressing . . . than the diversion of enemy troops from northern France'. There were, he added, 'some forty or fifty divisions in the United States ready for action', and these would be used 'only in France where they could be deployed more rapidly and on a broader front, and that none would be sent to the Mediterranean other than as a possible build-up for an attack on southern France'.

Marshall made it clear that whatever happened these troops would not be sent to south-eastern Europe. In effect, he was simply echoing the advice given to Roosevelt that the way to defeat Germany was 'to mount one big offensive and then slam 'em.'

Appreciating that the US Chiefs were clearly digging in their heels, General Wilson signalled the British Chiefs of Staff on the 19th, stressing the importance of creating a decisive threat to southern Germany before the end of the year. The current success in Italy was offering enticing strategic possibilities. In the last two weeks the Allies had pushed forward 160 km, but this momentum could not be maintained if seven divisions (a quarter of Alexander's land strength) were diverted to Anvil. Wilson also warned that a diversion of forces for Anvil would cause a break in offensive operations in the Mediterranean of at least six weeks, which would enable the Germans to establish themselves more strongly along the Gothic Line. Marshall was not impressed by such arguments, as he felt that once the Germans had been driven from their defences they could abandon the Po valley and withdraw into the Alps. He believed Alexander would be chasing thin air to no effect, but such reasoning was nonsensical in the light of the tenacious resistance the German Army had offered in Italy to date.

Indeed, the last thing Hitler wanted was Allied bombers operating from the Po valley and intensifying their strategic bombing campaign against his industries. Nor did he want the Allies forcing the head of the Adriatic and entering Yugoslavia where partisans were already holding down a dozen security divisions. He needed the Balkans' abundant raw materials and he did not want them exposed to the risk of Allied invasion. While Italy could serve as a shield for the Balkans, France was of much less value to his war effort now that the French railway system lay in tatters.

Wilson reasoned that if Alexander were given a free hand, he could reach the Po valley before Anvil was ever launched. Inadvertently Marshall then helped Hitler, for he and his colleagues were so dead set against operations in the Balkans that he decided to force the issue in favour of an invasion of southern France. To that end, once back in Washington Marshall sought the intervention of President Roosevelt.

Likewise, once the Allies' Normandy bridgehead was firmly established, de Gaulle's immediate concern was to ensure that Anvil was implemented. Although no date had been agreed, he was determined to make sure he was consulted and that French troops would play a major role. He flew to Algiers on 18 June and was informed that a breakthrough had been achieved in Italy and that General Juin's troops had distinguished themselves.

De Gaulle's only distraction was General Alexander, whose success in Italy was prompting him to call for a drive through the Brenner Pass to the Danube. This was sound strategic thinking and was in line with Churchill's vision; the only snag was that it would require Anvil's resources. De Gaulle flew to Rome and was partly swayed by Pope Pius XII, who expressed concern over future communist dominance of eastern and central Europe.

Nonetheless, Anvil remained a matter of honour for the French, and to regard southern France as a strategic irrelevance could only be seen as a national slur. De Gaulle stipulated to Alexander that French forces in Italy must be ready to depart from 25 July. He then flew to America to see Roosevelt on 6 July. Many expected their meeting to be a gruelling affair: the two men had first met at Anfa and it had not gone well, and since then they had been engaged in a ceaseless political duel. Quite remarkably, de Gaulle – a two-star general with few troops and head of a provisional government with no country, no capital and no constitution – retained the upper hand.

Momentum for Overlord could not be sustained as the weather began to deteriorate and on 19 June a storm blew up that halted all shipping in the Channel for three days. It was so severe that the two artificial concrete Mulberry harbours had begun to disintegrate by 21 June, and the one off Omaha beach was written off and cannibalised to repair the

British one at Arromanches. The build-up virtually ground to a halt, delaying 20,000 vehicles and 140,000 tons of stores, and a breathing space was thereby granted to the Germans.

By late June Eisenhower was beginning to fret as Montgomery's offensive plans in Normandy were repeatedly postponed due to the weather; his worries were exacerbated by the fact that on 14 June Anvil had reared its ugly head again as the Combined Chiefs asked him to reconsider launching it. On the 22nd Lieutenant-General J.H. Gammell, Wilson's Chief of Staff, came up from the Mediterranean to brief Eisenhower. Gammell found him in an agitated state, insisting that he wanted Anvil launched immediately regardless of the impact it would have on the Allied offensive in Italy and despite the fact that it would not provide instant dividends for Montgomery.

Eisenhower's agitation may have been caused at least in part by the fact that on that date, 22 June 1944, Stalin had upheld his promise made at Tehran and launched Operation Bagration, which was designed to liberate Minsk and drive the German Army out of Byelorussia. The near-total annihilation of Army Group Centre in the space of just under two weeks cost Hitler 300,000 dead, 250,000 wounded and about 120,000 captured. Only about 20,000 troops from Army Group Centre escaped unscathed. In addition, Hitler's forces lost 2,000 panzers and 57,000 other vehicles. Stalin's losses were 60,000 killed, 110,000 wounded and about 8,000 missing, as well as 2,957 tanks, 2,447 artillery pieces and 822 aircraft destroyed.

For Hitler, Bagration was a vastly more serious blow than the catastrophe at Stalingrad or the assault in Normandy. The destruction of Army Group Centre was a bigger and swifter disaster than the loss of Army Group B's 7th Army and 5th Panzer Army in mid-August 1944 at Falaise. Although overall total German losses in France were comparable to those in Byelorussia, the former occurred over a two and a half month period, not in a matter of weeks. Stalin's D-Day was a formidable achievement.

In India, despite Rangoon's vulnerability to British seaborne attack, the Japanese were preoccupied with their overland offensive into India. This was directed against both Imphal and Kohima, the capture of which would have forestalled General Slim's offensive into Burma. The Japanese supply lines, though, could not cope with such a major undertaking and the Japanese Army suffered a defeat from which it could never recover in that theatre of operations. By 22 June Slim had halted the four-month U-Go offensive, having killed, wounded or captured 53,500 Japanese troops from an original force of 85,000. Allied casualties were 16,700, about a quarter of them lost in the bitter fighting at Kohima. Nevertheless the Japanese were not broken and fell back to the Chindwin river, with the Allies conducting an indifferent pursuit.

'Wreck one great campaign'

Back in Normandy, Montgomery was never the easiest of personalities to deal with, but the row over Anvil tested Eisenhower's patience with him to breaking point. Major-General Simpson, Director of Military Operations at the War Office, noted Ike's telegram of 26 June sent to the Combined Chiefs of Staff: 'I attach such importance to the early launching of Anvil that I am prepared to do my utmost to ensure its success. Admiral Ramsey and General Montgomery share my conviction with regards to the importance of Anvil.'

That of course was completely untrue. Monty was furious and signalled Brooke on 1 July: 'Want to make it quite clear that I have had no discussion with him about Anvil and do NOT know what his views are.' He had not seen Eisenhower for two weeks, though he was due at Monty's headquarters on 2 July and Monty wanted to know if he should discuss it. In the event it mattered little, as Brooke recorded in his diary that day: 'COS met at 10.30am to discuss PM's proposed wire to President [Roosevelt] deciding to accept their decision to do Anvil. At 11am we met the PM and told him of the minor amendments which were wanted. He was in a good mood and they all went through easily.'

In fact Brooke knew that Churchill had already given in to Eisenhower over the telephone that day and counselled Monty not to raise the matter, as it would do more harm than good. Ike finally prevailed over his subordinate:

> Although in the planning days of early 1944 Montgomery had advocated the complete abandonment of the southern operation in order to secure more landing craft for Overlord, he now, in early August, agreed with me that the attack should go in as planned.

Churchill would not roll over so easily. In London Eisenhower soon detected Churchill's resistance to an invasion of mainland France:

It quickly became obvious that the Prime Minister was not over-sold on its value, at least in the early spring of 1944. He felt that it would be far better for the Western Allies to wait for more significant signs of a German collapse. Sometimes, in his contemplation of the possibilities before us, he spoke as if he were addressing a multitude. He would say, 'When I think of the beaches of Normandy choked with the flower of American and British youth, and when, in my mind's eye, I see the tides running red with their blood, I have my doubts . . . I have my doubts.'

Churchill had been working himself into the ground. General Brooke remarked of him on 7 May: 'He said that he could always sleep well, eat well and especially drink well, but that he no longer jumped out of bed the way he used to, and felt as if he would be quite content to spend the whole day in bed. I have never yet heard him admit that he was beginning to fail.'

Even on the eve of Overlord, Churchill did everything in his power to stop the invasion going ahead. He foresaw the war becoming a horrible slog, which it did in Normandy, but he greatly underestimated the Red Army, which, completely rejuvenated after its ghastly defeats of 1941 and 1942, was now making major inroads into German-occupied territories, with its eye firmly set on eastern Europe.

On the very day before D-Day Churchill called for an assault on the French Atlantic coast from Bordeaux to St Nazaire, employing up to fourteen assault divisions, with six of them withdrawn from Italy. Despite his undeniable skills as a grand strategist, Churchill clearly failed to appreciate – or perhaps simply ignored – the massive logistical effort required for modern warfare, as he felt that this second assault could be conducted within a few weeks of Overlord.

When the British Chiefs of Staff prevailed upon him not to raise this idea with Roosevelt, he reverted to his desire for victory in Italy with the capture of Trieste, a push through the Alps and the misnamed Ljubljana Gap, and the seizure of Prague and Vienna. Again Churchill was wilfully dismissing or simply optimistically ignoring the realities of the situation on the ground in Italy. It had taken Allied forces nearly a year to get to Rome, and the weather and the terrain would continue to limit their advance. General Brooke tried to point this out to Churchill, but the Prime Minister would not be swayed:

We had a long evening of it listening to Winston's strategic arguments . . . I pointed out that, even on Alex's [General Alexander]
optimistic reckoning, the advance beyond the Pisa-Rimini Line
would not start till after September; namely we should embark on
a campaign through the Alps in winter. It was hard to make him
realise that, if we took the season of the year and the topography
of the country in league against us, we should have three enemies
instead of one. We were kept up till close to 1am and accomplished
nothing.

It mattered little, as the Americans were having none of it. Eisenhower
put it bluntly to Churchill on 23 June: 'France is the decisive theatre.
The decision was taken long ago by the Combined Chiefs of Staff. In
my view, the resources of Great Britain and the US will not permit us
to maintain two major theatres in the European war, each with decisive
missions.'

In reality, Eisenhower really meant American resources, which he
was not prepared to divert to support Churchill's obsession with
breaking through in Italy. There was to be no more dithering;
Eisenhower was committed to a course of action and would not be
distracted. On the 24th the American Joint Chiefs of Staff issued orders
to the Chiefs of Staff and the British commander in the Mediterranean,
General Wilson, to release forces for Anvil. Churchill made the British
Chiefs of Staff reply that this was unacceptable, but the stony response
from the Joint Chiefs was that the subject was no longer open to debate.

Churchill now stepped up his campaign to derail Anvil and cabled
President Roosevelt, pleading: 'Let's not wreck one great campaign for
the sake of another. Both can be won.' But Roosevelt was adamant, and
on 29 June he cabled back: 'In view of the Soviet-British-American
agreement, reached at Tehran, I cannot agree without Stalin's approval
to the use of force or equipment elsewhere.' This, of course, was not
strictly true, but it meant that Churchill was essentially whistling in the
wind, though he refused to accept this to the last.

Roosevelt was a wily political player and at the end of June he pointed
out to Churchill that he would never weather any setbacks in Normandy
if it were known he had committed substantial forces to the Balkans
which could have assisted in the fighting in France. Churchill was

aghast and telegraphed back immediately, pointing out that at the Tehran conference:

> You emphasised to me the possibilities of a move eastwards when Italy was conquered, and specifically mentioned Istria. No one involved in these discussions has ever thought of moving armies into the Balkans; but Istria and Trieste in Italy are strategic and political positions, which you saw yourself very clearly might exercise profound and widespread reactions, especially now after the Russian advances.

Possibly out of a sense of fair play, or in an effort to find a casting vote, Roosevelt suggested raising the matter with Stalin. The British Prime Minister saw this as a pointless exercise, knowing full well that the Soviet leader would prefer the British and American armies to be tied up in France, leaving eastern, central and southern Europe to the Red Army.

Always a man of action, Churchill was all for seeing Roosevelt in person to persuade him of the merits of the Adriatic operation. Instructions were issued on 30 June for Churchill's personal flying boat and Lancaster bomber to be put on standby for a flight to Washington. He telegraphed Roosevelt on 1 July:

> What can I do, Mr President, when your Chiefs of Staff insist on casting aside our Italian offensive campaign, with all its dazzling possibilities, relieving Hitler of all his anxieties in the Po basin (*vide* Boniface), and when we are to see the integral life of this campaign drained off into the Rhône valley in the belief that it will in several months carry effective help to Eisenhower so far away in the north?

Churchill could not help adding, 'I am sure that if we could have met, as I so frequently proposed, we should have reached a happy agreement.'

On 2 July General Slim and Air Marshal Sir John Baldwin, Commander of the 3rd Tactical Air Force, met with Admiral Lord Louis Mountbatten, Supreme Commander in South-East Asia, to discuss operations after the victory at Imphal. The paucity of landing craft in the area again reared its ugly head. Among the options was Plan Z, the capture of Rangoon by an amphibious assault. Slim was of the view that this was 'strategically most attractive, but I doubted if we could get in time either the equipment or forces that would be required for an amphibious attack on a defended Rangoon. I thought our "Operation SOB" [Sea or Bust] would get us there at least as quickly.' He was right, for the resources for an amphibious attack would not be in place until 1945.

Churchill, now preoccupied with the fighting in Normandy, the menace of Hitler's V-2 flying bombs and the Red Army's sweeping advances, which had taken its troops into Poland, flew to Cherbourg on 20 July. He toured the Normandy battlefield and visited Montgomery. In the meantime, at the end of June General Wilson withdrew the bulk of the American units assigned to Anvil from the front lines in Italy, as well as the four French divisions, but all were exhausted and in need of rest and recuperation. Churchill was conscious that the Allied forces in Italy had already lost seven divisions (four American and three British), which were sent back to Britain for the cross-Channel assault, and the loss of a further seven for Anvil seemed the final straw. He feared that any further weakening of the Allied forces in Italy would render them unable to destroy the German armies there.

Half-way round the world the Americans launched an amphibious assault against Guam, the largest of the Marianas Islands, on 21 July. It took until 11 August to subdue the Japanese defenders; a month later they set about Peleliu. It would take a month of bitter fighting to secure this island. In total 50 per cent of all LST losses would occur in the Pacific, illustrating the intensity of the amphibious operations in that part of the world.

Driven to distraction

Throughout July Churchill bombarded Eisenhower with cables, driving the Allied Supreme Commander to distraction. In mid-July he drafted a petulant message to Roosevelt: 'This obviously cannot continue, and, with the greatest of respect, I must request a further and formal discussion upon the matter . . . We are entitled to press for better and more equal treatment. We have as many troops and forces on the whole in Europe, including both theatres, as you have yet brought into action.' He then went on to threaten to break up the Combined Chiefs of Staff structure and joint commands in the field. Luckily, Foreign Secretary Anthony Eden persuaded him not to send it.

Eisenhower recalled: 'This argument, beginning almost coincidentally with the break-through [in Normandy] in late July, lasted throughout the first ten days of August.' Even as late as the week before the landings Churchill sought to bully Eisenhower into getting his own way.

By early August Brooke, unlike Churchill, was ready to call it a day and acquiesce over American demands for Operation Dragoon (the name had been officially changed from Anvil on the 1st). He knew that the unending squabbling over the diverting of resources from Italy to southern France would ultimately prove to be counter-productive, and was sensible enough to appreciate that the campaign in Italy was a means to an end and not an end in itself. It dissipated Hitler's ability to strike back in northern France and in White Russia. The fact that the US Chiefs of Staff had opted to withhold naval power in favour of the Pacific, thereby stymieing attacks on Italy's exposed coastline and then by thwarting Alexander's victorious advance meant it would be unreasonable to view Italy as a decisive theatre of operations. He wrote to General Wilson on 2 August saying as much:

> It was a great pity that we were defeated over Anvil in the end: Alex's talk about his advance to Vienna killed all our arguments dead. It's a pity because I do not see Alex advancing on Vienna this year unless he does it in the face of a crumbling Germany and in that case he has ample forces for the task and greater than he will be able to administer over snow-covered mountain passes. However, I do not feel that Anvil can do much harm at this stage of the war, and it may well prove of some use in introducing French forces to reinforce the Maquis.

Brooke would later regret this, but he knew that General Alexander's performance had helped persuade Eisenhower and others that the advance in Italy should effectively be put on hold.

Churchill lunched with Eisenhower at his headquarters near Portsmouth on 5 August. With the Breton ports now within their grasp, Churchill argued that the capture of Marseilles was unnecessary, as the fresh divisions from America would now be able to come via Brittany.

This meant that those forces earmarked for Dragoon would be better employed in Italy and the Balkans. Eisenhower was not swayed, insisting that 'the maintenance and administrative position would never be equal to the final conquest of Germany until we have secured Antwerp in the north and Marseilles or equivalent port facilities on our right'. He also pointed out that the distance from Brest to Metz was greater than that from Marseilles to Metz.

Their relationship became particularly acrimonious when Churchill pitched up at Eisenhower's Normandy headquarters, codenamed Shellburst, near the village of Tournières, 20 km south-west of Bayeux, on 7 August. The Prime Minister still wanted Ike to shift Dragoon to Brittany or even the Channel ports, arguing fiercely that this would pile the pressure on the Germans in northern France. In reality, there was a lack of available ports as the German garrisons resolutely clung on to those they still held.

American troops arrived outside the well-defended Breton ports of Brest and Lorient on 6 and 7 August respectively. The German forces in Brest would hold out until mid-September, while the garrisons in Lorient and St Nazaire did not capitulate until the end of the war. This mattered little, as by August Le Havre and Antwerp held much greater allure for the Allies.

As Captain Harry C. Butcher recalled scathingly, it was not long before Churchill turned to his favourite diversionary operation during the meeting on the 7th:

> The Prime Minister had already opened the conference at lunch, telling us in phrases which only he can use so easily that history would show that Ike would miss a great opportunity if he didn't have Dragoon, formerly Anvil, shifted from the scheduled amphibious attack in the Toulon area to the ports in Brittany, notably Brest, Lorient and Saint-Nazaire, or indeed through the Channel ports where he assumed they could walk in like tourists. He had not given much thought to the probable demolitions to these harbours on the southern coast or to the great demand already made on Cherbourg or any other Channel ports we may capture. Such landings would quickly give the now rapidly travelling right flank of the Allied Armies a stronger force with which to sweep to France, in the view of Mr Churchill.

The arguments went on for some six hours, and this exchange clearly took its toll on Ike, as Butcher remembered:

> Ike said no, continued saying no all afternoon, and ended saying no in every form of the English language at his command. . . . Ike argued so long and patiently that he was practically limp when the PM departed and observed that although he had said no in every language, the Prime Minister, undoubtedly, would return to the subject in two or three days and simply regard[s] the issue [as] unsettled.

Meanwhile, the British Chiefs of Staff cabled General Wilson in the Mediterranean to alert him to the possibility of a quick change of plan for Dragoon, awaiting approval by the Combined Chiefs. By this stage, though, any change of plan was out of the question: if the LSTs and LCTs were to depart by 10 August for an attack on the 15th, there could be no meddling with the schedules.

Even Wilson pointed out that any build-up via Brittany would be slower than one via the Toulon area. 'Thus the PM also was rebuffed by his British Allied Commander,' concluded Butcher.

Eisenhower would have to endure more of the same when he called on the British Prime Minister at 10 Downing Street. Churchill remained unbending in his opposition to Dragoon when he met Ike on the 10th, as Harry Butcher again recalled:

> The PM was still a bit pouty over Anvil, favouring diversion into Brittany, despite our absence of satisfactory ports. So Ike went to 10 Downing Street to have a further talk with him. The Combined Chiefs of Staff have supported Ike completely. But now the PM was bemoaning the future of Alexander's campaign in Italy.

Churchill now played his ultimate card: with tears rolling down his cheeks, he threatened to resign if the Americans persisted with Dragoon; he said he might go to the King and lay down his mantle of high office. He also accused America of bullying Britain. Eisenhower was baffled by Churchill's unrelenting opposition to Anvil, to the extent he would endanger the alliance. He was also beginning to tire of the constant bullying by the pugnacious British politician.

The ever-present Butcher witnessed at first hand the problems that Churchill's attitude was causing:

> Ike has been increasingly concerned about the PM's attitude regarding Anvil and, above all, the feeling that the questioning and apparent dissension might cause a rift in the unity of the Allies at a time when success is almost in our grasp. The PM is upset over Ike's insistence for the landings in southern France, still set for 15 August. Mr Churchill knows that the American Chiefs – Marshall, King and Arnold – defer all questions in the European Theatre to General Ike. Consequently, the Prime Minister unlooses on Ike all his art of persuasion.

It was clear that Eisenhower was sick of it, but he was too diplomatic to say so; besides, everyone had better things to think of as the hard-fought Normandy battles were now coming to fruition around Falaise. Ike, although pushed to the brink of despair by his recalcitrant ally, would not budge; he was committed to making the Germans fight on as many fronts as possible. He pointed out that America had acceded to Britain's desire to invade North Africa first, thereby pushing the invasion of northern France back from the spring of 1943 to June 1944. The fall of Rome in June and the success of Operation Cobra in Normandy in July 1944 had finally convinced Eisenhower to give the green light to the secondary invasion.

Privately Eisenhower must have been very rattled that his decision to implement Dragoon could have brought down the British government. Indeed, he was clearly shaken by his encounters with Churchill and wrote to him:

> To say that I was disturbed by our conference on Wednesday does not nearly express the depth of my distress over your interpretation of the recent decision affecting the Mediterranean theatre. I do not, for one moment, believe that there is any desire on the part of any responsible person in the American war machine to disregard British views, or cold-bloodedly to leave Britain holding an empty bag in any of our joint undertakings . . . I am sorry that you seem to feel we use our great actual or potential strength as a bludgeon in conference.

Despite Churchill's antics, Eisenhower still held the British leader in high regard, affectionately describing him as 'a cantankerous yet adorable father'. Churchill, wily old politician that he was, also knew that despite his brinkmanship this was the high water mark of Britain's dominance of the alliance. Previously British and American Chiefs of Staff rarely disagreed on major issues, but from now on they would rarely see eye to eye and with Britain increasingly the junior partner it would rarely prevail.

While Overlord ultimately succeeded in defeating Army Group B, it failed to provide usable ports as quickly as the Allies had hoped. Eisenhower therefore convinced himself that he must have Marseilles, which is bigger than most of the Breton ports and all of the channel ports except Antwerp. Marseilles also had the advantage of being about 150km nearer to the German frontier than, say, Cherbourg. It could offer an entry point to those forces still in America and unable to enter Europe via the channel ports; the only potential alternative was Bordeaux and that would have meant diverting forces from Normandy.

Eisenhower also liked the idea of stretching the German Army from the North Sea to Switzerland. It seemed to him that Dragoon would also make better use of those American forces currently stuck in a slogging match in Italy and bring the French Army, re-equipped by America, back into the field. Ike and Marshall had won the day and Anvil now became Dragoon, employing the troops of General Alexander Patch's US 7th Army from Italy and General Jean de Lattre de Tassigny's French II Corps, his units having been built up in North Africa following the invasion there. The landings were scheduled for 15 August, ten weeks after D-Day. There would be no turning back.

Chapter Five

The Second Front –
Blaskowitz's Lost Divisions

The forces of the German commander in the west, Field Marshal Gerd von Rundstedt, Oberbefelshaber West (OB West), were divided into two army groups. In the south was General Johannes Blaskowitz's Army Group G with its headquarters in Toulouse; this group, totalling just seventeen divisions, consisted of General Kurt von der Chevallerie's 1st and General Friedrich Wiese's 19th Armies, stationed on the Biscay and Riviera coasts respectively. Wiese himself was based at Avignon, north-west of Marseilles.

Blaskowitz's Army Group G

General Blaskowitz was an experienced soldier with an unenviable task ahead of him. Born in 1883, he had commanded the German 8th Army during the invasion of Poland; however, his lacklustre performance meant he was the only army commander not elevated to the rank of field marshal at the end of the campaign. His appointment as Commander-in-Chief East lasted all of six months after his opposition to SS activities saw him replaced in mid-May 1940. However, he bounced back to command the 9th Army during the invasion of France, becoming Military Governor of northern France. In October he took over the 1st Army, which he controlled until May 1944, when he was appointed to command Army Group G. Blaskowitz first met his new staff on 16 May.

Blaskowitz found that his key armoured formations were Chevallerie's 11th Panzer and 17th SS Panzergrenadier Divisions, and Wiese's 2nd SS *Das Reich* and 9th Panzer Divisions. The latter, under Generalleutnant Erwin Jolasse, was desperately in need of a refit and rest; in March that year it had been sent to southern France, where it absorbed the 155th Reserve Panzer Division. Blaskowitz also discovered

74

that there were in fact only four infantry divisions of any note in the whole of southern France (the 708th, 242nd, 244th and 338th), as the rest were refitting or reforming and evidently substandard.

Although the 11th Panzer Division was nominally part of Wiese's 19th Army, it actually came under Hitler's direct command. A similar arrangement for the panzer divisions in Normandy had greatly hampered their timely intervention on D-Day. To make matters worse, not only was the 11th Panzer Division beyond Wiese's direct control, it was also based in the Carcassone-Albi area, some 240 km from Avignon and even further from the Marseilles-Toulon-Provence area.

The 11th Panzer Division was created in August 1940 under the command of General Ludwig Crüwell, and saw action during the Balkans campaign. It was then committed to the southern sector of the Eastern Front from June to October 1941, after which it was sent to the central sector, where it remained until June 1942 and then returned south. Generalleutnant Wend von Wietersheim assumed command in mid-August 1943. The division fought at Belgorod, Kursk and Krivoj Rog, and suffered significant casualties when it was encircled at Kresun, south of Kiev. The exhausted division was then transferred to France for refitting in June 1944, where it absorbed the 273rd Reserve Panzer Division. The latter was commanded by General Hellmuth von der Chevallerie from mid-November 1943 to 9 May 1944.

In the north, Field Marshal Erwin Rommel's vastly stronger Army Group B comprised General Friedrich Dollmann's 7th Army, consisting of sixteen divisions stationed in north-western France, and General Hans von Salmuth's 15th Army, consisting of twenty-five divisions stationed in Belgium and north-eastern France.

Rundstedt expected the Allies to invade the Pas de Calais, as this would offer the attacking force the shortest crossing-point of the English Channel, and it was just four days' march from the vital German industrial region of the Ruhr. The massing of the US 3rd Army and the Canadian 1st Army opposite the Pas de Calais convinced von Rundstedt, Rommel and Hitler that this reasoning was correct. The net result was that Oberkommando der Wehrmacht (the German High Command) gave priority to von Salmuth's 15th Army north of the Seine. Due to the Allies' successful deception efforts, Rundstedt's better units remained in the Pas de Calais area, which had a negative effect on Dollmann's 7th Army covering Normandy and Brittany. A phantom Allied 4th Army in Scotland also convinced Hitler of a threat to Norway, pinning down even more troops in Scandinavia.

General Georg von Sodenstern, commander of the 19th Army at Avignon until he was replaced by Wiese on 1 July 1944, tried to sound optimistic about the demands made by Rommel's Army Group B: 'One recognises the perplexity of a command which to close up one gap has to tear open another, and has trusted to the vague hopes of lucky developments in the south of France.' However, there would be no lucky developments.

Siding with von Rundstedt, Sodenstern had disagreed with Rommel's preference for keeping the panzer forces of Army Group B close to the Normandy beaches. This, he reasoned, was simply putting one's head on the anvil just as the blow was about to fall. Sodenstern also argued that any defensive success in the south of France would be pointless if they were defeated in Normandy. In his view it would be far better to withdraw from southern France and fight in front of the West-wall. Blaskowitz agreed with Rundstedt and Sodenstern; he favoured a withdrawal into the interior where Army Group G could fight a mobile battle. Hitler, though, could not make up his mind what to do about the defence of southern France.

In the Mediterranean the Allies ran a series of deception operations designed to mislead the Axis Powers as to the true strength of the Allied forces in the region, and then to convince the Germans that the Allies would attack Crete or western Greece from the Mediterranean, or Romania via the Black Sea. Clearly Churchill was in favour of thrusting into the Balkans, partly to forestall Stalin's plans for the region, and years later Eisenhower was to concede that this should have been their course of action.

'Fortress' Riviera

While the bulk of German defensive efforts were directed to northern France during the first part of 1944, the Mediterranean coast was not altogether neglected. The French Riviera, once a byword for luxury, was now host to German pillboxes, gun emplacements, mines and booby-traps, though Army Group G (or more precisely the 19th Army) was hardly in a fit state to defend it effectively. Altogether Blaskowitz had about 30,000 troops in the assault area, but within a few days' march there were over 200,000. By early June some 62,500 mines had been laid along the coast and almost a thousand permanent fortifications constructed; weapons pits, trenches, tank obstacles and road-blocks supplemented these.

Blaskowitz and the 19th Army's Chief of Staff Generalleutnant Walter Botsch knew that they had no Atlantic Wall on their hands: only one-third of the intended concrete defences were ever completed, and those built were in the first echelon on the beach zones. Blaskowitz was only too well aware that the defences around Marseilles, Toulon and the Gulf of Fréjus constituted little more than a thin crust that at best would hold the Allies up. Once inland, there was nothing to stop them other than natural geography and those units to hand.

The key naval port facilities at Toulon were outclassed only by its larger western civilian neighbour at Marseilles. Its defences against attack from the sea included batteries at Mauvannes and on the peninsula of St-Mandrier. Inland, Toulon is partly shielded by the hilly terrain and narrow river valleys running west of the port from Bandol to the Grand Cap Massif and the region west of Solliés-Ville. The eastern approaches running from La Valette to La Crau and Le Pradet are more vulnerable because of the coastal plain which provides the best route of attack. The 19th Army protected this area with two defensive belts. The outer ran from the coast south of Hyèrres blocking the main east–west road. To the north the town was protected by the Redon hills, and the German defences continued along the Gapeau river past La Crau and up to Solliés-Ville and Solliés-Pont. These defences were reinforced by the 700-metre-high Coudon rock overlooking the plains east of Toulon, which provided ideal artillery and observation positions.

The inner defensive belt was anchored on the Coudon foothills and the Touar and Pradet ridges running down to the coast near Le Pradet. These ridges, although low-lying, look out over the coastal plain and were guarded by German anti-tank guns and pillboxes. Making use of old French fortifications, the Germans also held the Faron feature overlooking northern Toulon. Just to the west of Faron, the Las River valley provides an entry point to Toulon, but this was screened by a fortification known as La Poudrière, which was based in old quarry workings.

Before the German take-over of southern France in November 1942, the French authorities, as a token of goodwill towards the Germans, had strengthened the coastal defences to safeguard Toulon from an attack from the sea by the Allies. Other preparations included plans for scuttling the fleet, in the event of a successful landing by the Allies. Now, on the peninsula in front of the harbour at Toulon, there was a complex of 340mm gun batteries mounted in turrets. In addition, some seventy-five medium-sized guns were strung out along the coast, including 200mm and 105mm Flak guns. Two massive 340mm guns from the scuttled battleship *Provence* had been moved by the Germans to the Cape Cépet battery on the St-Mandrier peninsula which forms Toulon's large bay. Originally there had been two twin gun turrets in the battery, but when the French fleet was scuttled they had also been damaged. The Germans managed to repair two of the guns, though one was sabotaged just before the landings.

Blaskowitz's principal commands in the south were the 58th Reserve Panzer Corps stationed in Toulouse (controlling the 2nd SS Panzer Division, 9th Panzer Division and 189th Reserve Infantry Division), and General Ferdinand Neuling's 62nd Reserve Corps at Draguignan north-east of Toulon (controlling the 157th Reserve Infantry Division and the 242nd Infantry Division). Created in France in 1943, the 58th Corps was transferred from Rambouillet to Mödling in Austria before taking part in the occupation of Hungary in March 1944. The following month it returned to France, this time to Toulouse, coming under Blaskowitz's Army Group G.

The 189th Reserve Division was raised in September 1942 and redesignated the 189th Infantry Division in December. It was then reformed in May 1943 in France and came under the command of Generalleutnant Richard von Schwerin from October 1943 until the end of September 1944. Formed in October 1942 from Division Nr 157, the 157th Reserve Division was stationed in France under Generalleutnant Karl Pflaum until the Italian surrender in September 1943. It then moved into Italy, taking 5,772 prisoners during two days. The 242nd Infantry Division came into being in July 1943 under Generalleutnant Johannes Bäßler, comprising the 917th, 918th and 919th Garrison Regiments and the 242nd Artillery Regiment.

The majority of the Luftwaffe units in southern France came under the direction of Fliegerdivision 2. This had its headquarters at Montfrin, about 17.5km east-north-east of Nîmes, and like all

Luftwaffe forces in France was subordinated to Luftflotte 3. Most of the formations had an anti-shipping role. Jagdfliegerführer Süd controlled the fighter defence of southern France. Its headquarters had been located at Chateau La Nerthe (near Chateauneuf-du-Pape, about 10km south-east of Orange and 11km north of Avignon) since 1 May 1944.

Nahaufklärungsgruppe 13 (NAG 13) with Fw 190 and Bf 109 fighters had been deployed in France since 1942, initially at Avignon and then on the Atlantic Coast. In April 1944 it was redeployed to the Riviera and the 2. *Staffel* was tasked with maritime reconnaissance between the Spanish border and Corsica. By mid-1944 NAG 13 was equipped with a mixed unit of Fw 190 A-3/U4s and Bf 109 G-8s, their armament reduced to two machine-guns and a single cannon respectively. By 1944 the anti-shipping *Stab* and III/Kampfgeschwader 100 were based on the airfields of Blagnac and Francazal, both near Toulouse.

Luftflotte 3 issued orders on 8 August that in the event of an Allied landing in southern France *Stab* and III/KG 100 would be placed under Fliegerdivision 2's control. In the event of a landing, Luftflotte 3/Fliegerdivision 2 planned to bomb the invasion fleet at first light with all available aircraft. However, the Allies had mastery of the air and all Blaskowitz could do was stand back and watch. On 25 June he may have witnessed 250 USAAF B-17 bombers attack the airfields near Toulouse with impunity.

The Kriegsmarine Admiral Commanding, France was dissolved to form part of the Marinegruppenkommando West command in Paris at the end of 1942 (the former had been based in Wilhelmshaven). This controlled all naval units in France and Belgium, and a final change took place with the addition of the Mediterranean sector in September 1943. This new command was integrated into two others to form Admiral Commanding, Southern French Coast; previously, since June 1943, only the western part (Languedoc region) had been under German control under the Admiral, Southern French Coast.

The Impact of Overlord
Around 0330–0400 on 6 June 1944 staff at Army Group G's headquarters at Rouffiac, outside Toulouse, were roused with the news that the Allies were invading Normandy and all coastal defence sectors were put

on high alert. It was not long before the fighting in Normandy started drawing in the German forces stationed in occupied France. However, Hitler ordered that the majority of the 15th Army's formations north of the Seine remain in place as he feared a secondary invasion was about to be launched at the Pas de Calais. This meant that the burden of providing reinforcements in Normandy soon fell on Blaskowitz's already inadequate Army Group G.

At the same time French resistance groups stepped up their efforts and many of Blaskowitz's units were urgently ordered north. Just one day after D-Day the 17th SS Panzergrenadier Division received orders to depart from its marshalling area and head for Normandy. Under Operation Mimose the division redeployed from the area of General Chevallerie's 1st Army south of the Loire to the sector of General Dollmann's 7th Army facing Lieutenant-General Omar N. Bradley's US 1st Army at the base of the Cotentin peninsula. General Heinz Lammerding, commanding the 2nd SS Panzer Division, was also ordered to Normandy, but his forces were bogged down fighting the Maquis or local resistance. Large areas were under the control of the Resistance fighters, leaving local German forces surrounded and cut off. Lammerding was soon signalling his corps commander General Krüger in Toulouse with his catalogue of woes; he was understandably annoyed that his panzer division was wasting valuable time fighting the Maquis, which was a role that should be handled by the local security divisions.

Chaos reigned. On top of the Maquis problem, only 40 per cent of Lammerding's panzers were serviceable and 70 per cent of his half-tracks and heavy trucks. Repeated calls for spare parts fell on deaf ears, which meant broken-down vehicles could not be moved and then required infantry to guard them. Six depots had to be set up for the stragglers and breakdowns, and efforts to commandeer local civilian vehicles produced few results. This was to be typical of the experiences of many of the units moved northwards to join the fighting.

In response to his dwindling forces, Blaskowitz asked the German High Command to provide him with troops to replace the 2nd SS Panzer Division once it had left Corrèze and the Dordogne. A Kampfgruppe from the 11th Panzer Division, comprising two infantry battalions, an artillery battalion and an anti-tank company, was duly assembled with instructions to contact the 2nd SS Division in Tulle. These forces arrived on 11 June and the panzers of the 2nd SS duly rolled north to Limoges. The following day Blaskowitz took personal control of the anti-partisan operations and requested that the German High Command formally declare the south-west a battle zone. The French Resistance now found itself at war with Army Group G.

General Krüger's 58th Reserve Panzer Corps staff were then ordered to Le Mans to help direct the fight against the Americans. Krüger was an experienced tank commander, having been in command of the 1st Panzer Division from mid-July 1941 to the beginning of January 1944. His corps dropped its reserve designation on 6 July and departed on the 27th, joining Panzergruppe West two days later, though it was subsequently subordinated to the 7th Army and Panzergruppe Eberbach.

By the second week of July German divisions from the Calais area were also finally arriving in Normandy. In order to keep them in the Caen sector and to avoid them gaining any sort of initiative that could dislodge the British and Canadians, the British 2nd Army attacked north of the city. On 7 July some 460 bombers flattened Caen, dropping 2,560 tons of bombs in an area 3.6km long by 1.3km deep. Then, at 0420 hours on the following day, three Allied divisions thrust hard into northern Caen, but the Germans held on grimly to the south and south-east of the city. From 10 to 15 July the British launched a series of attacks both west and east of Caen in order to keep the Germans tied down.

In the meantime, the Americans were battling to reach their start line ready for the break-out, Operation Cobra. On 17 July they had taken St Lo and reached the St Lo-Periers road, having advanced only 11 km in seventeen days at the cost of 40,000 casualties. The break-out could not be launched before 20 July because of the necessary build-up of supplies.

In order to gain Lieutenant-General Bradley more time, Montgomery decided to punch east of Caen. Operation Goodwood, launched on 18 July, made good initial progress until it ran into the in-depth defensive positions of infantry and armour. The punch soon became bogged down and degenerated into a slogging match, which succeeded in slowly grinding down the German panzer units. Two days later the offensive was called off, having gained the Americans time and prevented the transfer of any panzer units further west, at a cost of 4,000 British casualties and 500 tanks.

Three US infantry divisions of General Collins' VII Corps were assigned the task of spearheading the break-out, and they drew up on the Lessay-Periers-St Lo line. Initially scheduled for 24 July, the break-out had to be called off due to the bad weather. The following day the Americans withdrew 1.1km, while 2,500 bombers dropped over 4,000 tons of bombs on the German defences, in an area 6.5km long by 2.4km wide, just south of the St Lo-Periers highway. At 0230 hours the assault troops moved off again, only to be slowed up by determined German resistance.

On 27 July the 9th Panzer Division was put on notice to be ready to march north from the Avignon area. By 1 August it and six infantry divisions of varying quality were heading for the Normandy battlefield, now that it was clear to the Germans that Operation Cobra represented a very real threat. As they rumbled north, the panzers were set upon by the Maquis and by Allied ground-attack aircraft. Nonetheless, despite numerous air attacks, the division seemed to escape largely unscathed as it moved towards Normandy. In fact, this division never got to fight as a whole, owing to the belated destruction of the bridges over the Loire and the Allied landings in southern France. Elements of the support services never reached the division in Normandy and were not reunited with the parent formation until it had retreated to Metz following the defeat. However, it was clear that Army Group G was haemorrhaging units it could ill afford to lose.

While Lieutenant-General Patton waited for the US 3rd Army to become operational, he took over VIII Corps and drove southwards. By 29 July he had taken Coutances and Avranches. On 1 August the 3rd Army became combat operational, and, ignoring Bradley's orders to secure a wide corridor, Patton squeezed his seven divisions along the coast in 22 hours. He was now ready to sweep south-eastwards towards the Seine in order to trap the German armed forces in north-western France. The following day the Allies could see that their plans were almost complete. The Canadians drove through the south of Caen and headed for Falaise, while the Americans sped eastwards; the trap was rapidly forming. Montgomery ordered the Americans to make a long hook, in order to trap as many Germans as possible and prevent any crossing the Seine. The developing pocket could not be properly closed, because the Germans dug in north of Falaise and the Canadian advance was slower than expected due to determined German resistance.

The US 3rd Army and the British I Corps slowly headed for each other. The Falaise Pocket was steadily squeezed from all sides as the Germans fought valiantly to keep open the 'neck'. The pocket was only 32 km wide by 16 km deep by 17 August, but it contained about 100,000 Germans, remnants of fifteen divisions with elements from twelve others. The panzer divisions managed to hold the Americans and Canadians at bay, but the vast columns of retreating Germans were decimated by Allied fighter-bombers and artillery, the roads becoming choked with burnt-out vehicles, which only added to the chaos.

Blaskowitz's lost divisions

In early June Blaskowitz's army group totalled less than twenty divisions, including all those formations under its two panzer corps and in its area of responsibility. The rot had set in way before D-Day, though, with Blaskowitz losing units to Army Group B. For example, the 326th Infantry Division, raised in November 1942, was initially stationed in southern France, but in February 1944 was reassigned to the 15th Army. In total, Army Group G saw elements of thirteen of its divisions redeployed before Operation Dragoon commenced.

Critically, as the deadline for Dragoon loomed, Blaskowitz had very few panzers remaining in southern France. Most of his armoured formations – the 2nd SS, 9th and 17th SS Panzergrenadier Divisions, along with elements of the 271st, 272nd, 276th, 338th and 708th Infantry Divisions, as well as the 341st Assault Gun Brigade and all his anti-tank companies – had been drawn north to the bitter fighting in Normandy. Only the 11th Panzer Division remained in the south, refitting north-east of Bordeaux after being mauled on the Eastern Front.

On 1 August Blaskowitz's operations officer Colonel Horst Wilutzky was briefed by Field Marshal Günther von Kluge at the Commander-in-Chief, West's headquarters. Wilutzky and General von Gyldenfeldt, Blaskowitz's Chief of Staff, decided that 'there was no military justification for holding German units in southern France any longer'. Blaskowitz and von Kluge agreed, but Hitler insisted that Army Group G stay put for another two weeks, by which time it was almost too late.

Three days later Blaskowitz put his cards on the table about Army Group G's weaknesses and informed von Kluge that because of the 'release of men and weapons its defensive power has become considerably smaller and . . . a successful defence of the coast is no longer guaranteed'. On 8 August Kluge and his Chief of Staff, General Hans

Speidel, decided it was imperative that Blaskowitz be saved. 'It's time to abandon the south of France,' Kluge argued. 'Why leave the 1st Army on the Atlantic now we know the outcome of the war is at stake. Let us put Army Group G on the line Seine-Loire-Gien-Evers-Gex. Let's abandon Provence.' But Hitler would have none of it; his policy was never to give ground.

On Sunday, 13 August General Weise received a rare bit of good news, though it did little to alleviate his concern over Luftwaffe reports of up to 100 troopships in the area off Corsica. Major-General Walter Botsch, his Chief of Staff, announced that Army Group G headquarters had just phoned to say that Hitler had authorised the release of the 11th Panzer Division. The only problem was how to get it to the Riviera in time and unscathed by Allied air attacks. Most of the bridges over the Rhône were already down.

As well as losing elements of his fighting strength, Blaskowitz also found that his command staff structure had been severely weakened by the requirement to send a steady stream of reinforcements north. He had to give up one army headquarters, two corps headquarters and one panzer corps headquarters. Chevallerie's 1st Army was left with a single corps and Wiese's 19th Army was left with the 11th Panzer Division and some second-rate static infantry divisions. By mid-August Blaskowitz's army group consisted of just seven divisions (six infantry and one panzer), and four of his infantry units were not really combat ready. At the end of the month Wiese's 19th Army, the formation that would have to resist Dragoon, could only field four infantry divisions and one panzer division. Two weeks later, even with reinforcements, the 19th Army mustered just five infantry divisions, elements of two panzer divisions and a panzergrenadier division. This lack of manpower ultimately showed what little priority Hitler gave to defending the south of France.

The panzer units sent north suffered around 35,000–40,000 killed, wounded or missing during the Normandy campaign and none was reassigned to Blaskowitz. The 2nd SS Panzer Division fought doggedly during the battles in Normandy. Although it was not surrounded at Falaise, it lost upwards of 7,000 men, though many of these went missing and were subsequently able to rejoin the division. The far-from-complete 9th Panzer Division suffered about 3,500 casualties and the 17th SS Panzergrenadier Division some 8,000. The infantry divisions sent north endured comparable losses. The 271st Division moved to the Montpellier area in southern France after being created in the Netherlands in late 1943. It had 11,617 men on its roster by mid-1944 but they were not fully trained nor properly equipped. At the end of June the division was shipped to Normandy via Lyons and Rouen. In the subsequent fighting it lost up to 4,000 casualties, but also avoided being trapped in the Falaise Pocket. The 272nd Infantry Division fared slightly better. Having fought on the Eastern Front, it was shipped west in late 1943 and in April the following year joined the 19th Army. By mid-June it could field 12,725 men and in early July was shipped by rail from the Mediterranean to Normandy via the Le Mans area. Likewise avoiding the Falaise Pocket, it suffered about 1,000–2,000 casualties.

Formed in south-western France in 1943, the 276th Infantry Division totalled 13,362 men in early June, but again they were not combat ready. This division too was freighted to the Le Mans area, but in contrast was caught at Falaise, losing up to 6,000 men. The 277th Infantry Division, which came into being in Croatia in late 1943, arrived in southern France early in the New Year; it had a reported strength of 10,649 men by mid-June and was committed to the fighting in Normandy the following month. About half of the troops were caught at Falaise, sustaining losses of 4,000–5,000. The 708th Infantry Division was sent to defend the Bay of Biscay after being raised in May 1941. By early August 1944 it had a strength of 8,123 men; deployed to Normandy, it was caught up in the American Army's break-out and lost some 4,000 troops, most of whom were taken prisoner.

All Blaskowitz got in return was the 198th and 716th Infantry Divisions. The former was being organised and the latter was recuperating from Normandy. Raised in December 1939 from reserve troops in the Protektorat Böhmen-Mähren (Protectorate of Bohemia and Moravia), the 198th Infantry Division first saw action in Denmark and France, then served on the Eastern Front for three years until being transferred to France in June 1944. It consisted of three infantry regiments (Grenadier-Regiments 305, 308 and 326, containing two battalions each), an artillery regiment (Artillerie-Regiment 235), plus Fusilier-Bataillon 235 and Feldersatz-Bataillon 198, and a panzerjäger battalion. Generalmajor Alfred Kuhnert assumed command on 5 August 1944 and the division reportedly mustered just 3,800 infantrymen at the start of the campaign.

Blaskowitz faced a similar problem in terms of Luftwaffe support; by 1944 southern France had been drained of Luftwaffe units that were desperately needed elsewhere. At most he was backed by 200 aircraft in the region, but they would have to fend off 4,056 Allied planes. Likewise, the German Navy had just 75 small craft to confront 2,250 Allied vessels.

Chapter Six

Dragoon Hots Up

At the end of 1943 an Anvil planning group known as Force 163, headed by Brigadier-General Garrison H. Davidson, the US 7th Army Engineer, was established at the École Normal at Bouzareah just outside Algiers. Force 163 included a French component under Colonel Jean L. Petit. Toulon became their focus, along with the coast to the east of the port. The Alps Maritimes presented a challenge, though the valley of the Argens river formed a path through the mountains between the Massif de Maures and the Provence Alps. Allied headquarters sent a message to the US 7th Army's headquarters at Palermo, which showed that Eisenhower was determined to go through with Anvil. The telegram stated: 'An estimate is required as a matter of some urgency as to the accommodations which you would require for your planning staffs should you be asked to undertake the planning of an operation of similar size to Husky . . .'.

Following the Sicilian campaign, the US 7th Army had shrunk from six divisions to little more than the headquarters staff. They were now instructed that landings were to take place in the south of France in conjunction with Overlord, with early objectives of Lyons and Vichy, the location of the French government, and that the assault would be conducted by American and Free French Forces.

Patch takes over
The planning gathered pace in early January 1944 when Lieutenant-General Mark W. Clark replaced General Patton as the 7th Army's commander. While Overlord continued to slip behind schedule, owing to the enormous shipping requirements, and the fighting dragged on in Italy following Anzio, it became apparent that Clark could not cope with controlling the US 5th Army as well as directing Anvil. On 2 March Lieutenant-General Alexander M. Patch, a veteran of the Pacific campaign and Guadalcanal, took over the 7th Army.

The planning staff moved to Naples to work with the 7th Army and General Lucian Truscott's US VI Corps. Truscott understandably wanted reassurances that there would be no repeat of Anzio. A daylight attack was agreed upon, as the value of an accurate preliminary bombardment far outweighed the need for surprise. However, Patch could immediately see that conducting Anvil in early June alongside Overlord was a tall order. With Overlord soaking up all the landing craft and the fighting on the Italian front tying down Patch's assault forces, the proposed date for Anvil began to slip towards late July.

General Wilson, the Allied Supreme Commander in the Mediterranean Theatre, was presented with the outline plans on 29 April. These envisaged a three-battalion parachute drop to support an opening two-division assault, with Commandos and Rangers securing offshore islands and the flanks. Given that Toulon was the immediate goal, a landing area to the east of the port between Cape Cavalaire and the Bay of Agay was selected. To confuse the Germans about the exact location of the landings a preliminary bombing campaign would be conducted along the entire French coast from Spain to Italy.

General de Lattre had initially proposed landing on either side of Toulon, but he did not get his way. Not unreasonably, he also wanted French troops to be the first ashore, but their lack of experience counted against them and de Gaulle refused to commit the French parachute unit. De Lattre later fell out with his deputy, General de Larminat, when the latter refused to relinquish tactical control of his forward units. De Lattre also wanted his II Corps to move swiftly to trap the Germans, whereas Patch saw this as an excuse for French troops not to have to reduce the German garrisons in Toulon and Marseilles.

Two weeks later three other options were drawn up depending on the German response to the invasion; the first foresaw a partial German withdrawal, the second a complete German withdrawal and the third a complete German surrender, bringing a halt to all organised resistance. It was obvious that the most likely was the first option. The planners assessed that it was unlikely that the Germans would be able to hold the invaders on the beaches, so would offer a token resistance before abandoning the coastal zone and conducting a fighting withdrawal in the lower Rhône region.

Plans went ahead for a two-division landing east of Toulon, with a target date of early August. The key objectives remained Toulon and

Marseilles, followed by Lyons and Vichy. In light of the fact that there would be no Sledgehammer, on 1 August Anvil officially became Operation Dragoon. It has been said that this change was due to a breach in security about the Anvil codename, but others claimed the new name was chosen because Churchill had been 'dragooned' into the operation. After all the frustrations over Anvil and the many false starts, Eisenhower recommended it should be conducted no later than 30 August, with a target date of the 15th.

Invasion beaches

There were to be six invasion beaches. From north to south they were: Rosie (north of San Raphael), Camel (around San Raphael and Fréjus), Delta (around Ste-Maxime and St-Tropez), Alpha (at Cavalaire-sur-Mer), Garbo and Romeo (between Cavalaire-sur-Mer and Le

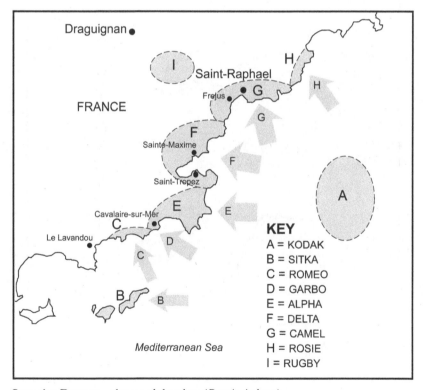

Operation Dragoon – the assault beaches. (*Dennis Andrews*)

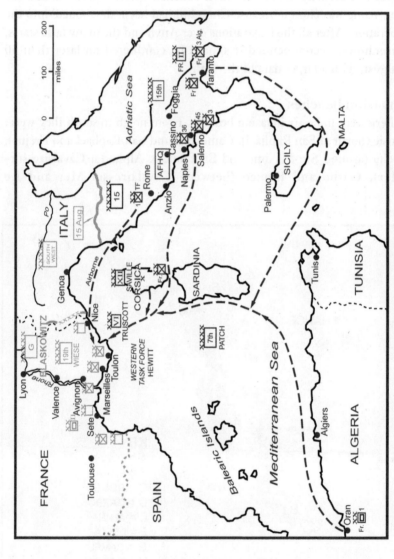

Operation Dragoon – the gathering of the invasion force. (*Dennis Andrews*)

Lavandou). Islands south-east of Le Lavandou were codenamed Sitka, while the invasion fleet assembly area was dubbed Kodak. The airborne drop zone south-east of Draguignan was codenamed Rugby.

Enemy defences on the islands of Port Cros and Levant were to be neutralised under the cover of darkness by Sitka Force, consisting of the 1st Special Service Force. Once this task had been achieved, it would secure the island of Porquerolles under the codename of Satan Force. Similarly, French special forces, notably the French *Groupe de Commandos*, dubbed Romeo Force, would neutralise German forces on the Cap Nègre, and were also to block the coastal highway and take the high ground 3 km to the north. Once this had been completed, they would be in a position to protect the left flank of the landings, and once a beachhead was established, the special forces would fall under US VI Corps control. Another French unit, the French Naval Assault Group known as Rosie Force, was to land the night before near Pointe de Trayas with the aim of disrupting the Cannes–San Raphael and Cannes–Fréjus highways before joining the right flank.

Kodak Force consisted of Truscott's US VI Corps' headquarters plus the US 3rd, 36th and 45th Infantry Divisions, supported by General du Vigier's 1st Combat Command from the French 1st Armoured Division. Sudre's Combat Command was to get ashore between Cape Cavalaire and Agay and link up with the airborne task force. Once de Lattre's French II Corps had come ashore, all French forces would be placed under his command. The first echelon, consisting of General Brosset's 1st Motorised Infantry Division and de Monsabert's 3rd Algerian Division, were to land within the first 24 hours, followed four to eight days later by General de Vernejoul's 9th Colonial Infantry Division.

The planners decided to commit an airborne force of divisional size, but no such force was available in the Mediterranean so a unit of comparable size was improvised from the 517th Parachute Regimental Combat Team (RCT), the 509th and 551st Parachute Battalions and the 550th Airborne Battalion. Other units in Italy were designated gliderborne and received instruction from the 550th and the Airborne Training Centre. By early July the concentration of airborne forces in the Rome area was almost complete and aircraft providing two troop carrier wings were en route from England. The 517th Parachute Regimental Combat Team came into being as part of the 17th Airborne

Division on 15 March 1943, with the division's parachute units comprising the 517th Parachute Infantry Regiment, the 460th Parachute Field Artillery Battalion and Company C, 139th Airborne Engineer Battalion, which was later redesignated the 596th Airborne (Parachute) Engineer Company.

During the fighting in Italy the 517th had been assigned to Major-General Fred L. Walker's 36th Infantry Division, which under the US IV Corps was operating on the left flank of the US 5th Army. On 17 June 1944 they had deployed south of Grosseto. After the Combined Chiefs of Staff issued a directive on 2 July to General Wilson to proceed with Anvil on 15 August, the 517th RCT was released from IV Corps and moved to join the gathering First Airborne Task Force in the Rome area.

The provisional troop carrier division was to lift the air assault with a total of 415 transport aircraft protected by Spitfires and Beaufighters all operating from bases in Italy. The first drops would take place just before dawn with the first resupply mission scheduled for the late afternoon.

On 19 and 20 July, in preparation for the invasion, forty-nine aircraft and crews comprising detachments from each of the 79th, 80th, 81st and 82nd Troop Carrier Squadrons, part of the 436th Troop Carrier Group based at RAF Membury, were dispatched to Votone Air Base in Italy. They returned to Membury on 23 and 24 August, by which time the 6th Tactical Air Depot units had moved to France.

By the end of July Patch's invasion force numbered 155,419 men with 20,031 vehicles. It was intended by D-Day plus 30 to have 366,833 men and 56,051 vehicles ashore, and by D-Day plus 65 some 576,833 men and 91,341 vehicles.

Truscott's US VI Corps

After the liberation of Rome the US VI Corps was pulled out of the line to prepare for its third and last amphibious assault of the war. Its three divisions had ample experience of such operations, having been blooded during the Italian campaign. However, the 36th and 45th Divisions received amphibious assault refresher courses at the Invasion Training Centre at Salerno, and the 3rd Division at Pozzuoli; once this was complete they were to move to Naples. It was not until 24 June that the 36th Infantry Division was finally allocated a role within Operation

Dragoon. In the meantime the French forces were to embark at Taranto, Corsica and Oran, in a slightly unwieldy arrangement.

The US 3rd Infantry Division had had a distinguished career, having come into being during the First World War at Camp Green in North Carolina in November 1917. Eight months later it was committed to the war in France with the American Expeditionary Force to Europe. After seeing action during the Aisne-Marne offensive, the division was assigned to defend Paris and then deployed to the Marne. While other units fell back, the men of the 3rd Infantry Division held their ground, gaining the nickname the 'Rock of the Marne' for their unit. More recently it had seen combat in the Second World War, having landed at Felada under General Jonathan Anderson on 8 November 1942 to help secure French Morocco. Brigadier-General Truscott took command of the 3rd Infantry Division in April 1943 and it was subsequently involved in the assault on Sicily on 10 July 1943, dramatically beating the armour to Palermo and racing on to Messina. Just nine days after the invasion of the Italian mainland, on the 18th the 3rd Division took part in the Salerno landings, driving on to the Volturno and to Cassino. Following the initial assault at Salerno, the commander of the US VI Corps, Major-General Ernest J. Dawley, was replaced by General John P. Lucas. Unfortunately, Lucas's determination to consolidate his beachhead before breaking out gave the Germans enough time to reinforce, resulting in a bloody stalemate. After a brief recuperation the division next landed on the Anzio beaches on 22 January 1944 as part of the US VI Corps. Allied forces were hemmed in for four months by German counter-attacks, and at this time Truscott replaced Lucas as commander.

That summer the 36th 'Texas' Infantry Division likewise was struggling up the Italian coast towards the Germans' Pisa-Rimini defensive line. This division was originally established as a National Guard unit from Texas and Oklahoma in July 1917. It was sent to Europe in July 1918 and was involved in the Meuse-Argonne offensive. Although disbanded at the end of the war, it was reactivated on 25 November 1940. Commanded by Major-General Fred Walker, the division had deployed overseas on 2 April 1943 and first saw combat on 9 September 1943 during the landing on the Gulf of Salerno at Paestum. Following its efforts against Cassino with the US 34th Infantry Division, the 36th Division held the Rapido river and was finally withdrawn on 12 March

1944 for rest and recuperation. It also took part in the Anzio landings, subsequently pushing north to take Velletri on 1 June; four days later its troops entered Rome.

The 45th Infantry Division, nicknamed the 'Thunderbird Division' after its insignia, was activated on 16 September 1940. It also saw action on Sicily, at Naples-Foggia, and during the Anzio and Rome-Arno operations. During the invasion of Sicily it became embroiled in the controversy surrounding the Biscari Massacre, during which seventy-six German and Italian prisoners of war were executed; as a result an officer and an NCO were court-martialled. Major-General William W. Eagles commanded the 45th Division from December 1943 until December the following year. Interestingly, its original divisional insignia had been a yellow swastika on a red diamond, but this had been changed to the Indian thunderbird on a red triangle, for obvious reasons.

While preparing for Dragoon, Truscott soon became a victim of French military pride when he fell foul of de Lattre. An agreement had been reached that Combat Command Sudre would be assigned to his corps after Brigadier Aime Sudre, of the French 1st Armoured Division, had visited him in July. With the approval of his superior, Sudre then suggested that Truscott visit them in Oran. When de Lattre heard of this meeting he was furious; he summoned Truscott to lunch and then proceeded to launch a tirade against him. The French general was clearly still smarting at the fact that his troops would not be the first ashore. Protocol had been violated and honour besmirched, and de Lattre now demanded prior sight of all orders to Sudre. Truscott, of course, could not agree to this.

Task Force Butler was created shortly before Dragoon on Truscott's orders, as he suspected that the on-going political squabbling with de Lattre would cost him control of Combat Command Sudre, the US 7th Army's only armoured force. Major-General Fred Butler was placed in charge of a hastily gathered ad hoc force consisting of a tank battalion, a tank destroyer company, a cavalry and reconnaissance squadron and an armoured field artillery battalion. Patch tried to reassure Truscott that he would have a free hand with Sudre's forces, but Truscott suspected they would revert to French command once ashore in the Riviera and he would lose them.

French Resistance

Patch, Truscott and de Lattre were also expecting support from the French Resistance. Before the German occupation of the southern Free Zone, Lyons in particular was a key centre for the Resistance organisations, hosting the Brutus network set up by de Gaulle. Marseilles similarly played host to two major resistance movements, the non-communist coalition known as *Mouvements Unis de Résistance* (MUR) and the French Communist Party's irregular partisan riflemen known as the *Franc-Tireurs et Partisans* (FTP). Of the two, the FTP was the stronger with up to 2,000 men, while the MUR had fewer than 800. Socialist Party members in the city made up an important component of the MUR, and lawyer Gaston Defferre was in command of the Socialist militia as well as head of the local Allied intelligence network. He was also a member of the *Section Française de l'Internationale Ouvrière* (SFIO – the French Section of the Workers' International) Socialist Party and a leading figure in the Brutus network.

A number of the city's Corsican crime syndicates also became central to the non-communist underground, which lacked the experience to carry out effective resistance work. Due to their anti-communist activities in Marseilles before the war, few of the resistance-minded Corsicans were accepted into the maligned communist underground.

Unfortunately, since the MUR supported the Allies' policy of denying the Communists arms, this stopped any meaningful co-operation between the various groups in Marseilles. While the communist and non-communist forces were superficially merged with the creation of the FFI in February 1944, the reality was that they remained at loggerheads until the FFI was absorbed into the regular French Army. An agreement was reached in the western Alps between the Head of Region 2 (Marseilles) of the MUR and the Italian *Resistenza* in Piedmont in May 1944, and a declaration of military and political solidarity made.

Corsica – an unnecessary diversion

After liberating Corsica, the French proposed an invasion of the island of Elba (Operation Brassard), using the 9th Colonial Infantry Division (9e DIC), two battalions of French commandos (*Commandos d'Afrique* and *Commandos de Choc*), a battalion and supplementary battery of the

Colonial Artillery Regiment of Morocco (RACM) and the 2nd Group of Moroccan Tabors (2e GTM). Taking Elba would permit the Allies to dominate not only the Piombino Channel but also the coastal road used by German transport on the Italian peninsula, both of which were vital transportation arteries for the supply of German forces in western Italy. The garrison on Elba was made up of just two infantry battalions manning the fortified coastal areas, as well as several coastal artillery batteries totalling some sixty guns of medium and heavy calibre.

Initially Eisenhower was not keen on the idea, viewing it as an unnecessary diversion of resources while preparations for Anzio were under way. But once the British general Sir Henry Maitland Wilson took over in the Mediterranean Theatre, attitudes at Allied headquarters changed and the operation was approved. By this time, though, the Germans had strongly fortified Elba, an island dominated by rugged terrain, making the assault considerably more difficult.

Nevertheless, at 0400 hours on 17 June 1944 the French I Corps commenced its assault with support from forty-eight Royal Navy commandos. The lightly equipped French *Choc* landed at multiple points before the main landing force and neutralised the coastal artillery batteries. The French initially encountered problems in the Gulf of Campo on the south coast because of the German fortifications and the extremely rugged terrain. Opting for an alternative plan, the landing beach was shifted to the east, near Nercio, and the 9th Colonial Infantry gained a beachhead there. The crest of the 400-metre Monte Tambone Ridge overlooking the landing areas was secured by French commandos within two hours.

The Royal Navy commandos boarded and seized the German Flak ship *Köln* and also landed to guide in other troops heading for the beaches. Tragically a German demolition charge killed thirty-eight of them. Portoferraio was taken by the 9th Division on the 18th and the island was largely secured by the following day. Vicious fighting in the hills continued between the Germans and the Senegalese colonial infantry, with the latter employing flamethrowers. Of the garrison, 1,995 were captured and 500 killed. French losses were 252 killed and missing, and 635 men wounded. British fatalities were 38 of the 48 commandos committed, with 9 others wounded.

Dragoon's naval support

The 8th Fleet was responsible for putting the Riviera assault force ashore and maintaining it there until such time as the French ports were secured. The Control Force was to look after supporting maritime operations while the Alpha, Delta and Camel attack forces were responsible for landing the 3rd, 45th and 36th US Infantry Divisions respectively. Vice-Admiral H. Kent Hewitt was to command the Western Task Force, consisting of some 505 US ships, 252 British, 19 French, 6 Greek and 263 merchantmen. The warships (5 battleships, 4 heavy cruisers, 18 light cruisers, 9 aircraft carriers and 85 destroyers) were to protect the 370 large landing ships and 1,267 small landing craft. They were allocated across the four attack forces, Task Force 84 Alpha, 85 Delta, 86 Sitka and 87 Camel.

The USS *Biscayne* was the flagship of Rear Admiral Bertram J. Rodgers USN, Delta Task Force Commander, while on *Bayleaf* was Rear Admiral Spencer S. Lewis in charge of Camel Force, supported by Rear Admiral Morton L. Deyo with responsibility for the bombardment warships. Rear Admiral Lyal A. Davidson on the USS *Augusta* was in overall command of Task Force Sitka.

The USS *Duane* served as the flagship for the commander of the 8th Amphibious Force. This had six flotillas of landing craft, each consisting of twelve craft divided into two squadrons, B and C, making a total of seventy-two tank landing craft. Each flotilla had a sick berth attendant (medic) attached and each squadron had a medical officer. In addition, the Americans proposed to employ the Sherman Duplex Drive (DD) amphibious tank that had been developed for Overlord. The 191st, 753rd and 756th Tank Battalions were trained in the Bay of Naples for their assault role.

Task Force 84 was overseen by a Coastguard cutter and a fighter control ship, while its assault group included two attack transports each capable of carrying almost 1,600 troops and a variety of landing craft, and three attack cargo ships. The landing ships, which had been wrangled over for so long, numbered 25 LSTs supported by almost 150 various types of smaller landing craft. Task Force 85 was directed by a destroyer and a fighter direction tender; its assault group included 6 troop transports, 24 LCT/LSIs and about 110 other landing craft. Task Force 87 had 6 transport/cargo ships plus 24 LSI/LSTs supported by about 90 landing craft. Lastly Task Force 86, which was to deliver the French special forces, was the smallest, with 5 destroyer/transports, 5 LSIs and 17 other vessels.

Hewitt was reliant on the aircraft carriers for his tactical air support. These were under the overall control of Rear Admiral Thomas Troubridge RN, with the American carriers commanded by Rear Admiral Calvin T. Durgin USN, who had commanded the USS *Ranger* in action during the North African landings. Troubridge's escort carrier Task Force 88 (TF88) comprised two groups. The first, Task Group 88.1, was made up entirely of British carriers and consisted of HMS *Attacker* (879 Naval Air Squadron (NAS) equipped with Seafires), HMS *Emperor* (800 NAS equipped with F6F Hellcats), HMS *Khedive* (899 NAS equipped with Seafires), HMS *Pursuer* (881 NAS equipped with F4F Wildcats), and HMS *Searcher* (882 NAS equipped with F4F Wildcats). This task group was protected by the cruisers HMS *Delhi* and HMS *Royalist* (flagship), plus five British destroyers and a Greek destroyer.

Task Group 88.2 comprised HMS *Hunter* (807 NAS equipped with Seafires), HMS *Stalker* (809 NAS equipped with Seafires), and two American carriers, USS *Tulagi* (VOF-01 equipped with F6F Hellcats) and USS *Kasaan Bay* (VF-74 equipped with F6F Hellcats). They were defended by the light cruisers HMS *Colombo* and HMS *Caledon* and six US destroyers. All the British carriers were by courtesy of Roosevelt's Lend-Lease and American shipyards, having mostly been handed over in 1943.

Brigadier-General Gordon P. Saville of the USAAF's 12th Air Force was appointed Air Task Commander, with the XII Tactical Air Command. The medium bomber and fighter elements of Saville's force were provided by Seafires from the seven British carriers and Grumman Hellcats from the USS *Kasaan Bay* and USS *Tulagi*. Hewitt, Saville, Patch and Truscott travelled together from Naples on the amphibious assault ship USS *Catoctin*. They were joined by Admiral André Lemonnier, Chief of Staff of the French Navy.

Employing over 880 ships, Dragoon was the largest amphibious operation ever conducted in the Mediterranean; in the Pacific only three operations were bigger, out of the forty amphibious assaults conducted there. During the Allied naval build-up the Luftwaffe kept General Wiese appraised of developments, though neither he nor

Blaskowitz knew exactly where the blow would fall; in any case, they had insufficient forces to defend the entire coastline.

Allied operations in the Mediterranean did not go unhindered by the Luftwaffe. On 20 April 1944 bombers attacked the ships of Task Force 66, escorting the convoy UGS-38 bound for the Mediterranean, soon after the vessels cleared Gibraltar. The convoy's flagship was the US Coastguard cutter USS *Duane*, which was shortly to play a role in Dragoon on her first assignment since being converted to a command and control vessel. Three ships from the convoy were lost, including the SS *Paul Hamilton*, which sank with 580 people aboard, and the destroyer USS *Landsdale*.

As the numbers of Allied escort vessels increased, and the threat from German U-boats decreased, the US Navy had decided that cutters like the *Duane* would better serve national security needs as command and control vessels for amphibious landings. The USS *Duane* had been assigned to the 8th Fleet in mid-1943 and had escorted convoys to the Mediterranean and back and also through the Caribbean before being converted to an amphibious force flagship by the Norfolk Navy Yard in early 1944. The conversion included the removal of most of the heavy armament, the addition of more anti-aircraft weaponry, and the construction of enclosed rooms for thirty-five radio receivers and twenty-five radio transmitters.

The air war hots up

Supporting the preparations for Dragoon were the 42nd Bomb Wing (Medium) and the 17th Bomb Group. The former first saw action during the invasion of Italy, where its units flew close support missions to stop the German counter-attack on the beachhead at Salerno. As the Allied forces progressed, the 42nd took a leading part in interdicting Axis road and rail transport, and later in the attacks against the monastery at Cassino.

The 17th Bomb Group, comprising the 34th, 37th, 432nd and 9th Squadrons, was involved in the reduction of Pantelleria and Lampedusa in June 1943, participated in the invasions of Sicily in July and of Italy in September, and took part in the drive towards Rome. Because of its renowned bombing accuracy, the group was selected to bomb targets in Florence, but with strict orders to avoid the art treasures there. The 17th also took part in the assault on Monte Cassino.

In 1943 a heavy bomb group had a total complement of 294 officers and 1,487 enlisted men to fly and support 48 heavy bombers, while a medium bomb group had 294 officers and 1,297 enlisted men for 63 medium bombers.

Air operations for Dragoon were to consist of four phases:

I – operations taking place before D-Day minus 5;

II – operations taking place between D-Day minus 5 and 0350 hours on D-Day (Operation Nutmeg);

III – operations between 0350 on D-Day and H-Hour at 0800 (Operation Yokum); and

IV – all subsequent operations (Operation Ducrot).

In Phase I, from 28 April to 10 August 1944, the Allied air forces unloaded 12,500 tons of bombs on the region. Nutmeg began on the 10th, and while concentrating on coastal defences and radar stations, encompassed the whole of the French coast in order to throw the Germans off the scent. On 7 August Army Group G reported that the 'systematic, especially heavy air attacks on the transportation links over the Rhône and Var rivers . . . point to a landing between these two rivers', and 'statements from agents confirm this suspicion'.

The following day Wiese conducted a map exercise at the garrison headquarters at Draguignan for all his generals. It soon became clear that the army was on its own and could expect no help from the Luftwaffe or navy. Wiese's reserves consisted of a single regiment from the 148th Division, and all he could do to strengthen his defences was to move an anti-tank gun battalion to San Raphael.

On the 11th, as the Dragoon assault force began to move from the Naples area towards the south of France, the USAAF 12th Air Force sent B-25 Mitchell and B-26 Marauder twin-engined bombers and P-47 Thunderbolt fighters to strike at German gun positions along the French and Italian coasts west of Genoa. The following day almost 550 fighter-escorted B-17 Flying Fortresses and B-24 Liberator four-engined bombers attacked targets in France and Italy, the B-24s striking gun positions in the Genoa, Marseilles, Toulon and Sete areas, while the B-17s bombed gun positions in the Savona area in Italy. At the same time more than a hundred P-51s strafed radar installations and other coast-watching facilities along the southern French coast.

During the night of 12/13 August twin-engined A-20 Douglas Bostons attacked targets along the Monaco-Toulon road, and fighter-bombers hit guns and barracks in the area; fighters strafed airfields at Les Chanoines, Montreal, Avignon, La Jasse, Istres-Le-Tube, Valence and Bergamo. On 13 August the 17th Bomb Group attacked the Toulon harbour gun complex twice, both times encountering intense and accurate anti-aircraft fire, which damaged a number of the attacking B-26 Marauders. The heavy Allied bombing of Toulon and other targets in the days before the landing alerted Blaskowitz to the fact that something was likely to happen in this area. Indeed, suspecting an imminent attack in the Marseilles-Toulon region, by the 14th Blaskowitz had moved the 11th Panzer Division and two infantry divisions to new positions east of the Rhône, just in case.

On the 14th nearly 500 B-17s and B-24s of the 15th Air Force bombed gun positions around Genoa, Toulon and Sete, and struck the bridges at Pont-St-Esprit, Avignon, Orange and Crest in France. In addition, thirty-one P-38 Lightnings dive-bombed Montélimar airfield, while other fighters flew over 180 sorties in support of the bombers. Also on the same day medium bombers blasted coastal defence guns in the Marseilles area. The Toulon-Nice area also came under attack, with American medium bombers hitting coastal defences and fighter-bombers pounding various gun positions, tracks, enemy headquarters and targets of opportunity; fighters also strafed radar installations and targets of opportunity along the southern coast as the Dragoon assault forces approached.

The final build-up
On the night of 10 August Churchill flew via Algiers to Italy to see General Alexander to discuss the on-going operations and his loss of resources. In Algiers Churchill saw his son Randolph, who was recovering from injuries received in a plane crash that happened while he was visiting partisan-held Yugoslavia. Almost inevitably, de Gaulle came up in their conversation and Randolph pressed his father to change his mind about his recent decision not to see the French leader. 'After all,' said Randolph, 'he is a frustrated man representing a defeated country.

You, as the unchallenged leader of England and the main architect of victory, can afford to be magnanimous without fear of being misunderstood.'

Churchill arrived in Naples on the 12th and stayed with General Wilson at the Villa Rivalta. While there he received a plea from the Polish Home Army, which was struggling desperately for survival in Warsaw; it urgently needed weapons to fight the Germans. Stalin, however, considered the rising in the Polish capital an irrelevance and refused to lend it his support, apparently believing that the Red Army and its Polish allies had done all they could to reach the city. So the RAF had to make a 2,250 km round trip from southern Italy to Warsaw to drop supplies and weapons although the Red Air Force was less than 80 km away.

After a visit from the partisan leader Tito, Churchill went by barge to bathe in the hot springs at a nearby beach. On the way he passed two convoys massing for Dragoon, and the troops recognised him and cheered. In return, he sent them a note wishing them good luck. Later he wrote, 'They did not know that if I had had my way they would have been sailing in a different direction.'

That night Roosevelt, perhaps trying to placate the British Prime Minister and with an eye to the future, sent him an invitation for a meeting in September in Quebec without Stalin. Churchill agreed. The following day he went to Capri and swam in the sea, guarded by American military police. On the 14th he went for a swim beyond Cumae, and after lunch in Naples flew to Corsica. In Ajaccio harbour he went aboard the *Royal Scotsman*, an old merchantman bearing six assault craft ready for Dragoon.

On 12 August, due south of Ajaccio, the Luftwaffe picked up two large convoys, each of about 75 to 100 merchant vessels and warships, including two aircraft carriers, heading north-east towards the harbour; already present in the harbour were another 20 vessels. As if to confirm that an invasion build-up was taking place, on the airfield were sighted 8 gliders and 5 multi-engine aircraft. Luftflotte 3 immediately ordered that reconnaissance efforts over these convoys be stepped up day and night.

Two days later an Fw 190 fighter of 2/NAG 13 and four Bf 109s were on convoy patrol in the area to the south of Marseilles-Toulon-Golfe du Lion, but no sightings were made. Subsequently, at 1915 hours, pilots of 2/NAG 13 reported numbers of landing craft stretching some 80 km west from Ajaccio Roads and at 2035 two convoys were sighted 160 km south of Menton, numbering over 100 landing craft as well as surface and air escorts.

In the meantime twelve P-38s of the 94th Fighter Squadron, 1st Fighter Group dive-bombed the headquarters of Jagdfliegerführer Süd at La Nerthe. At 1900 hours the base reported that its command post had been destroyed and that three personnel had been killed, three badly wounded and three slightly injured. The phone lines were down, rendering the base inoperable as a headquarters, and the base commander decided to set up an aircraft reporting centre in Courthezon (10 km south-east of Orange) the following day.

At noon on 13 August the main invasion convoy sailed from Naples through the Sardinia-Corsica Straits and deployed off the Riviera beaches at dawn on the 15th. The destroyer USS *Rodman*, assigned to protect part of the invasion convoy, sailed from Taranto on 11 August. Two days later French warships joined them, and the force arrived off the Delta assault area in the Baie de Bougnon also on the 15th. The naval guns and bombers bombarded the coastline as the landing craft were lowered and the first waves of troops were ferried towards the assault beaches. In Italy on the 13th Alexander's troops entered Florence, though their offensive strength was now exhausted and the Germans had been given time to entrench themselves more firmly in the Gothic Line. Indeed, the Allies were still stuck south of the Gothic Line ten days after the launch of Dragoon.

Chapter Seven

Dragoon – 'irrelevant and unrelated'

Early on 15 August, in the 15th Air Force's first mass night raid, 252 B-17 Flying Fortresses and B-24 Liberators took off before dawn to bomb the beaches in the Cannes-Toulon area in advance of Dragoon, while 28 other fighter-escorted B-17s attacked highway bridges over the Rhône river; other B-17s sent against coastal gun positions had to abort their mission owing to poor visibility. In the meantime, 166 P-51 fighters escorted the Mediterranean Tactical Air Force (MATAF) C-47 Skytrain transport aircraft carrying the airborne invasion troops.

By the evening of 14 August some 526 C-47s and 452 Horsa and Waco gliders had been gathered to ferry the airborne assault force. Le Muy, sited just inland from the landing beaches, provided some protection for the invasion area and access to the Argens valley corridor, and was therefore to be swiftly secured by Allied airborne troops. This parachute assault on the Le Muy-Le Luc area was conducted by the 1st Airborne Task Force, comprising the British 2nd Independent Parachute Brigade, the US 517th Parachute Regimental Combat Team and a composite US parachute/glider regimental combat team formed from the 509th Parachute Infantry Battalion, the glider-deployed 550th Airborne Infantry Battalion and the 1st Battalion, 551st Parachute Infantry Regiment. Between Marseilles and Toulon planes dropped radar-obscuring chaff and then several hundred parachute-borne dummies.

Within 18 hours of the air drop commencing at 0430 hours, no fewer than 9,099 troops, 213 artillery pieces and anti-tank guns and 221 vehicles had been landed behind enemy lines. Despite the landings being widely scattered, all missions were accomplished within 48 hours. The airborne task force losses included 560 killed, wounded or missing, with 283 jump and glider casualties. The 517th Parachute Infantry Regiment's losses included 19 killed, 126 wounded and 137 injured by D-Day +3. In addition, 357 of the 407 gliders employed were so badly damaged that they were written off.

104

At least five hours before dawn on the 15th Attack Force Sitka – comprising 2,000 members of the 1st Special Service Force, led by Colonel Edwin A. Walker – landed on the islands of Levant and Port Cros off the left Alpha flank. They quickly secured Levant, which was defended by perhaps 150 troops with fake artillery made to give the impression of formidable defences. Although the German defenders in the old fort on Port Cros would hold out for two days, the Alpha flank was quickly secured.

Meanwhile, 1,000 French commandos of Attack Force Romeo came ashore at Cape Negre, scaled the cliffs and headed inland to block the vital coast road. Things didn't go quite so well for the French Attack Force Rosie, charged with the same task on Camel's far right flank, which got caught in a darkened minefield and lost ten men to German machine-gunners.

At 0550 Saville's bombers moved in to soften up the German defences along a 72 km stretch of coast. The German flak reportedly remained quiet, stunned into silence by the weight of bombs. The USS *Tulagi*, deployed off the invasion coast, launched her first flight of Hellcats at 0546 in support of the assault forces. At 0600, two hours before H-hour (the assault's official start time), bombers of the 12th Tactical Air Force dropped their bombs along the invasion coast. The noise was deafening and the coast soon disappeared in a pall of smoke and dust. Over 4,200 sorties were flown that day.

The bombers departed by 0730 and the Riviera was still rumbling and smoking from their assault when Hewitt's battleships, cruisers and destroyers opened fire; some 400 naval guns, including those on the French battleship *Lorraine*, the British battleship HMS *Ramillies*, and the American capital ships USS *Texas*, *Nevada* and *Arkansas*, as well as a fleet of over fifty cruisers and destroyers, pounded the area even further, and then at 0755 the Allies' rocket ships unleashed 30,000 rockets on to the battered German positions. One of the major targets for the naval bombardment was the remaining gun from the scuttled French battleship *Provence* at Toulon; appropriately enough, this was blasted by the 340mm guns of the *Lorraine*.

The battleship USS *Texas* had arrived off St Tropez during the night. At 0651 she began her pre-landing bombardment on the defensive fortifications. She remained in the immediate region for two days to provide support until the assault troops had marched out of range of her guns, before leaving the French coast on the 16th and returning to New York for repairs.

USS *Augusta* fired 15 rounds at Port Cros island on the 15th, 63 the following day, and 138 on the 17th, and the German-held fort surrendered on the last day of the Allied naval bombardment. The *Augusta* remained in the area to provide naval gunfire support for Dragoon, and by the time the operation drew to a close she had expended over 700 203mm rounds.

Between 0430 and 0641 hours the American destroyer USS *Rodman* guarded minesweepers that were busy clearing the channels to the beaches and then spent two hours bombarding shore targets. Subsequently she was placed on fire support and anti-aircraft screening duties, roles she conducted until retiring to Palermo on the 17th.

Alpha's beach was bombarded by the combined firepower of a battleship, a cruiser, 5 light cruisers and 6 destroyers. Likewise Delta was subjected to heavy shelling by 2 battleships, 6 light cruisers and 8 destroyers. The bombardment group covering Camel consisted of a battle ship, a cruiser, 5 light cruisers and 11 destroyers. A battleship, a cruiser, 3 light cruisers and 4 destroyers covered the much smaller Sitka Force landings.

As well as the warships, fire support was provided by a variety of converted armed landing craft including the Landing Ship Medium (Rocket) and Land Craft Infantry (Gun) and (Rocket). Also there were Landing Craft, Support (Large) which were purpose-built gunboats based on the LCI, while Landing Craft Support (Small) were converted Landing Craft Personnel (Large) which could carry machine-guns and rockets. The formidable LCT(R)s carried 1,094 5-inch rockets with a range of 3,200 metres, and what these lacked in accuracy they made up for with sheer volume. Task Force Alpha was allocated 12 fire support craft, Task Force Delta 8 and Task Force Camel 7. All these vessels provided a further battering for the German defenders.

Churchill comes round

At 0800 on the 15th Churchill was ferried from the *Royal Scotsman* over to the destroyer HMS *Kimberley* heading towards the French coast. Brooke was delighted that his unrelenting taskmaster was now absent. 'Life has a quiet and peaceful atmosphere about it now that Winston is gone,' he wrote. 'Everything gets done twice as quickly.'

Always with an eye on history and his place in it, Churchill now accompanied the invasion fleet, but slept through the initial landings. Later he stood on the deck while passing American troops yelled 'Winnie, Winnie!', unaware that he had done everything in his power to derail Dragoon. Unimpressed, and perhaps still sulking, he retired to his cabin to read. He later noted bitterly: 'One of my reasons for making public my visit was to associate myself with this well-conducted but irrelevant and unrelated operation.' He viewed the whole operation as a waste of time and lives, and recorded: 'Here we saw long rows of boats filled with American storm troops steaming in continuously to the Bay of St Tropez. As far as I could see or hear, not a shot was fired either at the approaching flotillas or on the beaches. The battleships had now stopped firing, as there seemed to be nobody there.'

Just after midday, wrote Churchill to his wife, 'we found ourselves in an immense concourse of ships, all sprawled along twenty miles of coast with poor St Tropez in the centre. It had been expected that the bombardment would continue all day, but the air [attack] and the ships had practically silenced the enemy guns by 8 o'clock. This rendered the proceedings rather dull.' Nevertheless, Churchill later told King George VI, 'Your majesty knows my opinion of the strategy, but the perfect execution of the plan was deeply interesting.'

After the months of bickering over Dragoon, on the actual day there was an air of unreality to the proceedings, as Captain Butcher observed:

Today is D-Day for Anvil, but while the press conference was in progress, starting at 9.15, we had no word that it actually had taken place, although we were informed that H-Hour was 8 a.m. Ike merely told the reporters to listen to their radios during the day for interesting information. He was asked if he would have command of the invasion in southern France and he said 'Eventually', but asked them to 'lay off the subject for the time being'.

Clearly Eisenhower was trying to avoid rubbing salt into Churchill's wounds by immediately usurping General Wilson's authority in the Mediterranean. Once he had done so, it would be all too obvious that America was firmly in the driving seat. The last thing he wanted was the press trumpeting his leadership of both invasions of France.

Eisenhower's recollection of the situation was far more generous than Churchill's:

> As usual the Prime Minister pursued the argument up to the very moment of execution. As usual, also, the second that he saw he could not gain his own way, he threw everything he had into support of the operation. He flew to the Mediterranean to witness the attack and I heard that he was actually on a destroyer to observe the supporting bombardment when the attack went in.

It seems Churchill saw no further point in dragging out the issue. 'The Prime Minister has come around magnificently,' reported Ike's naval aide, 'and has sent Ike a glowing message, after watching the landings in southern France, that the results of all the Allies' efforts may eclipse the Russian victories.'

The latter, of course, was wishful thinking; nothing would eclipse Stalin's Bagration and Lvov-Sandomierz summer offensives, which had all but shattered the German armed forces on the Eastern Front. The scale and speed of the unravelling of Hitler's defences in France was nothing compared to the disasters that had engulfed his troops in Byelorussia, Ukraine and Poland.

Harry Butcher recalled:

> We have just heard from Major-General Alexander M. Patch, veteran of Guadalcanal, who commands the US 7th Army in the southern landings. He says the operation seems successful.
>
> Our old friend Lucian Truscott is commanding the VI Corps, which is comprised of the 3rd, 36th and 45th Divisions, which were the assault divisions. These were supported by airborne troops, Rangers, Commandos, French Commandos, and the 1st Special Service under Major-General Robert T. Frederick (formerly of the Operations Division). All assault divisions reported successful breaching of beach defences in [their] target areas and the attack was proceeding according to plan.

Riviera assault

The main assault on the beaches commenced at 0800 and there was no stopping the fleet of Allied warships and landing craft bearing the

American and French troops. Initially some twenty Sherman DD tanks were launched, all of which landed safely, but in the light of the weakness of the German resistance another sixteen were put ashore.

The US 3rd Infantry Division landed on the left at Alpha Beach (Cavalaire-sur-Mer), the 45th in the centre on Delta Beach (St Tropez) and the 36th on the right on Camel Beach (San Raphael). French commando units had already landed between Cannes and Hyères and secured the flanks. In the Alpha sector, Major-General J.W. O'Daniel's 3rd Division quickly picked its way inland and struck out in three directions. The 7th Infantry swept on to capture Cavalaire, while to the north troops of the 15th Infantry fought their way past minefields and machine-gun nests on their way into St Tropez. They arrived in mid-afternoon to be greeted by American paratroops (who had landed in the wrong place) and jubilant FFI soldiers, who had been fighting on and off for hours. The former had already captured the 240-strong garrison, along with two coastal batteries and an anti-aircraft battery. By nightfall the St Tropez area was clear of German troops.

In the 36th Infantry Division's sector the four assault beaches were codenamed Red, Yellow, Green and Blue. None of them was an ideal landing point. Red Beach was at the small port of San Raphael, which was the most important port in the entire US 7th Army's landing zone, because not only was it necessary for resupply of troops ashore, but also it was located near an airfield. Thanks to the local garrison, it was heavily defended by underwater obstacles, concrete pillboxes and gun emplacements, and immediately in front of the beach was a stone sea wall about 5 feet high. Inland from the beach and flanking it on the eastern side was the resort town of San Raphael itself and just beyond that the old stone city of Fréjus. The capture of Fréjus and San Raphael were priority missions that had to be accomplished swiftly.

Protected by submarine mine netting and flanked by extensive fire zones, Yellow Beach in front of the town of Agay was just a small horse-shoe-shaped inlet. Because of its defences any idea of a direct assault here was quickly abandoned. Enemy fortifications also obstructed Green Beach, a 250-metre-long rocky strip backed by a sharp incline near Cape Drammont. This was thought to be too small for a large landing, while Blue Beach, a few kilometres from Green, could accommodate only two small boats at a time.

It was decided that the 141st Infantry Regiment would attack Green

Beach with two battalions and Blue with one at H-Hour, in order to secure these beaches, capture Agay and protect the division's right. The 143rd Infantry was to follow up and push to the west to seize the heights overlooking San Raphael and Red Beach, thereby assisting the 142nd. The troops of the 142nd would land 6 hours later and, with the 143rd, would capture San Raphael, the airfield and Fréjus. Once off the beaches the troops were to strike inland to a depth of 20 km, resist any German counter-attacks from the Cannes area to the right, and push up the Argens river valley on the left to contact the paratroop force dropped near Le Muy.

At 0800 Colonel John W. Harmony's soldiers of the 141st began their assault. On Green Beach the 2nd Battalion struck to the right, the 3rd to the left. Miraculously, the defenders were taken by surprise and their machine-guns remained silent until the fourth wave had landed, by which time it was too late. Two hours later both Drammont and Cape Drammont, surrounding Green Beach, were reported clear. Casualties were light. Marching north through Agay, the 2nd Battalion encountered resistance from the defenders of Yellow Beach, while the 3rd Battalion seized the high ground directly north of Green Beach. On Blue Beach the Germans offered heavier resistance, with several anti-tank guns shelling the incoming landing craft of the 1st Battalion, 141st. However, this defence was soon neutralised and the battalion drove the Germans from the craggy dominating heights, with 1,200 men laying down their arms.

Colonel Paul Adams' 143rd Infantry, immediately following the 141st, came ashore in battalions on Green Beach, the 1st at 0945, the 2nd at 1000 and the 3rd at 1035. The 1st Battalion's immediate mission was to secure 'Grand Defend', the high ground to the north-west, and then the regiment pushed west, parallel to the shoreline, towards San Raphael.

On the far right the 36th Division ran into trouble. The landings at both Green and Blue Beaches went to plan, but Red Beach, where the 142nd Infantry Regiment was due to come ashore, was obstructed by mined concrete blocks, double rows of barbed wire, more mines and a combined trench and anti-tank wall that was 3.5 metres high. This wall was protected by German machine-gunners, while German 75mm, 88mm, 100mm and 105mm guns ranged in on the American minesweepers. Subsequent shelling by the fleet's battleships, cruisers and destroyers and bombing by a flight of B-24 Liberators failed to silence this German artillery. At 1100 hours the 142nd Infantry loaded into assault boats and headed for Red Beach, which they were due to hit at 1400. Here, though, the German defences had withstood all the bombing and those mine-clearing craft nearing the shore were shelled and sunk. To make matters worse, specially designed robot demolition boats, sent in just prior to the first wave, had clogged the beaches, which remained at the mercy of German flanking fire from San Raphael and the hills beyond Fréjus. With Green Beach open and undefended, the Naval Commander tried to order the 142nd Infantry to go there instead but communications between the admiral and the divisional commander were not working.

Heavy shore fire foiled the first landing attempt, after which Rear Admiral Lewis finally got through to redirect the 142nd Infantry east to Green Beach. The landing commenced at 1530. Colonel G.E. Lynch's regiment then swung in an arc north and west over the mountains between the 143rd and the 141st to attack Fréjus from the rear. The 143rd was ordered to clear Red Beach from the rear after it had seized San Raphael. There was to be no respite overnight as the troops hurried to broaden the newly won beachhead and secure their assigned objectives. Both Fréjus and San Raphael were cleared in the early morning by the 142nd and the 143rd. Red Beach was finally secured. Some 10 km inland the 141st surprised Germans travelling along the Cannes-Fréjus highway and placed blocks on all roads to Cannes near La Napoule.

While the Allied airborne landings suffered heavy losses (only 60 per cent of the paratroops landed on their drop zones and about fifty gliders were lost), the seaborne landings themselves were not opposed with much fervour and Allied losses amounted to just 95 killed and 385 wounded, a far cry from the huge casualties suffered during the Normandy D-Day landings. German forces by comparison lost over 2,000 men, with the bulk of them taken prisoner. There was no firing on the Allied fleet and 40 per cent of the prisoners taken were anti-Soviet Russians who had volunteered to fight Stalin, but had found themselves in the south of France on the receiving end of the Western Allies' offensive. Those who did offer token resistance were swiftly dealt with.

Over 94,000 men and 11,000 vehicles came ashore on that first day. The 3rd and 45th Infantry Divisions were soon pressing towards

Marseilles and the Rhône, while the 36th made their way towards the Route Napoleon and Grenoble. The follow-up forces, including the US VI Corps Headquarters, the US 7th Army Headquarters and the French II Corps (1st Armoured, 1st Motorised and 3rd Algerian and 9th Colonial Divisions) came ashore the following day and passed through VI Corps on the Marseilles road. Due to the rapidity of the advance, the lack of fuel became a greater impediment than German resistance. What followed was dubbed 'the champagne campaign'.

Meanwhile, Frederick's 1st Airborne Task Force pushed south and west, liberating local small towns and making contact with the FFI and Truscott's advancing forces, thereby sealing off the coast to the Germans. On 16 August units from the 509th Parachute Infantry and 550th Glider Infantry Battalions, with support from tanks of the 45th Division, drove the German defenders out of Le Muy. On the night of the 16th the 142nd broke the last German road-block before Le Muy in the Argens valley. Next day the paratroopers, who had landed nearby, were contacted and Draguignan was entered. In the town the local German corps commander, completely befuddled by the sharpness and speed of the Allied attack, was seized along with his entire staff. After two days on French soil VI Corps had secured a perimeter that extended some 32 km inland.

Blaskowitz's response

On the first day of Dragoon the Germans proved incapable of responding in a coordinated way, echoing the confusion that had confronted Operation Overlord on 6 June. At daybreak Botsch telephoned Blaskowitz's Chief of Staff General Heinz von Gyldenfeldt from the 19th Army's Headquarters at Avignon to say: 'The invasion fleet is approaching the coast off St Tropez. Therefore, we feel certain that the landings will take place there.' In fact the first reports of landings came from Marseilles.

General Wiese tried to establish a defence line using the 242nd Infantry Division in the Toulon area, the 244th guarding Marseilles with elements of the 189th and 198th as they came across the Rhône. Unfortunately for him the US 3rd Infantry struck on the boundary between the German LXII Corps' 242nd and 148th Infantry Divisions. The latter was formed at Metz in October 1942. Comprising the 8th and 239th Reserve Grenadier Regiments and a panzerjäger company, it had served in Italy and France under Generalleutnant Otto Schönherr.

General Baptist Kniess's LXXXV Corps controlled Generalleutnant Hans Schäfer's 244th and General Rene de l'Homme de Courbiere's 338th Infantry Divisions. The 244th was formed in September 1943 and consisted of three Grenadier regiments, the 932nd, 933rd and 934th, and an artillery regiment; Schäfer had assumed command in mid-April 1944. But Kniess's forces could achieve little and reinforcements summoned from other divisions amounted to little more than five battalions of men. They were unable to intervene quickly as the Rhône bridges were down following Allied air attacks. The following day two battalions would make a feeble attack towards Draguignan to try to reach LXII Corps' headquarters.

By the morning of the 15th General von Wietersheim's 11th Panzer Division was bearing down on the Allies' developing beachhead. Allied air attacks had missed a solitary bridge over the Rhône at Pont-St-Esprit 40 km north of Avignon. Von Wietersheim ordered his panzers to swing north from Avignon but his reconnaissance units were soon reporting that the bridge had just been destroyed in an air raid. Hitler had missed his chance by just 12 hours.

At Toulon it was now the German garrison's turn to scuttle the remaining French warships. They attempted to sink the *Strasbourg* and *La Galissonnière* in order to block the southern channel, but American Mitchell bombers sank them first.

All day during the 15th and through the night the Luftwaffe continually bombed the Allied fleet. A landing craft was sunk and at night German E-boats darted in and out of the ships doing quite a lot of damage. As early as 0100 hours Fliegerdivision 2 instructed KG 26 and III/KG 100 to attack the shipping in the Toulon-Marseilles area. However, the first raid did not occur until 0510, when JGr 200 scrambled a formation of about a dozen Bf 109s from its 1 and 2 *Staffeln*. Predictably enough, Allied fighters were waiting for them and they bumped into the P-38 Lightnings of 1st Fighter Group on 'Grapes' patrol (relays of twelve P-38s patrolling at 12–15,000 feet) between Fréjus and the Hyères Islands before they even reached the fleet. In the ensuing dogfight two Bf 109s were shot down and the rest of the force turned tail. In the meantime the Luftwaffe dispatched whatever reinforcements it could spare, with Luftflotte 2 sending some twenty-eight Bf 109s of II/JG 77 from Ghedi in Italy, bound for

Orange-Caritat, with the rest of the Gruppe following on the 16th.

Between 1838 and 1959 hours six Do 217 bombers of III/KG 100 attacked the landing craft, with the pilots claiming rather optimistically to have sunk a 7,000-tonne freighter and damaged the American destroyer *Le Long* and three LSTs, 312, 384 and 282. The Allies claimed glider bombs had accounted for two landing craft, while mines and shellfire were responsible for damage to other vessels.

Other attacks by Ju-88 bombers caused no damage. They had been ordered to carry out a torpedo attack at San Raphael while II Gruppe was assigned a target just east of Cap Nègre, where French commandos had come ashore. Bombs were to be dropped only south of the road since German troops were to the north of it.

During the 16th the Luftwaffe's main effort was simply reconnaissance. With airfields in the Rhône valley under continuous Allied attack, it was forced to withdraw assets to places of greater safety. Two days later Fliegerdivision 2 was subordinated with immediate effect to Luftflotte 2. The divisional operations staff were sent to Bergamo by the 20th, while a battle headquarters was established at Merate. Flying units were instructed to conduct the transfer flights either in the early morning or in the evening to avoid the attentions of Allied fighter-bombers.

The failure of the German Mortain counter-attack in Normandy and the developing Falaise Pocket meant that by the 16th it was imperative to save Army Group G before a more general collapse occurred in France. On the 17th Blaskowitz finally received his orders; abandoning Toulouse, he started withdrawing north. He had been instructed to move all his forces north-east except for the 148th Division in the Cannes-Nice area and a reserve mountain division at Grenoble, which were to move into Italy. The German High Command preferred to weaken the 19th Army rather than imperil the Italian front. Marseilles and Toulon were to remain German fortresses.

General Ferdinand Neuling at LXII Corps' headquarters just outside Draguignan, a few kilometres north-west of Le Muy, was not so lucky and found himself surrounded by enemy paratroopers. His two infantry divisions were trapped at Marseilles and Toulon. Friedrich Wiese sent the 189th Infantry Division to clear Le Muy and relieve LXII Corps, but the Americans easily fended off the feeble counter-attacks by elements of both the 189th and 148th Divisions.

LXII Corps had expected an airborne operation in the Marseilles area, and the Le Muy drop severely disrupted their communications. In particular, Neuling could not figure out what the goal of the paratroops was and did not know how to react. His command was reduced to a state of ineffectual chaos, while district commander Generalmajor Ludwig Bieringer could only muster 750 men to defend Draguignan. He radioed for reinforcements from 40 km away, but they did not come. Nor was he able to contact Neuling, the cabling between their two head-quarters having been cut. Fighting in the town was short-lived and the Americans quickly closed in on Bieringer's command post, and had soon seized the commander. The resistance by his headquarters was half-hearted following an American night attack. Bieringer had tried to raise Neuling on the phone but could get no reply, and while he was doing so his garrison surrendered. Shortly after, Neuling refused to accept an initial offer to surrender brokered by a young German lieu-tenant.

In the meantime Major-General Robert Frederick drove Bieringer down to Patch for interrogation; the German refused to disguise himself and was soon being pelted by locals and had to endure the humiliation of travelling the rest of the journey under a tarpaulin. In total, the 1st Airborne Task Force took a thousand German prisoners.

At 2100 hours on the 17th the U-boat *U-230* under Lieutenant Eberbach left Toulon and loitered near the Mandrier peninsula for two days before seizing an opportunity to attack the USS *Augusta*. The submarine tailed the battleship throughout the day on the 20th. Her captain claimed to have penetrated the *Augusta*'s destroyer screen and was about to launch four torpedoes when a shore battery opened up and bracketed the cruiser, which promptly beat a hasty retreat. The *U-230* ran aground that night and was abandoned by her crew.

Also on 17 August the Germans ordered the Vichy government to relocate to Belfort in eastern France with assurances that it would not be required to leave French territory. Pétain refused to go unless it was to Paris and three days later he was arrested by German troops. Pétain, Laval and the others were eventually sent to Sigmaringen in Germany.

Great hopes
After all the acrimony, even Brooke allowed himself an air of optimism on the 16th, recording:

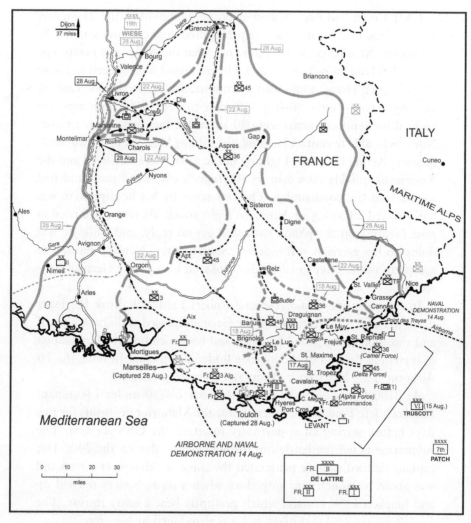

Operation Dragoon, 15–28 August 1944. (*Dennis Andrews*)

The landing near Toulon seems to be going well, whilst the operations in Normandy are working up towards a climax [at Falaise]. There are great hopes of delivering a smashing blow which might go a long way towards clearing the road for the rest of France.

The British Prime Minister Winston Churchill saw Operation Anvil/Dragoon as a waste of vital military resources. He threatened to resign over it and drove the Allied Supreme Commander General Dwight D. Eisenhower to distraction.

General Montgomery's meeting with Churchill in Marrakech on 31 December 1942 sowed the seeds of British opposition to the proposed Allied invasion of southern France.

Montgomery and Eisenhower, the architects of Overlord, pose for the cameras. For seven months in 1944 Ike endured unrelenting pressure from Monty and Churchill as they sought to strip away resources from Anvil/Dragoon, to divert the invasion or to cancel it altogether.

President Roosevelt did not trust General Charles de Gaulle, leader of the Free French, who was determined to manoeuvre himself into such a position that he would be hailed the saviour of France. The invasion of the Riviera was vital to de Gaulle's plans.

General Mark W. Clark (far right), commander of the US 5th Army in Italy, saw Dragoon as 'one of the outstanding political mistakes of the war'.

Eisenhower (standing, centre) and other Allied commanders visiting the Normandy beachhead. Operation Dragoon was originally supposed to coincide with Overlord.

Due to events in Normandy and following a row with General de Lattre over the French Combat Command Sudre, General Truscott was forced to set up Task Force Butler to provide armoured support for Dragoon.

Churchill with General Bradley in Normandy. On 7 August 1944 Winston spent the entire day lobbying Eisenhower to shift Dragoon to Brittany. Ike said no until he was 'practically limp'.

During the prelude to the Riviera invasion USAAF bombers, such as these Boeing B-17 Flying Fortresses, systematically struck the French and Italian Mediterranean coasts.

In Normandy and the south of France Allied airborne forces were assisted by the French Forces of the Interior (FFI) directed by Gaullist General Koenig.

The gathering of the invasion fleet in the Mediterranean and the preliminary bombing of Marseilles and Toulon soon alerted Generals Blaskowitz and Wiese to the prospect of an assault on southern France.

The cruiser USS *Philadelphia* pounding German coastal batteries from the Gulf of St Tropez on 15 August 1944.

American assault boats on the Riviera beaches. There were not enough landing craft to conduct Dragoon in parallel with D-Day, thereby ruining any diversionary value the operation may have had.

Although resistance on the Riviera was light, there were still 480 casualties.

On the first day of Dragoon some 94,000 men and 11,000 vehicles poured ashore.

Once the German 7th Army and 5th Panzer Army were trapped at Falaise in Normandy, it became imperative for Hitler to evacuate southern France as quickly as possible.

Apart from the 11th Panzer Division, General Blaskowitz had few armoured units in southern France. Most of his assault gun battalions were sent north to Brittany and Normandy.

French troops manhandle a captured Pak 40 anti-tank gun in liberated Toulon; this 'fortress' city yielded 17,000 German prisoners.

It was vital that General Blaskowitz held the Rhône crossings to ensure the escape of his 1st and 19th Armies. He conducted a remarkably orderly withdrawal.

Allied armour and Free French forces pushing towards Paris, making the Riviera invasion completely irrelevant to the liberation.

De Gaulle and General Leclerc (left) were adamant that French troops should take the credit for liberating Paris, despite the fact that the Americans, British, Canadians and Poles had borne the brunt of the Normandy fighting.

Just over a week after Dragoon, on the evening of 24 August elements of Leclerc's French 2nd Armoured Division slipped into Paris.

A French tank destroyer engages German troops on the streets of Paris. The German commandant initially refused to surrender, resulting in needless bloodshed.

Throughout France retribution against those who had collaborated with the occupiers was swift and often brutal. This French woman is escorted to an uncertain fate.

The retreating Army Group G, reliant on horse-drawn transport, was constantly vulnerable to Allied air attack. Blaskowitz's troops suffered 28,000 killed and wounded in southern France.

A devastated column of German horse-drawn wagons and lorries outside Montélimar. Blaskowitz's forces held the town until 28 August, when General Otto Richter was captured.

The fruits of victory. French Minister of War André Diethhelm, General de Lattre de Tassigny and Emmanuel d'Astier de la Vigerie, Minister of the Interior, review French troops during the liberation ceremony in Marseilles on 29 August.

Although dubbed the 'Champagne Campaign', the Allies' liberation of southern France was still a bloody affair. The Americans and French sustained about 10,000 casualties.

General Patton's US 3rd Army linked up with General de Lattre's forces on 12 September, three weeks after the German defeat in Normandy. This was just in time for the German counter-attack in Lorraine.

Forlorn German troops captured by the French 1st Army in Alsace. In total General Blaskowitz lost perhaps half of his 250,000 men in southern France.

Eisenhower in jovial mood. Despite his heated arguments over Dragoon, Ike kindly described Churchill as 'a cantankerous yet adorable father'. However, there could be no hiding the clear shift in the balance of power in the Anglo-American alliance.

Ultimately the only people who benefited from the invasion of southern France were de Gaulle and Stalin. In particular, the small French Army was able to take the credit for liberating the key cities of Marseilles, Paris and Toulon.

Events in the Falaise area during the second half of August and the subsequent liberation of Paris made Dragoon a pointless exercise. With the benefit of hindsight, Churchill felt his belief that Allied resources would have been better employed in Italy and Burma was vindicated.

Back in Naples the following day Churchill was soon distracted by events in the Aegean. Top secret German communication intercepts showed that a German withdrawal from Greece was imminent and Churchill was keen to get a military mission to Athens as soon as possible to prevent the Greek Communists seizing power. On the 17th Churchill visited the blasted remains of the monastery at Cassino and then flew to General Alexander's headquarters at Siena. Bad weather prevented him visiting the front on the Arno river until the 20th, after which he returned to Naples. He could not help but lament a lost opportunity, writing that the Allies:

> . . . could have broken into the Valley of the Po, with all the gleaming possibilities and prizes which lay open towards Vienna. That evening Alexander maintained his soldierly cheerfulness, but it was in a sombre mood that I went to bed. In these great matters, failing to gain one's way is no escape from the responsibility for an inferior solution.

On the morning of 18 August the 117th Cavalry Reconnaissance Squadron of General Dahlquist's 36th Infantry Division came ashore under Lieutenant-Colonel Charles J. Hodge. His armoured vehicles gathered near Le Muy and then drove through Draguignan heading for Salerns, Aups and Riez. They had only just got beyond the northwestern outskirts of Draguignan when they came under fire from a cave entrance on the nearby mountainside. A tank quickly loosed off several rounds of high explosive. A few German soldiers emerged from the cave, and then out staggered General Neuling, his corps headquarters having finally been captured. It now seemed only a matter of time before Army Group G suffered the same fate as Army Group B in northern France.

Chapter Eight

The 'Champagne Campaign'

General de Lattre, accompanied by his son Bernard, landed back on French soil on 16 August with a sense of optimism and anticipation. Two days later de Gaulle caused the Combined Chiefs of Staff concern when he announced that he intended to fly direct from Africa to France in a Lockheed Lodestar, which could carry barely enough fuel for such a trip, plus it was unarmed. The Americans offered him a plane plus fighter escort from England, but de Gaulle was adamant, provoking a polite reminder pointing out that if he did not coordinate his efforts with the Allies, they could not guarantee his safety. Now that Dragoon was firmly under way, the last thing Eisenhower wanted was an incident involving de Gaulle. However, behind the scenes there must have been some private reflection that life would be easier without this single-minded Frenchman, who by sheer will-power alone had made himself master of the Free French.

Late on the 18th the Luftwaffe made one last-ditch attack on the Allied fleet with 5 Do 217s, 10 Junkers and up to 15 torpedo Ju 88 bombers. One Ju 88 attempted to torpedo Fighter Direction Tender (FDT) 13 in the Delta Beach area, but its weapon detonated 250 yards short. Another Ju 88 dropped anti-personnel bombs on the same beach from 6,000ft. HMS *Colombo* and other ships of CTF 87 engaged a Ju 88 through gaps in the smokescreen, but observed no hits despite blasting away. Eleven Ju 88s attacked around St Tropez, while five passed over Camel and Delta Beaches in the Gulf of Fréjus at 9,000ft. At 2105 hours one of these straddled the USS *Catoctin*, Hewitt's flag-ship, with anti-personnel bombs. Two hit home, killing six men and wounding forty-two more, while others exploded near PT 208. Luckily General Patch had already gone ashore. After the attack three Ju 88s landed at Valence (two of them forced to belly-land after sustaining damage), another three at Montélimar and five at Orange-Plan de Dieu.

To the north in Normandy, meanwhile, by 18 August Army Group B's escape route at Falaise was only 8 km wide, though it was not completely sealed until the 21st. When the last pocket was finally overrun the Allies captured 334 armoured vehicles, 2,447 other vehicles and 252 pieces of artillery. Hitler lost 50,000 men captured and 10,000 killed, but significantly between 20,000 and 50,000 escaped to fight another day, although many of them would be killed before they crossed the Seine.

'Battle of Toulon Harbor'

With the weather remaining generally good carrier-based planes were able to conduct regular spotting missions and attack inshore targets, including gun emplacements and railway facilities, with impunity. Over the following week USS *Tulagi*'s aircraft flew a total of 68 missions with 276 sorties, inflicting considerable damage on the enemy. One squadron from the *Tulagi* alone reported a record of 487 motor vehicles ranging from staff cars to panzers destroyed and another 114 damaged. In the first week of Dragoon Blaskowitz lost 1,500 vehicles destroyed, mainly to air attack, as well as 200 vehicles captured and 1,500 horses killed. Losses in men comprised around 1,000 dead and 3,000 captured. During the fighting in the period 15–18 August the remnants of the 242nd Infantry withdrew into Toulon.

Brigadier-General Saville was full of praise for the air support effort from the carriers and wrote to Vice Admiral Hewitt to express his gratitude:

> I would like to express my appreciation for the outstanding work they have done and for their perfect cooperation. I consider the relationship and cooperation of this force to be a model of perfection and a severe standard for future operations. Today, I personally counted 202 destroyed enemy vehicles from 4 miles west of St-Maxime to 2 miles east of LeDuc. Well done and thanks.

Phases III and IV of Operation Dragoon's air war commenced on the 16th. The USAAF's 17th Bomb Group was called on to destroy the heavy guns at Toulon. Understandably the crews were sceptical of their ability to score direct hits on such small targets in the face of concentrated anti-aircraft fire. Pilots recalled it as one of the toughest targets of the war. The group was also tasked to destroy a number of bridges over the Rhône and Durance rivers. It was to lose five aircraft shot down and numerous others damaged during this phase of the air campaign.

The 37th Bomb Squadron, commanded by Captain Rodney S. Wright, from Washington state and a former RAF pilot, was the lead formation attacking the flak guns and emplacements around Toulon. Wright's number two on his right wing was Maurice Walton, piloting 'Red 34', a B-26 Marauder. The squadron was making its final approach when suddenly aluminium chaff (designed to distract enemy radar) began to flutter through the formation. This simply helped to highlight the exposed bombers as they made their run-in to the already fierce flak.

Red 34 had just released its bombs when the right engine was hit and caught fire. Luckily the co-pilot Don Hoover was able to feather it and this action, combined with a fire extinguisher, did the trick. Unfortunately tail-gunner Sergeant Jesse A. Ward was hit in the right arm. When he did not respond to the crew check, Staff Sergeant Brown, the waist gunner, went to assess Ward's condition and found him bleeding profusely. Bombardier Tom Richardson then crawled back and gave him an injection of morphine. Staff Sergeant Chuck Zahn, top turret gunner, helped move Ward to the radio compartment where Richardson administered first aid. The stricken bomber was forced to fly for two hours on one engine and in a desperate effort to lighten the load Sergeants Brown and Zahn threw out guns, flak vests, ammunition and anything else that was excess weight. All the while Don Hoover held the aircraft on course at about 170mph over the Mediterranean. Red 34 had suffered so much damage that it had to belly-land upon its return to base, and luckily it did not nose over as sometimes happened. Tail-gunner Sergeant Ward, who survived his injuries and the war, gained the Purple Heart and a Distinguished Flying Cross.

Sergeant Delbert F. Kretschmar, flying with the 95th Bomber Squadron, 17th Bomb Group reported things rather differently on 16 August: 'Mission was guns at south of Toulon. France. Mission was ok. Little flak and was inaccurate.' However, on 18 August another B-26 went down and two days later the 37th, 95th and 432nd Squadrons each lost an aircraft. During these missions the 17th Bomb Group encountered the heaviest, most accurate flak it had ever seen. Of the twenty-eight raids that the 42nd Wing conducted against this complex, just five succeeded in making a dent in the batteries. The so-called 'Battle of Toulon Harbor' cost the 42nd eight B-26s lost and resulted in damage to 125 others.

Fighting withdrawal

It was not long before the US 7th Army and French forces were pushing up the Rhône valley towards Avignon, Montélimar and ultimately Lyons. Blaskowitz had to time his withdrawal carefully so that units did not get ahead of themselves or fall too far behind, while drawing in his right flank (the 716th, 198th and 186th Infantry Divisions respectively west of Montpellier) and fending off the Americans and French on his left (the 148th and 242nd Infantry Divisions east of Toulon).

Overseeing the retreat up the west bank of the Rhône was General Petersen's IV Luftwaffe Field Corps, while Kniess's LXXXV Corps was managing things on the east bank. The plan was to coordinate their march on Lyons with the LXIV Corps heading from the Atlantic Coast via central France with the remains of two infantry divisions. This combined force would then move north towards Dijon and make contact with the retreating Army Group B. Blaskowitz must have looked at his situation maps with an air of exasperation, as all this had to be achieved with Patton's US 3rd Army on the verge of seizing Lyons or Dijon and the US 7th Army pushing up behind from the Riviera.

Both IV Luftwaffe Field Corps and LXXXV Corps had to protect vulnerable retreating headquarters staff, logistics and communications staff, field police units, Luftwaffe ground personnel and hospital staff. They numbered about 100,000, including 2,000 women, all of whom had little or no combat value. These forces had little more than rifles with which to protect themselves and were at risk from the vengeful Maquis. Indeed, the presence of the French Resistance ensured they could not flee north-east via the Massif Central, but had to detour via Poitiers and Bourges to Dijon. Giving the withdrawal order to the 19th Army was easy as it shared Blaskowitz's Avignon headquarters, but LXIV Corps could not be raised on the radio. A liaison officer, General Edgar Theisen, was sent by car to Toulouse, from where radio and courier messages could be sent out. Just to be on the safe side a plane was also dispatched to Bordeaux. Despite all this, none of the messages from Blaskowitz got through, although by good fortune the naval station at Bordeaux received the order via Berlin.

Before its departure LXIV Corps was obliged to leave behind the better elements of the 16th Infantry Division and the 159th Reserve Division to hold the fortresses of Bordeaux-Gironde and La Rochelle. The 159th formed the vanguard and the southern flank of this retreating corps, while the 16th acted as rearguard and screened the northern flank. Once en route Generalmajor Erich Elster, commanding the LXIV Corps rearguard, found that his wireless van could reach no one.

By 22 August the Luftwaffe's ability to influence the fighting in southern France was almost at an end. The evacuation of the airfields at Avignon and Lyons was ordered and Allied reconnaissance pilots reported that by the 23rd only 15 fighters and 10 tactical reconnaissance aircraft were occasionally observed north of Lyons. In places it became a 'turkey shoot' for the Allied fighter pilots.

The liberation of Toulon naval base

General de Lattre's original plan had been for his 3rd Algerian Infantry Division to conduct the main attack on Toulon from the north on 24 August, followed up by the 9th Colonial Division. Their flank was to be screened by the 1st Combat Command Sudre from the 1st Armoured Division and the 3rd Algerian Light Armoured Reconnaissance Regiment. The Germans' strong eastern defences were to be distracted by the 1st Free French Division. Once on the ground, though, accelerated landing schedules meant he needed to quickly rethink his timetable. Because the German coastal resistance was not as tough as expected, de Lattre had to decide whether to wait for his command to become fully assembled or risk a quick dash for Toulon. In light of the dogged German resistance in the Breton ports, de Lattre opted not to wait. National pride was also at stake, as if the French forces could secure Toulon and Marseilles swiftly they would be able to keep up with the Americans as they pushed northwards.

On the evening of the 18th, two days ahead of schedule, the 9th Colonial Division began to arrive. The initial units were sent to attack down the Solliés-Pont-La Valette axis almost immediately. The 9th

Division was instructed to open the French attack, supported by the African commando battalion (*Groupe de Commandos d'Afrique*) tasked with seizing the Coudon forts and silencing the artillery. In addition, shock commandos of the *Bataillon de Choc* were to take the defences on Faron.

General de Monsabert was ordered to traverse the inland heights and encircle Toulon, while General Brosset's men tackled the heavily fortified coastal approaches. The unexpected early arrival of General de Vernejoul's division meant that this was able to push along the San Raphael–Toulon road. On the afternoon of the following day de Monsabert launched his Algerians into the attack. The assault on the Redon was also opened and the next day French forces crossed the Gapeau river and captured it. The defences at Solliés-Ville and Solliés-Pont were likewise taken.

The German defenders were not given a minute's peace by the Allied warships or air forces. On the night of 19/20 August A-20s attacked lights and motor transport from the battle line north-west to the Rhône river; B-26s, joined by fighter-bombers and fighters, also hit the coastal defences in the Toulon area, while B-25s bombed the Rhône valley bridges and airfields, achieving especially good results at the airfield near Valence.

On the 20th the 3rd Algerian Infantry Division reached Mont Faron on the outskirts of Toulon, where General de Lattre ordered de Monsabert's forces to Ange Pass in preparation for an assault on Marseilles to the west. By the 21st Toulon was completely surrounded by de Monsabert's men. In the evening elements of the 3rd Algerian Light Infantry Regiment moved from the suburbs into Toulon itself and street fighting broke out. Meanwhile, de Lattre instructed the 1st Combat Command to deploy just east of Marseilles at Aubagne. He knew he must not become bogged down while the battle for Toulon was at its height: the Americans needed help in the Aix area and the French 1st Armoured Division was needed for the push up the Rhône.

A-20 bombers again struck at motor transport in the Nice area during the night of 21/22 August and hit industrial buildings in southern France during the day; fighters also attacked motor transport west of the Rhône and in scattered parts of south-east France; the 85th, 86th and 87th Fighter Squadrons from the 79th Fighter Group were deployed from Corsica to southern France with P-47s, and the 315th

Fighter Squadron from the 324th Fighter Group moved from Corsica to Le Luc, also with P-47s. At sea the USS *Rodman* fired on shore batteries at Toulon on the 23rd, and covered minesweepers in the Golfe de Fos on the 25th and in the Baie de Marseilles on the 26th.

In the eastern sector of Toulon's defences French troops attempted to capture La Poudrière, where the defenders employed old French tanks. French armour was brought up to seal off the quarry tunnels. On the 23rd attacks were stepped up on the Touar ridge, which was secured. By the evening the French were in force outside and inside the city and French troops took great pleasure in raising the tricolour over the Sous-Préfecture building. The following day they had only to clear the last of the Germans from their city strongholds, and the old Hôtel de la Subdivision was used to host de Lattre's headquarters. The capture of the Grignan barracks, the Sainte-Catherine and Lamalgue forts and the Arènes ridge yielded over 1,000 prisoners

The 9th Division commenced securing the huge naval base on the 25th. There was heavy fighting on Le Mourillon peninsula and inside the Arsenal Maritime. Fort Malbosquet surrendered after an artillery bombardment and most of the others followed suit, though the defenders of Fort Lartigues had to be threatened with assault. The arsenal at Le Mourillon was bombarded the next day before capitulating, followed by the Fort de Six-Four and the Bregallion battery south-west of Toulon at Cap Sicie. The defenders of Cap Eguillette, Fort Napoleon and the Balaguier battery offered flagging resistance.

While the firing was still going on, Admiral Lambert, keen to reassert French control over Toulon naval base, set up his headquarters at the Préfecture Maritime in the name of the Marine Nationale or French Navy. A triumphal parade was conducted through the streets on the 27th, with a march-past for the War and Naval Commissioners, to the sound of German guns still firing from the St-Mandrier peninsula. The 340mm guns had been repeatedly blasted by Allied bombers and nearby warships but continued to fire.

German attempts to flee Toulon by sea were futile. On the 27th the American destroyer USS *Ericsson* captured fifty German submariners attempting to escape on a fishing vessel, and the American motor torpedo boat *PT-552* sank four German explosive motorboats at the entrance to the harbour, though the control boat got away.

At 2245 hours Admiral Rufus, the City Commandant, agreed to

surrender unconditionally. The following day the garrison of 1,880 German marines laid down their arms. The nine-day battle for Toulon had cost the French 2,700 casualties but they had now secured the vast naval base for the Allies and taken 17,000 German prisoners of war, along with considerable quantities of weapons, including artillery.

Communists seize Marseilles

To the west in Marseilles the Resistance did not stand idly by. In particular, Gaston Defferre's Socialist militia was very active. During the twelve-day battle for the city, Corsican Barthélemy Guerini provided invaluable support to Defferre's forces, supplying intelligence, arms and men; he was subsequently awarded the Legion d'Honneur for his exploits. His brother Antoine, also an agent for Anglo-American intelligence, was responsible for smuggling arms into the city for the MUR after they had been supplied by British airdrop. When English intelligence officers were parachuted into the Marseilles area to make contact with MUR, they were hidden in the cellars of nightclubs belonging to Antoine Guerini. The communist-dominated Resistance took over the city's prefecture on the 23rd as de Lattre's troops closed in on the suburbs. The garrison could have easily overwhelmed them but seemed more concerned with the approaching regular French Army.

During the night of 23/24 August A-20 bombers hit motor transport and targets of opportunity in the Rhône valley and medium bombers attacked bridges at Montpellier, Avignon and Lunel and scored direct hits on gun positions in the Marseilles area; meanwhile roaming fighters bombed and strafed gun positions, vehicles, roads and bridges throughout south-east France. B-25 and B-26 bombers also attacked the Rhône river bridges at Avignon, Culoz, St-Alban-du-Rhône, Pont d'Ain and Loyes, and hit gun positions around Marseilles itself. Kretschmar with the 17th Bomb Group noted on 26 August, 'Mission was gun positions at Marseilles, France. Mission was milk run. Had little flak. . . . Altitude was 10,600 ft . . . was a morning run. Didn't drop bombs . . . had a rack malfunction. Was in No. 4 position.'

Initially General de Monsabert had been instructed only to clear Marseilles's suburbs, but with the Resistance rising up and the 1st Combat Command forcing its way towards the Old Port, de Monsabert's men moved to support them. He called on the German commander to surrender but he refused. His men were still firmly entrenched in Fort St Nicholas, an old fort by the harbour, and they held out there for four days. French artillery, though, soon made such a stand a futile exercise. On the 27th, just two days after the fall of Toulon and following an attack by the Algerians on the Notre Dame de la Garde feature, the Marseilles garrison surrendered.

On 29 August marines from the *Augusta* and the cruiser *Philadelphia* went ashore in Marseilles harbour to take the surrender of over 700 German troops who had fortified the harbour islands. Two weeks later the first supply vessels began to unload in the harbour. The American and French armies found Marseilles already in the hands of a Resistance-led left-wing administration. Initially cooperation between the American military and the French proceeded smoothly, but American plans for the port to be given over almost exclusively to American military requirements and their long-term presence soon strained relations. The Americans had also designated the coastal area as a rest and relaxation zone for their troops and this further aggravated the situation. In Cherbourg the requirements of the war effort meant the Americans were able to ride largely roughshod over French sens- ibilities, but in Marseilles the administration soon let its displeasure be known.

Remarkably, French and American forces had captured both Toulon and Marseilles in just fourteen days. Dragoon's planners, erring on the safe side, had assumed that these towns would not be secured until D-Day plus 40. Upon his arrival in Marseilles General de Gaulle took a dim view of the FTP, seeing it as a threat to his consolidation of power in the south of the country. Similarly he commented 'What a farce,' upon inspecting local resistance forces; in Toulouse he was even more scathing, remarking 'Can't you sew?' to one unfortunate resistance officer. To be fair, de Gaulle was simply exhibiting a northerner's traditional sense of rectitude in the face of southern exuberance, but on a more professional level he was displaying his clear dislike for the rag- tag militia the French Resistance had turned into. He was also not blind to the fact that the Resistance was now much bigger than it had been under Nazi occupation, as everyone sought to share in the glory of the liberation. Within a few months de Gaulle would ensure that these paramilitary units were no longer any threat to him by incorporating them into the French Army, where they were subject to military discipline.

With all his formations ashore, de Lattre's Army B was to become the French 1st Army consisting of I Corps under General Béthouart on the right and II Corps under de Monsabert on the left. De Lattre was now an army commander in his own right, effectively making Patch an irrelevance to French military thinking.

Meanwhile in Italy the Allies were trying to break the Pisa-Rimini Line. Alexander launched Operation Olive on 25 August, but the 8th Army had been weakened by the requirements for Dragoon and its momentum was slow. It took a month to reach Rimini. There it soon became apparent that the Po valley was not the excellent tank country that the British had supposed. The Germans were able to withdraw to another defensive line along the river Uso, and there were another thirteen rivers to cross before reaching the Po itself. With the British exhausted, having lost almost 500 tanks, the Germans were able to check Clark's US 5th Army.

In the Far East the Japanese armies in Burma were in retreat by August, and to hasten them on their way Operation Capital was designed to advance into central and southern Burma. The Japanese were reconciled to losing their land-bridge to China, but they still had 100,000 troops in Burma, who had as yet experienced no maritime threat to their left flank. Operation Dracula, the amphibious assault to take southern Burma, would now have to wait, thanks to Dragoon.

Defeat at Montélimar

In order to avoid the errors of Anzio, it was decided that it was imperative for Truscott's US VI Corps to thrust northwards as quickly as possible even as the bridgehead was being consolidated. The Gap or Gate of Montélimar provided him with the best way of blocking Route N7 and trapping Wiese's 19th Army. The river Rhône flows in an almost straight north–south route over 200km between Lyons and its entrance to the delta at Avignon. Beyond Orange it narrows greatly, and at Montélimar, some 70km north of Avignon, the Montélimar Plain and the Valence Plain are divided by the Cruas Gorge, also known as the Gap of Montélimar. The west bank of the river is bordered by cliffs, while on the east deeply forested hills slope up to some 400 metres.

To exploit this breach at the Gap, Truscott ordered his deputy corps commander Brigadier-General Frederick Butler to spearhead the push with his task force (comprising the 753rd Tank Battalion, the 2nd

Battalion, 143rd Infantry from the 36th Division, the 59th Armoured Field Artillery Battalion, the 117th Reconnaissance Squadron, plus tank destroyers and supporting combat engineers). The 36th Division was to follow up towards Grenoble through Castellane and along the N85, while the 3rd and 45th Divisions pushed up the Argens corridor towards the Rhône. The 3rd Division rumbled along the N7, forcing its way into Aix-en-Provence on the 21st. Everywhere the Germans seemed in disarray or were gone. The 45th Division secured the crossings over the Durance by clearing Barjols, which enabled the 3rd Division to shift right to join the march on Grenoble. Their job, if all went well, was to herd the fleeing Germans into the arms of Task Force Butler and the 36th Division at the Gap of Montélimar. The trap was set.

Futile German attempts to reinforce their troops facing the beach-heads were soon thwarted once Task Force Butler had taken the Col de la Croix Haute mountain pass, 1,179 metres up on the N75 north of Apres. Similarly, with the aid of the FFI, the Gap was taken along with 1,000 German prisoners. This meant that the German 157th Reserve Division at Grenoble could not dispatch further troops south. Butler swung west to block the Germans' escape routes up the Rhône valley. North of Livron his men caught a German convoy of thirty vehicles but around La Coucourde ran into superior German forces. By this stage the Germans had established themselves on Ridge 300, the high ground dominating the roads heading north and east. However, on the 21st the Americans reached the hills overlooking the Rhône valley north of the Gate of Montélimar. From here, reconnaissance units from the Butler Task Force watched enemy traffic stream up the main valley road, and blocked enemy armour trying to get there through Puy-St Martin. Along the floor of the valley itself the Germans had grouped the 11th Panzer Division, while opposing them were the 636th Tank Destroyer Battalion and the 753rd and 191st Tank Battalions. The task force opened up on the fleeing Germans below. A tank crewman attached to the 143rd Infantry Regiment recalled:

We fired our guns continuously without stopping, and the recoil system got so hot that the system was slowing down. Norris, my loader, was pushing shells into the breach with his fist, and due to the fast fire, his skin began to peel off his hand. I exchanged places with Norris for a while, and I also lost some skin. We fired until we were out of ammunition and had to order more.

Just seven days after the landings the 36th Infantry Division had penetrated as far as Grenoble, 400 km into France. Truscott instructed the division to obstruct the German withdrawal up the Rhône, as well as counter any German reinforcements that might be pushing south. However, the 36th Infantry Division was spread over four widely separated sectors, at Grenoble, Gap and Guillestre, Digne, and in the beachhead. This meant that to escape, Wiese's German 19th Army would have to barge the American troops out of the way. By 1700 hours on 23 August a battalion from the 141st Infantry Regiment had got to within a kilometre of Montélimar before small-scale counter-attacks developed along its flanks. By midnight enemy infiltration threatened its supply lines and the battalion was forced to withdraw. The following day the entire division deployed to the region. The 142nd Infantry Regiment moved swiftly from Gap and Guillestre to defensive positions near Nyons, south-east of Montélimar, while the 143rd hurried down from Grenoble.

Behind the 11th Panzer Division, reinforced and backed by fresh units, came the entire 198th Infantry Division. As the soldiers of the 198th mounted a full-scale attack to drive the 141st out of its positions north-east of Montélimar and force its artillery to withdraw out of range of the highway, the 142nd and 143rd Regimental Combat Teams raced up from the south. By 24 August the 142nd had reached the battle-ground and occupied defensive positions in a zone some 40 km long; they were soon followed by the balance of the 143rd.

From 25 to 30 August the 36th Division was attacked daily, with the main German effort pushing along a spur valley which ran north-east from Montélimar in an attempt to cut the 36th's supply routes and encircle the defenders. In addition, the Germans constantly subjected the division's long defensive perimeter to spoiling attacks designed to prevent the 36th Division from launching any attacks of its own. On the evening of the 25th Route 7, several kilometres north of Montélimar, was severed by the entire 141st Regimental Combat Team, reinforced by elements of the 143rd. In the process they beat off German infantry and armour. This attack cut the valley road at a narrow neck of the Rhône south of La Coucourde. Lieutenant-Colonel Charles Wilber's mission was to hold the block as long as possible. In the event of the Germans breaking through, he and his men were to fall back eastwards to Crest and hold the town at all costs, blowing up the bridges as a last resort. Subsequent German counter-attacks broke through the road-block soon after midnight. German armour was soon being reported north and north-west of Crest, in the vicinity of Banlieu and near Grance. The northernmost road-block, manned by the 36th Cavalry Reconnaissance Troop, was forced back at daybreak by overwhelming German power. Reinforcements in the shape of the 157th Infantry Regiment of the 45th Division were deployed north of Crest.

Now, although the 36th Division had almost surrounded the 19th Army, the Germans were on three sides of the division. Artillerymen turned their guns 180 degrees to pummel German armour threatening Grance and Crest to the north. The 36th Division salient at Montélimar thrust towards Route 7 several kilometres north of the city. Running through Condillac, Sauzet and Cleon, and anchored at Crest, the snaking lines of supply and communication ran from the south to Crest. At first the Germans held the initiative and certainly if they had conducted a bold oblique thrust to the east, they might have disrupted the whole of VI Corps, cutting the only artery up from the beaches. General Dahlquist decided to hold the little Rubion stream-bed (in front of a vital supply road) on a flat bowl-shaped plain backed up by a wall of hills. His divisional artillery was deployed on to the hills, opening up in a great arc to the south, west and north. Key terrain held by the infantry allowed gun positions to be disposed in such a manner that the route of German withdrawal along the Rhône was under fire for 25 km.

Long German convoys were destroyed, and the entire zone was literally covered with a mass of burned vehicles, trains, equipment, dead men and dead animals. German attacks, initiated simultaneously from three directions, were hammered and repulsed by the same paralysing barrages. On the Rhône side of the line the 36th Division attempted to put the final seal on the main valley highway. Also American P-47s swooped in, pounded and destroyed all bridges across the river, forcing the enemy to remain on the east bank. Trapped in the developing pocket were three German divisions determined to hold open their escape route. On two successive days regiments of the German 198th Division surged against the centre of the Rubion line at Bonlieu but were thrown back by battalions of the 143rd and 142nd. The 141st, in the hot corner near the Rhône, faced incessant enemy attacks trying to drive them away from Route 7.

Further efforts to seize La Coucourde and to recapture and block Route 7 were not completely successful, although much damage was inflicted on the enemy. The 3rd Battalion of the 143rd held the vital Magranon Ridge near La Coucourde, overlooking Route 7, during three days of critical fighting. Cut off and isolated into small groups at one time, the battalion fought on resolutely and eventually defeated the German forces decisively. Towards the end divisional forces were shifted northwards to strike again along the Drome river valley. For nine days the Germans fought the Americans before retreating north to Lyons. In particular, on the 25th the 11th Panzer Division and supporting units launched five attacks. Two days later the bulk of the 11th Panzer Division and most of the retreating infantry had crossed the Rhône north of Drome, having lost 2,500 men taken prisoner, and leaving the Montélimar region in the hands of General Baptist Kniess's newly arrived LXXXV Corps.

General Otto Richter's 198th Infantry Division, plus a rearguard engineer detachment to the south, remained at Montélimar. On the night of 27/28 August Richter led his remaining two regiments and other survivors in a bid to escape. They ran straight into the US 36th Division's push on the town; the general and some 700 of his men were captured, but not before the Americans had suffered around 100 casualties.

On the 29th the 143rd Regiment shattered the German forces around Loriol, taking over a thousand prisoners in the final mop-up. On the same day the 142nd Regiment seized Livron but straggling groups of Germans continued to resist strongly until the 30th. Then elements of the 3rd Division, pressing the Germans from the south, contacted the 141st Regimental Combat Team near Clary.

Despite the terrible destruction wrought on the 19th Army, even on the last day of battle Colonel Paul Adams, commanding the 143rd, reported to headquarters, 'I'm expecting a hell of a fight.' At 0600 the last German counter-attack had formed in the vicinity of La Coucourde, but in an hour the drive had been repulsed and the attackers destroyed or captured. It was the American artillery at Montélimar that counted most and turned the tide of battle. During the eight days of fighting the 36th Infantry's 131st, 132nd, 133rd and 155th field artillery battalions fired well over 37,000 rounds at the confined and retreating German troops. Supporting fire from attached battalions, the 41st, 977th and 93rd Armored, brought the total number of rounds expended to considerably more than 75,000.

The US VI Corps' newspaper *The Beachhead News* reported triumphantly:

> Under the 36th Division command . . . such a great force of artillery was directed on the Germans that more than four thousand vehicles, one 380mm and five other railroad guns were destroyed, and the main escape gap for the fleeing German army was under constant fire and attack . . . the Division moved in and finished off the kill.

By the time the battle of Montélimar ended on 28 August the US VI Corps had suffered 1,575 casualties, having inflicted five times that number on the Germans. The highway for 18 kilometres north and south of the town was a smoking double-column of knocked-out vehicles, dead horses and dead men. There was no stretch of the road that did not display some sort of destruction. In total, the Germans suffered 11,000 casualties and lost 1,500 horses. The Americans took some 5,000 prisoners at Montélimar and wrecked more than 4,000 vehicles, as well as destroying the 189th and 338th Divisions. A number of captured 280mm and 380mm railway guns provided the French with considerable volumes of scrap iron. To date, the 19th Army had lost 57,000 PoWs.

The Allies had now secured the region between Nice and Avignon as far north as Briançon via Grenoble to Montélimar, effectively destroying General Wiese's 19th Army mainly through artillery and air strikes as it sought to flee. As a result, the Germans were unable to draw up a defensive line until the Americans had crossed the Moselle river.

In Italy Operation Olive had commenced on 25 August and the Gothic Line was penetrated by both the 8th Army and the 5th Army, but there was no decisive advance. Churchill had hoped that a breakthrough in the autumn of 1944 would open the way for the Allied armies to advance north-eastwards through the Ljubljana Gap to Vienna and Hungary to prevent the Red Army advancing into eastern Europe.

Allied link-up

The battered remains of Wiese's command streamed north to join Chevallerie's 1st Army, which was evacuating south-western France and heading for the strategic Belfort Gap – the gateway to Germany just north of the Swiss border. The 11th Panzer Division conducted a fighting retreat to Alsace to defend it. Alsace forms the pass between the French Jura and Vosges mountains and the Germans knew that if they lost control of it, Strasbourg and all of Württemberg to the east would be exposed.

Meanwhile the retreating Germans conducted various delaying actions, notably in the Autun and Dijon regions, but ultimately they were now being driven from the whole of France. The IV Luftwaffe Field Corps reached Lyons on 30 August, to find that the city's anti-aircraft defences had been fending off French troops to the west. The Corps was then transferred to the east bank of the Rhône, where it joined elements of the 11th Panzer Division. At the same time elements of IV Corps straggling behind were marshalled on the west bank to cover the LXXXV Corps.

On 2 September 1944 Truscott was promoted to lieutenant-general. In Lyons the 36th Infantry Division found the Maquis and the Milice, the Vichy police whom the French hated as much as the Germans, battling it out. The factories on the city's outskirts were ablaze and all the bridges had been destroyed except one. While the fighting in the industrial area was on-going, across the river liaison patrols were greeted by great cheering crowds of civilians. The jeeps were surrounded by masses of men and women who just wanted to shake an American hand or stare curiously at their liberators. Pretty girls threw flowers, while children climbed on the vehicles and sat there.

The US 7th Army liberated Lyons on the 3rd and another 2,000 Germans were captured; enemy forces were driven out of Besançon four days later. There were two days of celebrations in Lyons and all sorts of parties in honour of the Americans, not least drinking bouts in which the French and their guests vied with one another in paying extravagant compliments. Every private home threw open its doors to the liberators.

On the eastern flank the German 148th Reserve Division delayed the Americans once they were over the Var river. Their task was greatly assisted by the Maritime Alps, which run northwards to the Cottian and

Graian Alps south of Geneva. The Germans had established defensive positions along the Menton–Sospel–Breil road, the Nice–Ventimiglia highway and the Turini Pass. The division was eventually incorporated into the new LXXV Corps tasked with defending north-west Italy and preventing the Allies turning the Italian front. By 8 September the Americans had pushed west of Nice and reached Menton and the Italian border. The advance then came to a halt as there was some concern that the US 5th and British 8th Armies might drive the Germans out of Italy via the Franco-Italian border. On 12 September a German *Kamptverbande* naval unit, operating out of San Remo, amassed up to forty one-man submarines to attack Allied warships providing fire support. In the event, only ten were launched and no Allied ships were damaged.

The victorious Allied forces in southern and northern France linked up at Châtillon-sur-Seine on 12 September when de Lattre's troops made contact with Leclerc's French 2nd Armoured Division, which formed part of Lieutenant-General George S. Patton's US 3rd Army. The French II Corps, now formally under the French 1st Army, along with the US 7th Army became part of Lieutenant-General Jacob Devers' recently activated US 6th Army Group.

Blaskowitz's losses were considerable. It has been estimated that he sustained up to 7,000 dead in southern France and about 21,000 wounded, but in total he lost perhaps half of his 250,000 troops. Some 31,000 German prisoners were taken at St Tropez, Toulon and Marseilles, and another 2,500 round Montélimar, while 12,000 surrendered during the Allied drive north from Lyons and another 20,000 were cut off west of Dijon. He lost an additional 10,000 men to Patton's US 3rd Army and another 25,000 were left trapped in the Atlantic garrisons. In contrast, the Americans suffered about 4,500 casualties and the French slightly more. In comparison, in northern France the Germans suffered a total loss of 450,000 men (240,000 casualties and 210,000 prisoners), as well as losing most of their equipment, including 1,500 tanks, 3,500 pieces of artillery and 20,000 vehicles. Crucially, though, both Army Group G and the 19th Army escaped as coherent formations.

Unfortunately the French 2nd Armoured Division's actions in liberating Paris unwittingly helped to prolong the war, for the delay round the city also enabled the greater part of Army Group G's 1st Army to escape intact over the Rhine. Luckily for Blaskowitz, Patton's US 3rd Army was starved of gasoline in favour of supplying Montgomery's men. Patton's men came to a halt at Verdun and for five days waited there just 110 km from the Rhine.

Howard Katzander, a staff correspondent with *Yank*, recalled how the French celebrated the eviction of Army Group G: 'They called it the "Champagne Campaign", this war in the Maritime Alps, because of the way the champagne flowed in the celebrations of the liberated people at Antibes and Cannes and Nice during the pursuit of the Germans.'

Chapter Nine

De Gaulle Stakes his Claim –
the Liberation of Paris

In early August 1944 another massive diplomatic row erupted among the Allied High Command over how and when German-occupied Paris should be liberated. Naturally both General de Gaulle and General Leclerc had very set ideas on the matter. In the meantime the Communist-led Parisians had risen against the German garrison. In the wake of D-Day the liberation of the French capital was always going to be controversial, and in the event the American Army, Free French forces and the French Resistance were all to be involved. However, it was de Gaulle and Leclerc who marched triumphantly down the Champs Elysees claiming the credit as the saviours of France.

Leclerc's Shermans

In preparing for the Normandy invasion the Allies tried to spare Paris, but its rail marshalling yards and nearby factories made it a prime target. On 21 April 1944 Gare de la Chappelle was bombed and 640 civilians were killed. Following D-Day the Resistance also went to work, disrupting German communications in Normandy and Brittany. Paris itself remained quiet until the end of June, when Pétain's propaganda secretary was shot dead at his official residence. Throughout July the city became increasingly restless, though the Germans largely left it to Joseph Darnand's *Milice Française* to keep order. On 20 July the city's garrison became briefly embroiled in the plot to kill Hitler. Count von Stauffenberg, who planted the bomb at Rastenburg, assumed Hitler was dead and called Lieutenant-Colonel Caeser von Hofacker, Chief of Staff to General Heinrich von Stülpnagel, the German military governor of France. Field Marshals Erwin Rommel and Günther von Kluge were also aware of the intention to kill Hitler. While the plotters attempted to seize control of Berlin, supporters also attempted to do the same in Paris. On the orders of Stülpnagel and under the cover of an exercise the German garrison briefly arrested Police Leader for France SS-Gruppenführer Karl Oberg and 1,200 members of the Nazi security apparatus until it became apparent that Hitler had survived. Both Stülpnagel and von Hofacker were later hanged.

There is no evidence that General Blaskowitz or any of his staff at Army Group G were involved. To make sure there was no question over their loyalty, both Blaskowitz and his Chief of Staff, General Heinz von Gyldenfeldt, rang C-in-C West's headquarters to express their disbelief that such an outrage had been attempted. Blaskowitz then sent the obligatory telegram repledging his allegiance to the Führer. As word began to spread about what had happened at Hitler's Rastenburg head-quarters, it cannot have helped the morale of those troops stationed far away in the south of France.

Leclerc's armour did not come ashore on Utah Beach until 1 August; along with three American divisions, it then formed the US Army's XV Corps under General Wade H. Haislip. The initial advance, covering 110 km in four days as far as Le Mans, was fairly uneventful. Then the US 3rd Army swung north to help trap the retreating German Army in the Falaise Pocket. Unfortunately, near Argentan Leclerc let his enthusiasm run away with him and his tanks clogged a road that had been earmarked for petrol supplies. The ensuing chaos gave the Germans a much-needed breathing space. Tantalisingly, Leclerc and his men were just over 160 km from the French capital.

After the loss of some tanks, Leclerc's division successfully established a bridgehead over the river Orne and was then placed under the command of Lieutenant-General Courtney H. Hodges' US 1st Army's V Corps, and Leclerc became answerable to Major-General Gerow. The two men instantly took a dislike to each other. De Gaulle was concerned that the French Communists would liberate Paris and gained an undertaking that Leclerc could enter the city. However, at this stage Eisenhower felt it best to by-pass Paris altogether, and of course once the river Seine was crossed the city would lose all strategic importance.

General Dietrich von Choltitz, the new garrison commander in Paris, was under strict instructions to deny the city to the Allies, even if it meant razing it to the ground. Hitler told Choltitz the city 'must not fall into the hands of the enemy; if it does, he must find there nothing but a field of ruins'. The weak garrison consisted of the 325th *Wach Paris* (Paris Alert Security) Division under Generalmajor Brehmer, a company of light tanks, and six batteries of 88mm anti-aircraft guns from the Luftwaffe's 1 Flak Brigade under Oberst Egon Bauer with inexperienced teenage crews, supported by sixty aircraft. This amounted to just 5,000 men, supported by perhaps 20 mostly elderly French tanks and 256 flak guns of various calibre. Such a force was just about adequate to contain any insurrection, but nothing else. Hitler had promised two skeleton panzer divisions from Denmark, but they had not materialised. The German armed forces were in no position to assist; between 6 June and 19 August 1944 they lost all their panzers in the Battle for Normandy.

Hitler wanted any insurrection in Paris crushed, just as the Warsaw rising had been crushed. The Warsaw rising, or 'Burza', had begun when Polish Resistance forces launched a national uprising to coincide with the arrival of Soviet forces from the east in the summer of 1944 after the spectacular success of Operation Bagration. Unfortunately Soviet help did not reach the city and the Warsaw rising was brutally put down by the Waffen-SS. The Polish Home Army had secured most of Warsaw by 4 August 1944, although its lack of heavy weapons and ammunition meant it was unable to consolidate its three main defensive enclaves within the city. The Germans counter-attacked on 10 August and four days later the Home Army had been divided into six enclaves. The desperate Poles held out for two months before surrendering on 5 October. Fortunately Choltitz was a cultured man, who had no intention of going down in history as the man who torched Paris.

Parisian insurrection

Since early August Parisians had made the city ungovernable, though the Resistance forces were under instructions from de Gaulle not to rise up until the arrival of Leclerc and his 2nd French Armoured Division. Between 10 and 12 August the city was paralysed by a rail strike, then on 15 August some 20,000 police went on strike, supported by the Communist-dominated FFI. Two days later, as shooting broke out, Vichy supporters began to flee Paris. Pétain and Darnand fled to Germany. The Germans then began disarming the troublesome French police.

Inside Paris Choltitz could muster at most 20,000 troops by the third week of August. About 5,000 were attached to the Security Division, giving it a total strength of 10,000. Brehmer's division had four regiments but two had been sent to Chartres. Bauer's 1 Flak Brigade comprised three regiments with about two dozen flak battalions; there were also seven railroad flak battalions, twelve semi-mobile battalions and four fixed battalions, all of which could be used in a ground-support role. The Fallschirmjäger Flak Regiment 11 also had three battalions protecting the air bases at Brétigny, Villacoublay and Villaroche in the southern suburbs. Choltitz could not rely on any Luftwaffe support except from some of the flak units. Luftflotte 3 had decamped from Paris to Reims and all the airfields in the Paris area had been destroyed by the withdrawing Luftwaffe on the 17th.

De Gaulle was determined the city would not escape his control, and when Koenig's military delegate General Chaban-Delmas arrived on the scene he was followed closely by the Gaullist Charles Luizet, who was to take command of the police. On the 19th almost 2,000 police staged a general rising, but Colonel Rol, leading some 600 Communist-dominated Free French forces, was annoyed that they had acted without his orders and stolen his leadership's thunder. The Germans made a half-hearted counter-attack with a few tanks against the Police Prefecture building located on the Île de la Cité near Notre Dame, but fortunately they withdrew before things turned really ugly for the French. The Free French forces also liberated the Palais de Justice and Hotel de Ville, and almost 400 barricades were erected throughout the capital.

When it was suggested to Choltitz that the Free French revolt was directed at Vichy rather than his garrison, he remarked: 'Perhaps. But it's my soldiers they are shooting at!' A truce was agreed but Rol's Communists did not observe it, accusing General Chaban-Delmas of being a coward. His faulty intelligence indicated that the Germans had 150 Tiger tanks to hand and he did not wish to see the lightly armed Free French slaughtered or the city's historic buildings damaged. In fact, all the Germans could actually muster were some old French light tanks and a dozen Panther tanks at most.

In the meantime, at 1030 on 20 August an eager Leclerc presented himself at Hodges' US 1st Army headquarters near Falaise. 'His arguments, which he presented incessantly,' recalled Hodges irritably, 'were to the effect that, roads and traffic and our plans notwithstanding, his division should run for Paris at once. He said he needed no maintenance, no equipment, and that he was up to strength – and then, a few minutes later, admitted that he needed all three.'

General Omar N. Bradley, commander of the US 12th Army Group (US 1st and 3rd Armies), also found himself under siege by the international press demanding to know when the French capital would be liberated. He explained that the plan was to pinch off the city so that it would fall without a shot having to be fired and that the plan was for Paris not to be entered until 1 September. When asked which division would be given the honour of liberating the city, Bradley quipped: 'You've got enough correspondents here to do it.'

Ignoring his orders, Leclerc sent a reconnaissance group, consisting of 10 tanks and 10 armoured cars, towards Paris on 21 August. A furious Gerow ordered him to recall them, but Leclerc refused. Bradley prevailed on Eisenhower that they had little choice but to act or cause a diplomatic incident. Bradley then signalled Hodges, who recorded:

> Paris since Sunday noon, he said, had been under control of the [Gaullist] Free French Forces of the Interior, which, after seizing the principal buildings of the city, had made a temporary armistice with the Germans, which was to expire Wednesday noon. General Bradley said that higher headquarters had decided that Paris could be avoided no longer, that entry of our forces was necessary in order to prevent possible heavy bloodshed among the civilian population, and he inquired what General Hodges could dispatch at once.

General de Gaulle reached Rambouillet by the 22nd, the last stage before his triumphant entry into Paris. Since the Overlord and Dragoon landings his position had altered radically. The Allies had recognised the Provisional Government of the French Republic as the de facto authority in liberated France. Since landing in Normandy Leclerc's 2nd Armoured Division had been hastening towards the French capital via the Chevreuse valley, while de Lattre's divisions were busy securing Marseilles and Toulon and fighting their way north. De Gaulle was determined that France would achieve equal status among the Allies and that her sovereignty would be fully restored and recognised despite the actions of the Vichy government.

The Communist Resistance and the French police had forced Eisenhower's hand. 'Throughout France the Free French had been of inestimable value in the campaign,' Eisenhower recalled. 'So when the Free French forces inside the city staged their uprising it was necessary to move rapidly to their support. Information indicated that no great battle would take place and it was believed that the entry of two Allied divisions would accomplish the liberation of the city.' Just as de Gaulle was arriving at Rambouillet, Eisenhower authorised Leclerc's armour and General Barton's 4th US Infantry Division to drive on Paris the following day.

Leclerc of course was determined to get to Paris before Barton. His division, totalling 16,000 men equipped with 200 Sherman tanks, 650 pieces of artillery and 4,200 vehicles, converged on the city in three columns. The Americans were dismayed at the antics of the French soldiers, who treated the advance as one big party, kissing and hugging everyone en route. A furious Gerow phoned Hodges to complain that the French troops were stopping at every town for a celebratory drink, with predictable results, and that they were holding up the traffic. At about 1700 hours a light aircraft swooped over the besieged Police Prefecture building and dropped a canister. When the ill-equipped defenders opened it, they discovered it contained a message from Leclerc that read: 'Hold on, we're coming.' While this was welcome, the question remained, when?

As the Allied forces neared Paris the German resistance became more vigorous. Leclerc's main thrust was launched from the south, with a feint from the south-west. Outlying German defences consisted of small numbers of tanks supported by anti-tanks guns holed up in the villages and at the crossroads. At Jouy-en-Josas three French Shermans were lost in tank-to-tank engagements. Stiff resistance was also met at Longjumeau and Croix de Berny south of Paris. German 88mm guns at Massy and Wissous accounted for more of Leclerc's tanks. An 88mm gun sited in the old prison at Fresnes, blocking the Paris road, held off three of his Shermans for a while. The first was knocked out, but the second destroyed the gun and the third ran over it. The French lost another four tanks to anti-tank guns trying to outflank Fresnes. Despite Gerow's complaints, the push on Paris proved no picnic, costing Leclerc's division 71 killed and 225 wounded, with 35 tanks, 6 self-propelled guns and 11 assorted vehicles disabled or destroyed.

Generalmajor Hubertus von Aulock, who was in command of a Kampfgruppe tasked with defending the western and southern approaches to Paris, fell back before Leclerc's advance. Choltitz ordered Kampfgruppe Aulock's 2,000 men to withdraw back across the Seine and they ended up west of the Eiffel Tower near the Boulevard Suchet.

In the evening of 24 August a French patrol comprising 3 light tanks, 4 armoured vehicles and 6 half-tracks slipped into the city through the Porte Gentilly. By nightfall the tanks were within a few hundred metres of von Choltitz's headquarters at the Hotel Meurice. The next day, as the division entered in force, cheering Parisians mobbed the tanks crossing the Seine bridges. Elements of the 2nd Armoured Division reached the Police Prefecture at 0830. The Germans, though, were not ready to give up just yet. During five hours of fighting to clear the German defenders from the foreign office building on the Quai d'Orsay, another Sherman tank was lost. At the Arc de Triomphe a French tank silenced its German counterpart at a range of 1,800 metres. Three Shermans were then lost after they drove into the grounds of the Place de la Concorde with their turret hatches open and a grenade was thrown into each one.

A note from the 2nd Armoured Division was sent to Choltitz demanding that he surrender or face annihilation; bravely, he refused even to receive the note. Unfortunately he felt that he should put up at least token resistance before capitulating. Choltitz then went through the farce of urging his men to fight to the last, even as Leclerc's Shermans closed in on the Hotel Meurice. Choltitz himself was soon captured and driven to the Prefecture to see Generals Leclerc, Barton and Chaban-Delmas, as well as Luizet and Colonel Rol. The latter wanted joint signature on the surrender document with Leclerc. While the liberation had cost the 2nd Armoured Division 130 dead and 319 wounded, the Free French forces bore the burden of the casualties, losing up to 1,000 dead and 1,500 wounded. Rol felt they deserved the credit. Nonetheless Leclerc, feeling he was the ranking officer, signed on behalf of everyone. Afterwards Choltitz requested a glass of water. Alarmed, an interpreter asked: 'I hope you've no idea of poisoning yourself.' Irked at the idea of such dishonour, the general replied: 'No, young man, I wouldn't do anything like that. I have to take medicine for a heart ailment.'

Understandably the Communist Resistance leaders felt aggrieved, after weeks of fighting the Germans, so a second surrender document was drawn up, this time giving prominence to Colonel Rol's signature. De Gaulle and the Allies were displeased at this piece of diplomacy, which failed to acknowledge that Leclerc had been acting as a subordinate of the Allied High Command. At 2130 hours teams of Free French and German officers went out to pass the word to the remaining German strongpoints that were still holding out.

De Gaulle's triumph

De Gaulle made his official entry into the city on 26 August. On hearing that he intended using the 2nd Armoured Division, Gerow ordered Leclerc to disregard this and get on with cleaning up the city. There remained 2,000 German troops in Paris, Kampfgruppe Aulock continued to represent a potential threat and fighting was still taking place. But when de Gaulle insisted, Eisenhower had little choice but to give way. Triumphantly de Gaulle, Leclerc, Koenig and Chaban-Delmas, surrounded by French officials, walked from the Arc de Triomphe to Notre Dame with Leclerc's 2nd Armoured Division proudly lining the route.

Afterwards Gerow ordered Leclerc to clear the Germans from the northern suburbs, but de Gaulle wanted to keep the division in Paris to counter the Communists. He then wanted the division to join de Lattre's 1st Army pushing up from the south of France, but instead Leclerc found his force reassigned to XV Corps moving towards Alsace. During September Leclerc's Shermans bested a German armoured formation near Epinal and by the end of the month had liberated Strasbourg. They then drove, appropriately enough, on to Hitler's former lair of Berchtesgaden in Bavaria.

Chaos reigned in Paris as de Gaulle manoeuvred to place himself in ascendancy and ultimately grasp the French Presidency. Both Gerow and Koenig considered themselves to be the temporary military governor of Paris. Gerow flew to Hodges' headquarters and demanded: 'Who in the devil is the boss in Paris? The Frenchmen are shooting at each other, each party is at each other's throat. Is Koenig the boss, is de Gaulle the boss? Am I, as the senior commander, in charge?' In addition to Leclerc's, Barton's and Choltitz's men, there were now 50,000 self-proclaimed Free French forces running about the city.

The Council of National Resistance wanted de Gaulle to proclaim the Republic from the Hotel de Ville. His haughty response was emphatic: 'The Republic has never ceased to exist . . . Vichy was, and remains, nothing. I am the President of the Government of the Republic. Why should I proclaim it?'

On 28 August de Gaulle acted to remove the threat of the Communist Resistance as an independent force. The Free French forces were dissolved and any useful units absorbed into the regular French Army. De Gaulle requested thousands of American uniforms for them and additional military equipment with which to organise his new French divisions. Perhaps more worryingly, de Gaulle asked for the loan of two American divisions to help establish his position in Paris. Eisenhower was bemused: not even in North Africa had the French requested Allied troops to reinforce their political authority. Nonetheless, in response to this request, on the 29th two American infantry divisions marched down the Champs Elysees on their way to the front.

Eisenhower, Gerow, Koenig and de Gaulle stood on the reviewing stand as the troops trudged past. De Gaulle, though, left before the parade was finished, a deliberate snub that was not lost on the American generals. To make matters worse, de Gaulle's actions in liberating Paris helped prolong the war, for the delay around the city enabled the greater part of the German 1st Army to escape over the Rhine. The parade, though, had achieved de Gaulle's aim, which was to send an unequivocal warning to the various Free French factions: look at my powerful friends. His political coup was now complete. De Gaulle, not the Resistance nor the Americans, would be remembered as the saviour of Paris, and ultimately of France.

On 3 September Eisenhower reminded de Gaulle of the French Army's significant debt to US industry in a radio broadcast:

From this battle front American fighting troops send their grateful thanks to the workers of America for having made this the best equipped fighting force in all history. In this expression of our gratitude we are joined by our gallant Allies. The British units include in their category of weapons many types that you have produced. The French divisions now fighting in southern and in northern France are equipped <u>exclusively</u> with the products of your toil and skill. Each of you justly shares in the credit for the tremendous successes the United Nations have gained on this important front.

However, five days later, Eisenhower tacitly and probably grudgingly recognised de Gaulle's achievements:

> I address my words to the people of Paris. Two weeks ago French and Allied troops made their entry into the city. They came to give the coup de grace to the last elements of the enemy remaining here. But the liberation of Paris was already nearly complete. A week before, armed with courage and with resolution, the men of the French Forces of the Interior, who for four years, under the inspiration of General de Gaulle, had never ceased to struggle against the enemy, went into the streets to drive out the despised invader. The glory of having largely freed their capital belongs to Frenchmen.

De Gaulle was incensed by Hitler's actions in needlessly causing 1,169 casualties in Paris with several futile terror raids using the Luftwaffe and V-2 flying bombs. Hitler gave frantic orders for the French capital to be retaken or obliterated, but the reality was that it was already firmly under the control of de Gaulle, with General Pierre Koenig appointed as Governor.

Once de Gaulle had secured his power base in Paris, he set about an extensive tour of the country to reinforce the authority of his government, especially in the south where many of the Resistance movements and liberation committees contained Communists who were reluctant to recognise him. In de Gaulle's mind he had thwarted a Communist takeover of France, and he implied as much in his memoirs. The reality was that the Communists had had no such intention; they simply did not have the strength to take power, though regionally they could have made life difficult for de Gaulle by defying Paris. Ultimately, though, he was the one who commanded the loyalty of the regular army divisions.

Vengeance was soon exacted upon the wretched supporters of Vichy France, with up to 10,000 summary executions. De Gaulle, though, on reviewing the 7,037 death sentences passed by the French courts, commuted all but 767 of them, and among those eventually spared was Pétain. While de Gaulle accepted the need to purge the country of collaborators, he did not wish it to turn into a witch-hunt, and felt that the purge should be carried out in a manner that would not tear the country apart again.

While Eisenhower had been committed to the liberation of Normandy and the Riviera, his hand had been forced over the Parisian sideshow. It was now evident that Ike and Roosevelt's concerns over de Gaulle's political ambitions had come to pass. Meanwhile, after the heady success of the Riviera landings, de Lattre's victories at Belfort and Colmar were to be much more drawn-out and costly affairs.

Chapter Ten

The Battle of the Belfort Gap

In the south of France, with the Germans being pressed from the west and the south, the only remaining resupply and escape route lay through the network of roads and rail lines located in the 24 km-wide Belfort Gap between the Vosges Mountains to the north and the Jura Mountains to the south-east. Since the days of the Roman Empire this had formed a strategic corridor connecting the Paris basin to the Rhine valley. This area also holds the principal tributary of the Rhône, namely the headwaters of the Saone-Doubs river. The latter's river valley formed the natural route that Patch's US 7th Army would have to follow north. The region was also ideal for guerrilla activity by the Free French forces as the hilly and heavily forested countryside was criss-crossed with numerous streams and rivers, providing ideal locations for ambushes and acts of sabotage. The Vosges Mountains consist of the High and Low Vosges, divided by the Saverne Gap. The Belfort Gap lies at the southern end of the High Vosges, the main route of approach to the Plain of Alsace. The lynchpin of the High Vosges is Epinal on the Moselle, which has two major routes through the mountains, one to Strasbourg and the Rhine and the other to Colmar and the Alsace Plain.

The advance of the seven divisions of General Jean de Lattre de Tassigny's French 1st Army and the fourteen divisions of the US 7th Army was quite remarkable. Bypassing Toulon and Marseilles, the lead elements of the 7th Army had reached Grenoble by 22 August, with the objective of linking up with elements of Patton's US 3rd Army near Dijon and pressing eastwards down the Belfort Gap.

'An enigma'
It was now the duty of General Friedrich Wiese's 19th Army to bar the way to the pursuing enemy. Indeed, Blaskowitz hoped and intended that Wiese's men would form a loose cordon that would permit the

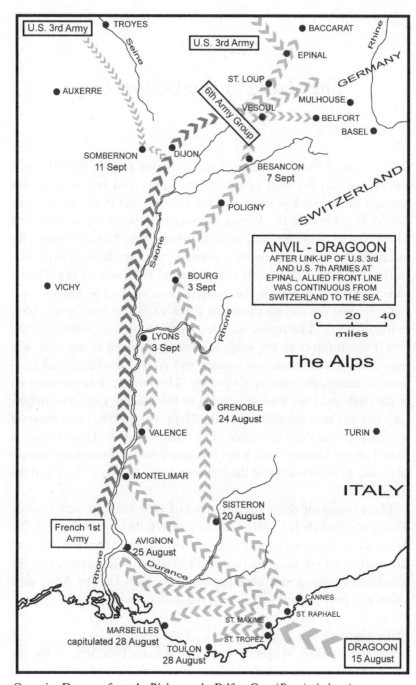

Operation Dragoon: from the Riviera to the Belfort Gap. (*Dennis Andrews*)

remaining elements of his depleted army group to retreat safely north-eastwards into the Belfort Gap.

The 11th Panzer Division rolled into Besançon on the evening of 5 September to cover the first units from the 19th Army moving into Belfort. Allied intelligence intercepts showed that the 11th Panzer Division was hardly a viable rearguard as by this time it consisted of just 9 panzers and 6 old French tanks, supported by 5 88mm guns with 400 rounds between them. Back in August, this division had fielded 79 Panther tanks, but by 1 September its numbers had fallen to just 30, plus 16 Panzer Mk IVs and 4 old Mk IIIs. It was subsequently strengthened by Panzer-Brigade 113, which brought the numbers up to a more respectable level, with a total of 40 Panthers, 19 Mk IVs and 4 Mk IIIs. Despite these welcome additions, the 11th Panzer Division's inventory was far below its authorised strength of 91 Panzer Mk IVs, 79 Panthers and 21 StuG III assault guns.

With the exception of the 11th Panzer Division, most of Wiese's combat forces were essentially improvised Kampfgruppen or battle groups made up of the remnants of his infantry divisions and fleeing rear echelon units. To help bolster his army, the German high command ordered the 30th Waffen-SS Division to move to France for anti-partisan duties. This unit arrived in Strasbourg on 18 August with instructions to hold the entrance to the Belfort Gap and counter any Free French units operating in the area. The division's 102nd Battalion deployed to the northern end of the gap and reached Vesoul on the 20th, with responsibility for the narrow plateau area between Noidans-les-Vesoul and Echenoz-la-Meline just to the south-west. Men of the 118th Battalion deployed to Besançon at the southern end of the gap on the 19th and then moved to Camp Valdahon, about 32 km south-east of Besançon.

The French Resistance's 9th Battalion *Franc Tireurs et Partisans* 'Adam Mickiewicz' with the Chariot Group successfully attacked the retreating Germans on 8 September at Autun (65km south-west of Dijon), inflicting damage to both their morale and the transport network. Also on the 8th Allied fighters strafed the Belfort area, hitting ten trains with good results, and a horse-drawn vehicle convoy near Strasbourg; the following day motor transport and rolling stock were bombed and strafed with particular success in the Belfort-Mulhouse-Freiburg areas. On the 10th the XII Tactical Air Command's fighters and fighter-bombers blasted communications in the Belfort and Dijon areas, cutting railroads and hitting several trains. They also cut the tracks in the Belfort, Basel and Freiburg areas.

De Lattre's French I Corps was counter-attacked west of Belfort along the Doubs river by German forces in the Montbeliard area on 8 September and the French were repelled. Also on the 8th the German 1st Army returned to Blaskowitz's control and his command became a full Army Group once again. This, though, was simply a formality as most of the units earmarked for Hitler's planned counter-attack came from the 1st Army anyway. However, Blaskowitz was granted a much-needed breathing space while the Americans and French regrouped. This gave him time to create an effective defensive line. General Wiese recalled: 'It was an enigma to the army why the enemy did not execute the decisive assault on Belfort between 8 and 15 September 1944 through a large-scale attack.' The tired American and French troops had lost their window of opportunity.

The construction of German rear area defences, which were soon to become the front line, was the responsibility of local Nazi Party officials. It was not long before Blaskowitz was at loggerheads with Gauleiter (District Leader) Adolf Wagner, who answered directly to SS-Reichsführer Heinrich Himmler. The Todt Organisation did not start work until September, by which time their efforts were largely too late. While the front-line troops fought delaying actions, little was achieved behind them despite their sacrifice. An exasperated Blaskowitz sent Generalmajor Hans Taeglichsbeck to assess the situation between Nancy and Belfort. He found that even the strongpoints necessary for holding the mountain passes were only at the preliminary stage. This was news that Blaskowitz did not want to hear. It also seemed that Himmler intended to take direct command of these defensive lines behind Blaskowitz, thereby hampering the operational chain of command. Blaskowitz's vocal protests understandably upset both Himmler and Wagner.

By early September it was evident that those senior Vichy politicians at Belfort would have to be moved. On the 8th Pétain arrived at Sigmaringen on the upper Danube. The castle there became the haunt of the most unsavoury Vichy collaborators, including Joseph Darnand, the former head of the reviled *Milice*. On the 20th Pétain was moved again by his captors, this time to Schloss Zeil, north of Wangen. De

Gaulle keenly hoped he would die before the Allied landings, but to the embarrassment of all the old marshal clung on. Clearly there would have to be a messy and doubtless acrimonious trial once Pétain was captured.

The Free French forces now numbered 560,000 men under arms, rising to a million by the end of the year, with men fighting in Alsace, the Alps and Brittany. On 1 September the headquarters of the French I Corps was assembled at Aix to command troops as a subordinate corps of the French 1st Army. It was now under the command of Lieutenant-General Émile Béthouart, who was a veteran of the 1940 campaign in Norway and had aided the Allied landings in French North Africa in November 1942. The I Corps' main component divisions were colonial formations, consisting of the 2nd Moroccan Infantry Division (2e DIM), the 9th Colonial Infantry Division (9e DIC), and the 4th Moroccan Mountain Division (4e DMM) supported by the 1st Armoured Division (1re DB). It was not until the end of the month that Army B was officially redesignated the French 1st Army.

The US 45th 'Thunderbird' Division moved into position opposite Épinal on 20 September, between the French 1st Army on its right and the 36th Division and Patton's US 3rd Army's XV Corps, forming the US 7th Army's left flank. The 36th 'Texas' Division crossed the Moselle on the night of 20/21 September near Éloyes and by the 24th, despite German resistance, had secured a bridgehead from Remiremont to Jarmenil, which had Bailey and pontoon bridges respectively. The 45th Division went over on the 21st/22nd and after some tough fighting seized Épinal. The 3rd Division was instructed to cross in the Rupt area to take Gerardmer near the Schlucht Pass and by a stroke of good luck seized a bridge before the Germans could blow it. By the last week of September the whole of VI Corps was over the Moselle.

Although Patch was reinforced by Patton's XV Corps (US 79th Infantry and French 2nd Armoured Divisions), the weather conspired to bog down the US 7th Army's advance; also it was short of fuel and ammunition. To make matters worse, both it and the French 1st Army lacked artillery as the Italian Front had been given priority. In the meantime the German defences had been improved, and beyond the Forest of Parroy were trenches, anti-tank ditches and concrete bunkers. Some 2,000 troops from the 15th Panzergrenadiers had entrenched themselves within the forest, and it would take the Americans a week of bitter fighting to drive out the defenders.

On 28 September the men of the US 79th 'Cross of Lorraine' Infantry Division entered the forest and came under attack by Panzer Mk IVs; they endured close-quarter fighting with enemy infiltration groups. The Americans pushed forwards about a kilometre and during the night came under constant German artillery fire, with splintered trees causing horrific injuries. Attempts to cut off the southern end of the woods on 1 October were met by an infantry attack supported by six panzers, and seven days later the Germans were still tenaciously clinging on. The following day the Americans launched an all-out push to finally subdue the remaining stubborn panzergrenadiers.

Heavy rain now further slowed the Americans' advance as they approached the next layer of German defences, which were some 3–5 km deep, extending from the swamps beyond the Forest of Parroy to the High Vosges. With the Allied air forces grounded by the weather, the Germans were able to bring up reinforcements unhindered by air attack. The exhausted US 79th, which had been continually in combat for four months, was relieved by the US 44th Infantry in mid-October. They were followed by the 100th and 103rd Infantry and 14th Armored.

To the south the US VI Corps launched its renewed attack on 20 October, following deception operations to convince the Germans that the assault would fall west of Le Tholy, south of Ramnervillers. The US 3rd Infantry Division came under heavy counter-attack and artillery bombardment, but by the end of the month it had captured 5,000 prisoners along with the high ground overlooking the Meurthe river valley in the St Die area. While this battle was under way, on the 23rd the 1st Battalion, 141st Regiment from the US 36th Division had been dispatched through the forest east of Bruyères. It soon came under counter-attack and was surrounded; two days later attempts to reach the 240 trapped men failed. Only on the 30th did the Japanese-American 442nd Infantry (*Nisei*) Regiment manage to cut their way through. By now the US VI Corps' main tasks were to bring its left and right flanks up through the 3rd Division's salient along the Meurthe, commit the newly arrived US 100th 'Century' and 103rd 'Cactus' Infantry Divisions and then penetrate the Vosges passes and push to the Rhine.

Problems for de Lattre

Unfortunately for the French, by early October the weather had begun to close in as conditions became wet and cold. The adverse weather, plus manpower and supply problems, combined to bring a halt to I Corps' advance that month. Also it was at this point that the French high command decided to replace its 'Senegalese' troops with Free French volunteers and send the colonial troops south. By the end of the year de Lattre was having increasing problems with his brave colonial forces. They were exhausted and ill-equipped, and French replacements were not forthcoming; they also viewed the ill-disciplined Free French forces with disdain. Many of the units had already endured one winter in Italy in 1943/4 and had been fighting continuously ever since. Among the Algerians there was a growing perception that their colonial masters were exploiting them. Where was the metropolitan or mainland French Army, many asked.

The 9th Colonial Division, as with other French divisions originating from the Francophone African colonies, lost its colonial troops in response to the 'climatic conditions' in France. Three 'Senegalese' regiments from the division were replaced with white Free French troops in November and the units were retitled Colonial Infantry Regiments. Similarly the 2nd Moroccan Division replaced one of its colonial regiments with a Free French-raised regiment. The 1st *Division Française Libre* or 1st Motorised Infantry Division had five battalions from Cameroon, Djibouti and French Equatorial Africa replaced by Free French recruits during September and October. In February 1945 the whitening process was extended to the black African, Caribbean and Pacific units. Inevitably the incorporation of Free French battalions into the 1st Army created friction, especially when the men of the North African divisions found themselves handing their weapons over to white French troops.

De Lattre not unreasonably wanted Frenchmen to liberate France, but this ultimately led to ugly accusations of racism. The huge numbers of Free French had to be brought within the French Army, particularly the 1st Army, and by November 1944 75,000 men had signed up, followed by another 65,000 by May 1945. However, Roosevelt and Eisenhower's original equipment shipments could not cater for such a massive influx of men. The Americans came up with light weapons and equipment for 52,000 men, but the shortfall meant that the French Army also had to rely on old French and captured German weaponry (including Czech and Russian arms). This caused a standardisation problem and such weapons were useless once available ammunition stocks had been exhausted.

In total, FFI units were used to create 8 infantry, 2 colonial and 1 armoured division, plus some 36 unaffiliated infantry regiments. Only about half the divisions ever saw any action, with the 10th and 25th Infantry involved in the fighting in Alsace. The Americans also requested 120 battalions of French troops to protect their lines of communication throughout France.

Battle for the Belfort Gap

The defection of Ukrainian recruits from the 30th Waffen-SS Division brought the Free French forces more than 1,200 trained men with all their weapons and equipment; they were duly inducted into the FFI as the 1st Ukrainian Battalion (*Batallion Ukrainien*, or BUK). On 26 September, attired in French black berets and German uniforms, they marched from Chateau de l'Abbeye to take part in the attack on Belfort. In their last action as the 1st BUK, on 3 October they assaulted and secured Hill 736 near the town. Afterwards the French took the unorthodox step of recruiting the whole of the 1st BUK into the 13th Demi-Brigade of the French Foreign Legion in order to avoid having to repatriate them. This was the only time in the history of the Legion that an entire foreign unit was embraced in such a manner.

The Allies' logistics situation was improving by early November, coinciding with orders from Eisenhower, now in charge of all Allied forces in north-western Europe, calling for a broad offensive along the entire French front. In the meantime the inactivity of the French I Corps misled the Germans into believing it was digging in for the winter and they reduced their forces in the Belfort Gap to a single under-strength infantry division. Just before the Vosges campaign commenced the 198th Infantry Division was reinforced with men from six different battalions and five regiments and companies, including troops from two Kriegsmarine units, 8. Schiffs-Stamm-Abteilung and leichte Marine-Artillerie-Abteilung 687. None of these did much to enhance the division's lamentable combat capabilities.

The French attacked the Belfort Gap on 13 November, killing the German divisional commander near the front lines; the commander of the German IV Luftwaffe Field Corps narrowly escaped capture. Six days later French armour pushed through the Belfort Gap and reached the Rhine at Huningue. The defenders were split into isolated pockets, particularly in Belfort itself, and French troops of the 2e Division *d'Infanterie Marocaine*, 9e Division *d'Infanterie Coloniale* and 1re Division *Blindée* were able to move through the German lines. By the 24th the German 308th Grenadier-Regiment was trapped, forcing its men to surrender or intern themselves in Switzerland. The following day I Corps liberated Mulhouse after a surprise armoured drive, and Belfort was assaulted and captured by the Moroccans.

General de Lattre, appreciating that the Germans were conducting an almost entirely static defence, directed both his corps to advance on Burnhaupt in the southern Vosges Mountains to encircle the German LXIII Corps (formerly the IV Luftwaffe Corps). By the 28th this operation had been completed, capturing over 10,000 German troops and crippling the LXIII Corps. French losses were serious enough that plans to clear the Alsace Plain had to be shelved while both sides reorganised and regrouped for the next round of bloodletting.

After forcing the Belfort Gap, General Jean de Lattre de Tassigny's French 1st Army reached the Rhine in the region north of the Swiss border and south of the town of Colmar. In the meantime the French 2nd Armoured Division, spearheading the US 7th Army (VI and XV Corps) in the northern Vosges Mountains, forced the Saverne Gap and also reached the Rhine, liberating Strasbourg on the 23rd. The net result of this was to compact the German presence in southern Alsace into a semi-circular bridgehead that became known as the 'Colmar Pocket'.

Trapped in the Colmar Pocket

The Colmar Pocket contained the now exhausted German 19th Army. Forming the southern boundary was the French I Corps, facing the Rhine at Huningue. The French soldiers launched an offensive to destroy the Pocket, but this operation was thwarted owing to the requirement to cover more of the Allied front line as US units were shifted north in response to Hitler's Ardennes Offensive. Hitler was also determined to hold the Colmar Pocket, and during the first half of December reinforced it with 8,000 men; these represented no less than 80 per cent of the total reinforcements sent to fight the US 6th Army Group. His intention was for them to strike north through the French to attack the US 7th Army. The 19th Army deployed nine divisions to try to halt French attempts to develop the pocket into a threat against Strasbourg.

On 1 January 1945 the Germans launched Operation Nordwind, which was aimed at retaking Alsace. Only after the US 7th and French 1st Armies had contained and turned back this offensive were the Allies able to resume their efforts to reduce the troublesome Colmar Pocket. On the 20th the French I Corps led a fresh attack northwards but met stiff German resistance and the advance stalled after the first day as the German 19th Army fed in reinforcements. It would take three long weeks for the French and the US XXI Corps (US 28th and 75th Infantry and 12th Armored Divisions) to overwhelm the 19th Army, fighting in extremely cold weather over ground that offered the attackers little or no cover, against stubborn defenders who put up fierce resistance.

Notably the 2nd and 4th Moroccan Divisions from General Émile Béthouart's I Corps were assigned to take Ensisheim, with secondary attacks on the right flank of the corps north of Mulhouse carried out by the 9th Colonial Division. Armoured support was provided by the French 1st Armoured Division. The heavily wooded and urban terrain again favoured the defenders. Attacking in a snowstorm, the French I Corps initially achieved tactical surprise against General Abraham's LXIII Army Corps. This attack forced General Siegfried Rasp to commit his only reserves, consisting of the 106th Panzer Brigade, the 654th Heavy Anti-tank Battalion and the 2nd Mountain Division. In reality, Panzer Brigade 106 was not up to much and had been already mauled in the fighting in Lorraine.

Formed in July from the remnants of Panzergrenadier Division *Feldherrnhalle*, which had been destroyed on the Eastern Front, two months later Panzer Brigade 106 was deployed in reserve in the Lorraine sector with the German 1st Army. On 8 September its forty-seven armoured fighting vehicles were involved in the counter-attack against Patton's US 3rd Army in the Luxembourg sector. The brigade was routed after one day's fighting, with 750 men captured and 21 panzers and tank destroyers and more than 60 half-tracks lost. With three-quarters of its combat effectiveness gone, the brigade was no longer capable of any offensive operations.

On the night of the 20th, German counter-attacks managed to stall I Corps' advance, and the Germans' in-depth defence, the poor weather and the exposed geography all combined to mar the French advance and limit its success. Notably the French 1st Armoured Division's 1st Combat Command lost 36 of its 50 medium tanks to mines, and losses in other tank units were also high. It was evident that the Germans had no intention of giving up the fight.

General de Monsabert's French II Corps with the US 3rd 'Rock of the Marne' Infantry Division and Brossel's 1st Infantry Division launched its attack southwards on 22/23 January. To the south of the 3rd Division, the US 28th 'Keystone' Infantry Division (whose battle honours included the liberation of Paris) held its sector of the front with the French 2nd Armoured Division in reserve. General John W. O'Daniel's 3rd Infantry Division attacking to the south-east aimed to cross the Ill river, bypass the city of Colmar to the north, and open a path for the French 5th Armoured Division to cut the vital railway bridge at Neuf-Brisach that was used to resupply the Germans in the Colmar Pocket. The pressure from the French and American forces was so intense that by the end of the month the Germans were forced to redistribute their troops. Then I Corps struck again in early February, moving north to link up with the US XXI Corps at Rouffach, south of Colmar, after pushing through weak German resistance and reaching the bridge over the Rhine at Chalampé.

The pocket was sealed by 9 February, and although the Germans lost 22,000 men taken prisoner, the bulk of the 19th Army escaped over the Upper Rhine. Those remaining German forces in the I Corps area retreated over the Rhine into Baden. From now on the thrust of the Allied offensive moved to the north, and I Corps was assigned the defence of the Rhine from the area south of Strasbourg to the Swiss frontier until mid-April.

Colmar cost the French 13,390 casualties and the Americans 8,000. Total German losses were put at 38,500.

Chapter Eleven

Lorraine and the Southern Push
to the Rhine

After retreating through France in August and September 1944, the German 1st Army fought a protracted defensive battle in Lorraine. With Army Groups G and B streaming eastwards, the German High Command had to do something dramatic to stop the rot. In particular, they needed to gain valuable time in which to strengthen the West-wall defences before the Allies launched their assault on Germany itself.

Despite the failure of the Normandy/Mortain counter-attack, Hitler remained convinced that his panzers could successfully envelop the advancing Allies. This view he derived from the German Army's performance on the Eastern Front, where time and time again it had managed to snatch victory from the jaws of defeat; it was most certainly not based on the reality of the situation in France, where Operations Overlord and Dragoon were backed by overwhelming firepower on the ground and in the air.

By early September Blaskowitz's 1st Army, now under General Otto von Knobelsdorff, was safely behind the Moselle and Wiese's 19th Army was holding Army Group G's front from Nancy to the Swiss border and stretching westwards as far as the Loire. After the collapse in Normandy Field Marshal Walter Model's Army Group B, with four armies, was defending the region from the North Sea down to Nancy and trying to stabilise the situation. Following his successful withdrawal from southern France, Hitler became convinced of Blaskowitz's tactical abilities: he was the right man to oversee the much-needed counter-offensive.

With the Allies now preoccupied in the south of France, Hitler did not need to worry about the Italian Front. In fact, Field Marshal Kesselring was directed to relinquish his 3rd and 15th Panzergrenadier Divisions to France and the Hermann Goering Panzer Division to

Poland. These two panzergrenadier units would form the core of Hitler's opposition to the push on the Upper Meuse by Patton's US 3rd Army.

Counter-attack in Lorraine

Indeed, Hitler was hoping to counter Patton, who was spearheading the Allies' eastwards drive into Lorraine, posing a direct threat to the German West-wall defences. However, until General Jacob L. Devers' US 6th Army Group pushing up from the south of France could nip off the remaining bulge formed by the German 19th Army, Patton's left flank was precariously exposed. Hitler realised that a decisive blow against Patton would stop him getting into Germany and would prevent Devers' forces from linking up with Bradley's 12th Army Group. To this end he gave priority to his forces in Lorraine. In contrast, the Allies were now at the end of their supply lines and Eisenhower's attention was increasingly focusing on Operation Market-Garden, which was intended to take Montgomery's 21st Army Group through the Netherlands and over the Rhine. Operations in the south were now just an unwanted distraction, though Patton was constantly calling for more fuel and ammunition.

Hitler's forces in Lorraine were on the whole under-strength and of poor quality. Only the 16th Infantry Division with about 7,000 men was worthy of note; all the rest had either been mauled in the fighting during the summer or were newly raised Volksgrenadier divisions of questionable value. Frightened recruits and weary veterans were hardly an ideal combination. In contrast, Patton's divisions were largely up to strength and eager to press on.

It was apparent that Hitler needed to act quickly. Gathering together a number of newly raised panzer brigades, he planned to surround Patton with the battered 5th Panzer Army, which had only just recently escaped from the chaos of Normandy. At the same time Blaskowitz was ordered to commit his only panzer force, the veteran 11th Panzer Division, which was defending the Belfort Gap. Hitler, as always obsessed with counter-attacking when such action was not feasible, felt that the bridgehead west of Dijon would not only provide a haven for LXIV Corps but also offer a suitable jumping-off point for an attack on Patton's southern front. Looking at the situation reports, Blaskowitz doubted whether the counter-attack could succeed, and was even more concerned about his forces' ability to hold on until LXIV Corps arrived. However, he knew that Hitler's orders could not be ignored and on 4 September he instructed XLVII Panzer Corps to move into the Neufchateau region. This, though, proved impossible in the face of attacks by the US XII and XX Corps.

Now under General Hasso von Manteuffel, the 5th Panzer Army was redeployed from Belgium to Alsace-Lorraine. The counter-attack was initially to involve three panzergrenadier divisions, the 3rd, the 15th (brought up from Italy) and the 17th SS (from Normandy), together with the new Panzer Brigades 111, 112 and 113. They were to be supported by elements of the Panzer Lehr, the 11th and 21st Panzer Divisions, and the new Panzer Brigades 106, 107 and 108. On paper at least, it seemed to be a credible force.

In fact, Blaskowitz and Manteuffel were able to muster at most about 350 tanks, amounting to barely three weak panzer divisions or a panzer corps – hardly sufficient for Hitler's optimistic plans. Against them Patton could field 1,122 M4 Sherman medium tanks and M10 and M18 tank destroyers. In addition, the 19th Army had just 165 artillery pieces; the rest lay scattered about southern France. The two German generals could see only one outcome. Colonel Hans von Luck from the 21st Panzer Division, a veteran of the brutal fighting in Normandy and around the ancient city of Caen, bumped into Manteuffel in the Vosges on 9 September. In their conversations Manteuffel did not mince his words:

> The US 6th Army Group, including the French 1st Army, is approaching from southern France and is supposed to join up with Patton. The remains of our retreating armies from the Mediterranean and Atlantic coast are . . . still holding a wedge that extends as far as Dijon, but for how much longer?
>
> The worst of it is Hitler is juggling with divisions that are divisions no more. And now Hitler wants to launch a panzer attack from the Dijon area to the north, in order, as he likes to put it, 'to seize Patton in the flank, cut his lines of communication, and destroy him'. What a misjudgement of the possibilities open to us.

Certainly Manteuffel's own army was far from reconstructed following its defeat in Normandy and the panzer forces were in a poor state. For example, the 17th SS Panzergrenadier Division, after suffering losses in Normandy, had been boosted with reinforcements from units as far away as the Balkans and Denmark. It was able to field just 4 Panzer Mk IVs and 12 StuG III assault guns. The 21st Panzer Division had also been seriously mauled in Normandy and could muster only a few assault guns.

The 11th Panzer Division was regarded as the best armoured unit in the region, but it too had lost a number of its tanks during its withdrawal from the south. For the Lorraine offensive it would be able to field about 50 panzers, over half of which were Panthers. However, it would have to redeploy before it could have any bearing on the fighting. In contrast, both the 3rd and 15th Panzergrenadier Divisions were in good order and up to strength. The former had a battalion of assault guns and the latter could field 36 Panzer Mk IVs, while both also had a battalion of Panzer IV/70 tank destroyers.

While German industry soon alleviated the critical shortage of panzers on the Western Front following Falaise, there was little Hitler could do about his complete lack of experienced tank crews. In addition, his senior generals could see little point in raising new panzer brigades when the replacement panzers would have been better issued to the existing depleted panzer divisions. The bulk of these new panzer brigades were raised from units that had been destroyed when the Red Army crushed Army Group Centre in Operation Bagration in June. For example, Panzer Brigade 106 was created around the tattered remnants of Panzergrenadier Division *Feldherrnhalle*. Also the first batch of brigades consisted only of single tank battalions.

Nevertheless Hitler planned to stop the US 3rd and 7th Armies linking up by cutting off those forces pushing towards the Belfort Gap. This was to be achieved by a counter-attack from Pontalier towards Plateau de Langres, scheduled for 12 September. In the event, with the Americans converging on Dijon, these plans were quickly abandoned. Likewise, American military activity in the Nancy area soon thwarted Hitler's plans for an armoured counter-attack in Lorraine, as Blaskowitz struggled to contain the US forces spilling over the Moselle. Although Hitler's counter-attack was intended to cut off the US 3rd Army, Blaskowitz was more concerned that it should prevent an American wedge forming between his 1st and 19th Armies.

Hitler's lost panzer brigades

Nancy was the lynchpin, and in the subsequent fighting for the city Blaskowitz was forced to commit all his available armoured forces. Between Metz to the north and Nancy lay the 3rd and 17th SS Panzergrenadier Divisions, while the 553rd Volksgrenadiers defended Nancy itself. Just to the south were deployed the 15th Panzergrenadiers, and beyond them Panzer Brigade 112, the 21st Panzer Division and Panzer Brigade 111. Panzer Brigade 113 and the 11th Panzer Division were near Belfort.

Under the growing strain, it was not long before Blaskowitz and Manteuffel fell out. The 5th Panzer Army had to share control of the front with Blaskowitz's 1st and 19th Armies, causing administrative headaches for von Knobelsdorff and Wiese. Nor were there enough telephones for command and control of the three armies, creating a far from ideal situation. When Manteuffel visited Blaskowitz on 11 September, both knew Hitler's ambitious intentions were nonsense. In addition, the US 1st Army was bearing down on the German city of Aachen, obliging Field Marshal von Rundstedt to redirect all available forces to that area, including Panzer Brigades 107 and 108. This meant that a third of the panzer brigade counter-offensive force was lost already. Rundstedt had been sacked after the disaster in Normandy, but had then found himself reappointed as Commander-in-Chief West in early September.

Panzer Brigade 106 was destroyed while trying to stop the Americans from reaching the Moselle on 8 September. Two days later the US 4th Armored Division and 35th 'Sante Fe' Infantry Division crossed the river south of Nancy in the face of fierce resistance from the 15th Panzergrenadier Division. The next day the US 80th 'Blue Ridge' Infantry Division crossed to the north of the city and on the 13th was counter-attacked by the 3rd Panzergrenadiers with ten assault guns. That day, with his defences ruptured, Blaskowitz gave the order to start evacuating Nancy, with the 553rd Volksgrenadier Division covering the withdrawal.

Elements of Leclerc's French 2nd Armoured Division then crushed Panzer Brigade 112 at Dompaire, south-west of Nancy and north-west of Belfort, on 13 September. His Combat Command Langlade slipped between Kampfgruppe Ottenbacher and the 16th Infantry Division and took control of the high ground overlooking Dompaire. Following an

American air strike, Panzer Brigade 112's Panthers were hemmed in on three sides, although German reinforcements in the shape of 45 Panzer Mk IVs from Panzer Regiment 2112 almost threatened to trap one of the French battle groups.

Luckily a French road-block formed by armour and anti-tank guns beat off the reinforcements and by the end of the day the panzer brigade had lost 34 Panthers and the panzer regiment 28 Panzer Mk IVs. In total, Panzer Brigade 112 was reduced from 90 tanks to just 21, and suffered 1,350 men killed and wounded; the survivors were placed under the 21st Panzer Division. Blaskowitz and Manteuffel had now lost four panzer brigades before their counter-offensive had even started.

With the German garrison at Nancy under threat of encirclement, Blaskowitz threw the 3rd and 15th Panzergrenadier Divisions into the counter-attack, but they suffered heavy casualties and the US 80th 'Blue Ridge' Division rolled into the city on the 15th. When Manteuffel's counter-offensive finally got under way on 18 September Panzer Brigade 113 ran straight into the Americans at Lunéville south-east of the city and was forced to disengage. The brigade was then redirected to attack towards Arracourt, east of Nancy, along with Panzer Brigade 111, but the latter became lost. During the 19th American tanks and artillery knocked out 43 tanks, but Blaskowitz ordered Manteuffel to renew the attack the following day.

General von Mellenthin noted:

> Our Panthers were superior to the American Shermans, but the enemy had very strong artillery and anti-tank support, and when the fog lifted enjoyed all the benefits of overwhelming air power. The German attack cost nearly fifty tanks and achieved nothing.

Despite Blaskowitz's orders, Panzer Brigade 113 did little and Panzer Brigade 111 committed only a few companies to the fighting. There was now a danger that Patton would drive a wedge between the 5th Panzer Army and the 1st Army and force his way to the Rhine.

Blaskowitz gets the sack

Blaskowitz held Manteuffel responsible for this sorry state of affairs, while the latter blamed his poor performance on his inexperienced panzer brigade crews. Hitler was so angry that his new panzer force had been squandered to no effect that he abruptly sacked the unfortunate commander of Army Group G. Blaskowitz's other crime was quarrelling with Hitler's right-hand man Heinrich Himmler about the second-line defences. General von Mellenthin recalled with some distaste:

> On 20 September 1944 General Balck and I arrived at the head-quarters of Army Group G, then situated at Molsheim in Alsace. It was our unpleasant duty to relieve the army group commander, General Blaskowitz, and his chief of staff, Lieutenant-General Heinz von Gyldenfeldt. As we drove up to the headquarters, with the wooded crests of the Vosges rising above, I thought of my last visit to this region – the breakthrough of the Maginot Line, . . . now I was chief of staff of an army group, which had barely escaped annihilation and was facing as difficult a crisis as could be imagined.

Hermann Balck had been told by Hitler that Blaskowitz lacked offensive spirit; Balck now was to fight for time while Hitler prepared for his counter-offensive in Belgium. Under no circumstances would those earmarked forces be diverted to Army Group G. Balck found Army Group G deployed as follows: General von Knobelsdorff's 1st Army in the Metz-Château-Salins area; General Hasso von Manteuffel with the 5th Panzer Army defending the northern Vosges between Lunéville and Epinal; and Wiese's 19th Army holding the southern Vosges and the Belfort Gap.

Balck threw the 1st Army into the attack on the 24th, spearheaded by the 559th Volksgrenadier Division and the remains of Panzer Brigade 106 west of Château-Salins. This advance was thwarted by heavy American air attacks. By 25 September the 11th Panzer Division had arrived, but with the new panzer brigades cut to pieces, Manteuffel could only muster 50 tanks. For the attack north of Arracourt that day the 11th Panzer Division had only 16 panzers and two regiments of panzergrenadiers, but it fought on tenaciously for another four days against the US 4th Armored Division. The 559th Volksgrenadiers were also obliged to renew their attack against the US 35th Infantry Division.

The remains of Panzer Brigades 111 were assigned to the 11th Panzer

Division, 112 to the 21st Panzer Division and 113 to the 15th Panzergrenadiers. The US 3rd Army had now gone over to the defensive and American withdrawals enabled Manteuffel to occupy Juvelize and Coincourt east of Arracourt. German attacks on the 27th to take Hills 318 and 293 ultimately ended in failure, despite the best efforts of the 11th Panzer Division, which lost 23 panzers.

By the end of the month this messy fighting in Lorraine between Balck's Army Group G and Patton's US 3rd Army had become a stalemate. From an overall force of 616 panzers and assault guns committed in the area only 127 remained operational, though another 148 were repairable. Balck visited von Rundstedt at Bad Kreuznach on the 29th and informed him that Army Group G needed a minimum of 140 panzers as well as artillery otherwise all its offensive operations would come to a standstill. Rundstedt made it clear, however, that Hitler was currently preoccupied with Aachen and Arnhem, and that there would be no reinforcements. In response Balck instructed Manteuffel to break off his attacks and withdraw the exhausted 11th Panzer Division in order to husband his dwindling resources. Thus ended Hitler's attempts to cut off Patton's spearhead.

In October Army Group G lost the tough 3rd and 15th Panzergrenadier Divisions, which were sent to the Aachen area, and was given an ill-equipped security division as a replacement. Manteuffel's 5th Panzer Army was also withdrawn ready for the major Ardennes offensive in December. The army group now had just 100 panzers with the 1st Army. The latter mustered some 86,000 men, with seven of its eight divisions covering a 120 km front; the battered 11th Panzer Division acted as the only reserve, with just 69 tanks. Patton had a huge numerical superiority: at least three-to-one in men and eight-to-one in tanks, not to mention a huge advantage in artillery. His forces struck on 8 November between Nancy and Metz with all the strength they could muster. Although the Germans were taken by surprise, bad weather slowed Patton's armour. The 11th Panzer Division counter-attacked two days later, claiming 30 American tanks destroyed. Having rescued the shaken 559th Volksgrenadier Division, it then withdrew on Morhange.

The panzers counter-attacked again on the 12th, capturing an entire American battalion. Although the Germans abandoned Morhange, the Americans were forced to call a halt. On the night of 17/18 November the 1st Army withdrew, leaving the ill-equipped 10,000-strong Metz garrison to its fate. The last of the city's forts did not surrender until 13 December, and in the meantime Leclerc's tanks rolled into Strasbourg on 24 November.

Over the Moselle and Rhine

By 1945 the Germans were expecting a big Allied push over the Rhine and did everything they could to stiffen the defences of this vast natural barrier. They believed that the Allies would strike downstream of Emmerich, so Blaskowitz, now commander of Army Group H, deployed there the stronger of his two armies, the 25th under General Günther Blumentritt. General Alfred Schlemm's battered 1st Parachute Army was left to cover the 72 km between Emmerich and Duisburg.

On 8 February Montgomery launched Operation Veritable, thrusting the Canadian 1st Army under General Henry Crerar, supported by the British 2nd Army under General Miles Dempsey, into the Rhineland. Attacking through the Reichswald, Lieutenant-General Sir Brian Horrock's British XXX Corps came up against Schlemm's 1st Parachute Army. This attack was followed by Operation Blockbuster, which took the Canadians to the Rhine itself. The Americans hoped to launch Operation Grenade across the Rhine to the south, but this was delayed for two weeks by flooding. Eleven days after Veritable commenced, Lieutenant-General William H. Simpson pushed his US 9th Army forwards from Geilenkirchen to the Rhine around Dusseldorf. At the same time Patch's US 7th Army advanced to the Upper Rhine.

By 10 February the German 19th Army's LXIV and LXIII Corps had sustained in excess of 22,000 casualties and lost 55 armoured fighting vehicles and 66 artillery pieces. The LXIV Corps' five divisions (2nd Mountain, 198th Infantry and the 16th, 189th and 708th Volksgrenadiers) all suffered heavy losses, in particular the 2nd Mountain Division, which lost 5,700 men killed, captured or wounded. The 198th Infantry Division escaped with just 500 combat troops, over 1,000 having been captured. Only the 708th Volksgrenadiers escaped largely intact. To the south LXIII Corps' divisions (the 159th Volksgrenadier and the 338th and 716th Infantry) suffered similar fates. The long-suffering 19th Army was all but spent.

Operation Plunder was the codename for the principal attack across the Rhine, but during the Malta Conference Eisenhower announced additional crossings south of the Ruhr. It was almost as if the Americans were intent on stealing Montgomery's thunder. At the beginning of March they launched Operation Lumberjack, striking between Koblenz and Cologne using Hodge's US 1st Army and Patton's US 3rd Army. A week later Hodges' VII Corps was in Cologne, though the Germans had brought down the Hohenzollern Bridge over the Rhine.

More importantly, just an hour's drive to the south the armoured Combat Command B of the US 9th Armored Division supported by elements of the US 78th 'Lightning' Infantry Division reached Remagen at the same time. Dramatically they seized the Ludendorff railway bridge, the only remaining span over the Rhine, before the Germans could destroy it. The Americans had secured a bridgehead two weeks before Montgomery was ready to go. Ironically this bridge had originally been constructed during the First World War to move men and material to the Western Front. The bridge had two rail lines and a footpath, but one line had been boarded over to allow road traffic. The Americans wanted Simpson's US 9th Army to cross at Urdingen, but Montgomery refused, perhaps smarting that he had lost the opportunity to breach the Rhine defences first. Ten days after its capture, the battered Ludendorff Bridge fell into the Rhine, killing twenty-eight American soldiers. Its loss mattered little as by the 21st the Americans had five pontoon bridges over the Rhine at Remagen. In contrast, its loss cost Field Marshal von Rundstedt his job as Commander-in-Chief West. He was replaced by Albert Kesselring, a very able general and hero of the Italian front, but there was little he could do.

Operation Undertone – the offensive to clear the Saar-Palatinate triangle south of the river Moselle, representing the third stage of the Allies' advance on the Rhine – was launched on 12 and 15 March by Patton and Patch respectively. This triangle was a major German salient jutting out into the Allied line, and was held by Army Group G, now under SS-General Paul Hausser. He had lost control of the 19th Army after its evacuation from Colmar, but still retained General Hans Felber's 7th Army and General Hermann Foertsch's 1st Army.

Patch, reinforced by the 42nd and 63rd Infantry and 10th Armored Divisions, opened his attack with the 3rd and 45th Divisions, along with the 3rd Algerian Infantry. In a parallel assault known as Operation Earthquake the 3rd Division attacked near Rimling and within half an hour had passed into German territory.

The US VI Corps' job was to clear northern Alsace and drive along the Rhine valley, and the 42nd, 103rd, 36th and 3rd Algerian Divisions, supported by the 14th Armoured Division, duly struck across the Rothbach and Moder rivers. Three days later the 42nd and 103rd Divisions crossed the German frontier. The 3rd Algerian Division, supported by the French 5th Armoured Division, was given the job of seizing Lauterbourg and the crossings over the Lauter.

Patton's 3rd Army crossed the Moselle on 13 March, then on the night of the 22nd he further stole Montgomery's thunder by throwing the US 5th 'Red Diamond' Infantry Division across the Rhine at Nierstein and Oppenheim south-west of Frankfurt. Hitler immediately declared this a greater threat than the bridgehead at Remagen, as this section of the Rhine was virtually unguarded. Hitler wanted to send a panzer brigade but all he had available were five disabled panzers at the tank depot at Sennelager. By the evening of the 24th Patton had seized 19,000 prisoners.

South of Koblenz Patton's US VIII Corps pushed the US 89th 'Rolling W' and 87th 'Golden Acorn' Divisions across the Rhine at Boppard and St Goar at 0200 hours on the 26th. The powerful 89th Division was supported by the 748th Tank Battalion, the 811th Tank Destroyer Battalion, the 550th Anti-aircraft Battalion (AW) and Company A of the 91st Chemical Mortar Battalion. Altogether the division plus supporting and attached forces numbered well over 23,000 men. To oppose this steamroller, the Germans had a number of Luftwaffe anti-aircraft battalions fighting as infantry and Volkssturm home guard. They were armed with small arms, machine-guns, 20mm and 88mm anti-aircraft guns, some field artillery and a few panzers.

The US 354th and 353rd Infantry Regiments spearheaded the crossing, with the 355th in reserve. The 354th attacked with its 1st Battalion towards Wellmich and its 2nd towards St Goarshausen from St Goar. Over a company and a half of the 1st Battalion (Companies A and C) reached the east bank in the first wave with little resistance during the crossing, but they came under heavy fire from the hillside behind Wellmich once ashore. To make matters more difficult, the swift current and the machine-gun and 20mm fire prevented the assault boats from returning to the west. On its way over, the 2nd Battalion faced point-blank fire just above the water from machine-guns and 20mm anti-aircraft guns. Nonetheless, a pontoon bridge was completed between St Goar and St Goarshausen the following day and over 2,700 prisoners were eventually taken.

By late March Patch's US 7th Army, in conjunction with Patton's push from the north, had overrun the Saar-Palatinate triangle. The region was in chaos and the German 1st and 7th Armies had lost 100,000 men taken prisoner in the space of two weeks. They had gone from controlling twenty-three divisions to losing 75 per cent of their combat effectives in one stroke. In the meantime the US 7th Army's zone west of the Rhine had been cleared of German resistance. They crossed at Worms on 26 March, allowing a break-out towards Darmstadt.

By early April the 19th Army was of little more than divisional strength, with about 10,500 combat effectives; it was still holding the Siegfried Line and the Black Forest, but was at risk of being outflanked. The German 1st Army was facing the US VI and XXI Corps with just 7,500 troops. The German 7th Army was in even more dire straits, with a combat strength of just 4,000; it, too, was forced back by the US 3rd Army and US 7th Army's XV Corps.

With the end now in sight, the only real front line on the Western front ran from the Löwenstein Hills to Nuremberg. This was defended by a motley collection of 15,000 men supported by 100 panzers and self-propelled guns and twenty battalions of artillery. On 22 April the Americans and the French 1st Army reached the Danube, and this advance was followed by an attack on the city of Ulm.

By 1 May 1945 the German 1st Army under General Foertsch could muster fewer than 500 combat effectives, supported by about 7,000 SS troops. Likewise the 19th Army, commanded by General Erich Brandenberg, was just 3,000 men strong and had no divisions capable of effective defensive combat. The latter formally surrendered at 1500 hours on 5 May to the US VI Corps and the French 1st Army; on the same day Foertsch also surrendered his command to the US 3rd Infantry Division.

Between August 1944 and May 1945 Patch's US 7th Army suffered 15,271 killed and 58,342 wounded. The Americans had advanced some

1,450 km since landing on the Riviera on 15 August 1944. During this period the French I Corps alone sustained losses of 18,306, including 3,518 dead. The French Army suffered another 43,670 casualties helping clear the German forces from Tunisia and in the Italian campaign.

By now, partly thanks to Roosevelt's and Eisenhower's efforts, de Gaulle's French forces constituted the fourth largest Allied army after the Soviet Union, the USA and the United Kingdom, with 1.3 million men under arms. These forces included seven infantry and three armoured divisions fighting against Germany. From a standing start in 1943 this was a considerable achievement and was testimony to de Gaulle's ambition that France should sit as an equal with the 'Big Three'.

Chapter Twelve

Churchill and Monty were Right

'As we had intended it to be,' wrote de Gaulle after the war, 'the Allied battle of France was also the battle of Frenchmen for France. The French were fighting "a united battle for a united country".' It was he who had ensured that de Lattre and Leclerc had been involved in the defining moments of the liberation of France. After all, it was they who had driven into Marseilles, Paris and Toulon to the frantic cheers of their fellow Frenchmen. De Gaulle had placed himself at the head of the liberation of France and would reap the benefits in post-war France. There was nothing Roosevelt or Churchill could do about it.

With a profound sense of occasion Winston Churchill announced the liberation of France to the House of Commons on 28 September 1944:

> What a transformation now meets our eyes! Not only Paris, but practically the whole of France, has been liberated as if by enchantment . . . the foul enemy . . . has fled, losing perhaps 400,000 killed and wounded, and leaving in our hands nearly half a million prisoners. Besides this, there may be 200,000 cut off in the coastal fortresses or in Holland . . .

Churchill then went on to discuss the battles for Normandy, Arnhem and the Channel ports, before turning to the contribution made by Operation Dragoon:

> While this great operation [Market Garden] has been taking its course, an American and French landing on the Riviera coast, actively assisted by a British airborne brigade, a British air force and the Royal Navy, has led with inconceivable rapidity to the capture of Toulon and Marseilles, to the freeing of the great strip of the Riviera coast, and to the successful advance of General Patch's army up the Rhône valley. This army, after taking over

171

80,000 prisoners, joined hands with General Eisenhower, and has passed under his command.

Although Churchill had swallowed his pride and publicly admitted that Dragoon had been a success, he could not help but put in a rejoinder pointing out that it was D-Day that had ensured its success. He also omitted to mention that he had opposed the operation with a vengeance:

> When I had the opportunity on 15 August of watching – alas, from afar – the landing at St Tropez, it would have seemed audacious to hope for such swift and important results. They have, however, under the spell of the victories in the north, already been gained in superabundance, and in less than half the time prescribed and expected in the plans which were prepared beforehand. So much for the fighting in France.

Churchill then paused for effect as the gathered British Members of Parliament listened intently to his measured oration before adding:

> We have, I regret to say, lost upwards of 90,000 men, killed, wounded and missing, and the United States, including General Patch's army, over 145,000. Such is the price in blood paid by the English-speaking democracies for the actual liberation of the soil of France.

We can only wonder if Churchill, looking around at the gathered faces, posed himself the question as to whether de Gaulle and France would be grateful for this sacrifice. Both Britain and France would soon have empires to reclaim, although the Americans had said all along that they would not and could not support this. Nevertheless, the reality was that American-supplied weapons would help France in her attempts to cling on in Indochina and Algeria.

Military historian Philip Warner was altogether dismissive of the achievements of Operation Dragoon, subscribing to Churchill's strategic school of thought:

> The aim of this operation was to clear southern France of Germans, which it did, thus providing ten more divisions for use

against the Allied advance in the north. The south of France was of no tactical value to the Allies and the troops they used in its invasion would have been more usefully employed in Italy, from which most of them had been taken. Tactically it would have been far more sensible to leave those ten German divisions in the south of France waiting for an invasion which never came. This represented one of the many divergences in Allied opinion on strategy.

Warner's argument certainly has some merit, especially in light of Hitler's obsession with not giving up ground and his constant orders to his generals to stand fast. Inevitably, of course, those remaining divisions in the south of France would have been drawn northwards and back to the German border regardless. Churchill knew from Enigma decrypts of German top secret signals that they would not fight for the south of France with any great vigour, whereas in contrast they would defend the Italian passes leading into Austria at all costs. This fighting would also inevitably bring in German reinforcements from elsewhere.

Churchill was right

In Churchill's own version of events he gave the impression that he had favoured Normandy, and was simply worried about timings and casualties there. After the disaster at Dieppe, one can perhaps forgive such fears. But contemporary documents paint a different picture: his intention was always to see through his Mediterranean strategy rather than commit to a direct assault on Nazi Germany. His desire to enter central Europe was supported in 1943 by military considerations rather than just political ones. Churchill's hope had always been that an invasion of Germany would only be conducted in the wake of a military and political collapse.

In the event Churchill's concerns about Overlord proved largely groundless; only at Omaha Beach were casualties excessively high. Further inland, though, events did not pan out as hoped. Despite the Allies' overwhelming superiority the Germans hung on grimly and had to be ground down by costly frontal assaults. Ultimately, though, it was a contest that Hitler could not win.

However you look at it, in strategic terms Dragoon was a nugatory exercise. It was not conducted in parallel with Overlord owing to shortages of amphibious transport, thereby losing its diversionary impact. In addition, the success of Overlord meant Army Group G would have been forced to withdraw from southern France anyway to avoid being cut off, regardless of an invasion in the south. The timing of Dragoon meant it did not take any pressure off the Allies fighting in Normandy, since Blaskowitz's better units, especially his panzer divisions, had already been drawn north by 15 August. By then Army Group B's 5th Panzer Army and 7th Army in northern France were already trapped in the developing Falaise Pocket along with Blaskowitz's armoured units redeployed from the south. Flight over the Seine became an imperative regardless of what was taking place in the Riviera.

Dragoon clearly had no discernable impact on the fighting in Normandy. In mid-August 1944, even as part of Field Marshal Walter Model's Army Group B was being overwhelmed in the Falaise Pocket, far to the south Patton's US 3rd Army was driving all out for the Seine to create a much bigger trap. His forces were on the line Orleans–Chartres–Dreux facing little or no opposition the day after Dragoon commenced. He pressed on, hoping to swing north and trap the Germans against the river. This hope was thwarted in part by the Allies themselves and in part by the Germans' quick thinking.

It seemed as if Hitler's forces in Normandy were on the verge of a second and much bigger disaster than Falaise. Unfortunately for the Allies, determined German resistance held up the US XV Corps as Model's retreating troops fought desperate rearguard actions along the Seine. After the Falaise Pocket had been overrun, Model conducted a highly successful rearguard operation at Rouen at the end of August to save the survivors of his exhausted and scattered command. In no small part thanks to the rearguard action at Rouen there was no second Falaise Pocket; frustratingly for the Allies, the bulk of Army Group B west of the Seine – some 240,000 troops, 30,000 vehicles and 135 panzers – escaped over the river.

The surviving staffs of the 5th Panzer Army and the LVIII Panzer Corps were pulled out of the line and responsibility for the front was assumed by 7th Army once more. After Falaise, German armoured vehicle losses were modest considering the rapidity of the Allies' advance: only 60 panzers and 250 other armoured vehicles were left on the west bank of the Seine, and only about another 10,000 troops were captured. Most of the survivors of the 5th Panzer Army, the XLVII and LVIII Panzer Corps and the I SS and II SS Panzer Corps were withdrawn to Germany behind the relative safety of the long-neglected Siegfried Line. There was nothing Dragoon could have done to influence these events.

Despite Operation Dragoon, the rest of Army Group G also withdrew in good order, blocking the strategic Belfort Gap until almost the end of the year. The failure of Dragoon to trap Blaskowitz's forces in the south of France meant that Army Group G was able not only to hold the Belfort Gap but also to obstruct the Allies' efforts to secure Metz and Nancy. If Dragoon had not taken place, the German forces in southern France would still have been able to withdraw largely unmolested. The requirement to smash these divisions would inevitably have fallen on the Allied air forces, and as they had not managed to achieve this feat in Normandy it is unlikely they would have been any more successful in the south.

Having escaped Dragoon, Blaskowitz's forces contributed to what the Germans dubbed 'the miracle in the west', playing a key role in stabilising the German front line before the West-wall, despite the failure of Hitler's Lorraine counter-offensive. In just short of thirty days Blaskowitz had withdrawn Army Group G with some 240,000 men up to 800 km, and two-thirds of his combat troops had escaped. They in turn were able to counter-attack the pursuing enemy and establish a continuous defensive line.

After Operation Market Garden had failed in September, Eisenhower opted for a broad-front strategy, leading to costly fighting along the entire length of the Franco-German border, involving those forces who had pushed up from the south. The Allies never did achieve a decisive breakthrough in Italy, proving in Churchill's mind that he had been right all along. Then, following the defeat of the Germans' surprise Ardennes offensive, Eisenhower was unnecessarily distracted by the Colmar Pocket.

'Great strategic mistake'
Eisenhower's ultimately decisive support for the seizure of a port in southern France was based on the notion that a broad-front campaign would be fought from the North Sea to Switzerland. He was also

swayed by the bloody stalemate that prevailed in Normandy during late June and through July. He did not altogether appreciate Montgomery's belief that a single thrust in Normandy would break through the German defences after they had become unbalanced. Anzio clearly weighed heavily on his mind, but by the time Dragoon was implemented it was an academic exercise.

As far as Stalin was concerned, Overlord was of great strategic value but Dragoon was simply of political significance. After the sweeping success of Operation Bagration and the follow-up operations in June–August 1944 that cut great swathes through central and southern Europe, the Western Allies' invasion of southern France was irrelevant to his ambitions. By early September the Red Army was rolling into the Balkans. Only an invasion in the Adriatic might have spoiled Stalin's plans, but with the Allies bottled up in Italy he was given a free hand.

Overlord offered him real support by forcing Hitler to fight on two fronts (although he was already doing so in Italy) and by keeping two SS panzer corps with four battle-hardened panzer divisions in France at a critical time for the Red Army. These were only redeployed to the east in the spring of 1945, by which time the Red Army was more than ready for them. In contrast, German forces in Italy were able to spare divisions to bolster the Eastern Front.

Hanson Baldwin, a contemporary military analyst for the *New York Times*, commented on the first day of Operation Dragoon, 'The troops involved could have been more profitably employed in strengthening our forces in Normandy and Brittany.' After the war he would reaffirm his belief that 'the invasion of southern France two months after the Normandy attack had little military, and no political, significance'. Ultimately Dragoon failed in its primary objective of giving 'the greatest possible assistance to Overlord by destroying or containing the maximum number of German formations in the Mediterranean'. By the time Overlord had secured a footing in Normandy, the mere threat of an invasion in southern France was keeping ten divisions tied up on the Mediterranean coast. It had always seemed to the British that little would be gained by turning the threat into a reality.

Launching the invasion two months after Overlord meant that Dragoon was well past its sell-by date. By this point Hitler knew where the Anglo-American centre of gravity lay, so what cared he about events in the distant south of France. In the weeks following Dragoon and the German collapse in Normandy, stabilising the front east of the Seine became the key priority.

Montgomery's verdict, given with the benefit of hindsight, was damning:

> I personally had always been opposed to Anvil from the beginning, and had advocated its complete abandonment for two main reasons. First, we wanted the landing craft for Overlord; and secondly, it weakened the Italian Front at the very time when progress there had a good chance of reaching Vienna before the Russians. (Failure to do this was to have far-reaching effects in the Cold War that broke out towards the end of 1945.)
>
> But Anvil . . . in my view was one of the great strategic mistakes of the war.

It is interesting that Montgomery persisted with Churchill's optimistic view that the Allies could have broken through in Italy.

There can be no denying that Dragoon was an unwanted planning distraction for Eisenhower. It should have been cancelled or simply maintained as a threat, much as Operation Fortitude had convinced the Germans that the Allies would land in the Pas de Calais area as well as Normandy. If this had been done, then all the resources in terms of vital landing craft, logistical, naval and air support as well as the assault troops could have been committed to Overlord and this would have ensured that it could have been conducted in May 1944.

It should also be borne in mind that the dispute over Dragoon was not based on nationality. Eisenhower's Chief of Staff General Walter Bedell Smith agreed with Montgomery over Dragoon, while Major-General Francis de Guingand agreed with Eisenhower. Indeed, Bedell Smith supported Brooke, while Admiral Andrew Cunningham, the Naval Commander-in-Chief in the Mediterranean, supported Eisenhower. Brooke ultimately shared Churchill's and Montgomery's misgivings about the utility of Dragoon. Even ten years after the war ended he remained unconvinced, remarking with great understatement:

It was a relief to feel that at last these landings were taking place and could no longer produce heated arguments. The Americans' original idea was to launch them in May before Overlord and seriously at the expense of operations in Italy. Coming as they did now, they could no longer do all the harm they would have done at an early date. But I still wonder whether we derived much benefit from them.

In Italy, of course, the Allies never did break through, and the German armies there did not give up until the end of the war. There was an interesting postscript to the Italian Front involving Blaskowitz. On 10 February 1945 he and von Rundstedt's Chief of Staff Lieutenant-General Siegfried Westphal held a meeting near Stuttgart with Alexander Constantin von Neurath, the German Consul at Lugano. American intelligence reported:

> The three frankly discussed the possibility of opening the Western Front to the Allies. . . .
> Neither Westphal nor Blaskowitz made definite suggestions. They appear however, (a) to be working with Kesselring, (b) to have uppermost in their minds the idea of opening up the Western and Italian Fronts to the Allies, and (c) to be approaching the point where they might discuss an arrangement on purely military lines with an American Army officer.

However, they knew the Waffen-SS and other Eastern Front veterans were prepared to fight to the bitter end and would not countenance surrender.

The Allies did not reach Milan, Turin and Trieste until 2 May 1945; four days later they arrived at the Brenner Pass, the gateway to Austria. Nor was the amphibious left hook of the Anzio operation repeated. Churchill's dreams of getting into Austria or Yugoslavia came to nothing, which suited Stalin.

General Clark, commander of the US 5th Army in Italy and subsequently American High Commissioner in Austria, offered a judgement that was as damning as Monty's:

> The weakening of the campaign in Italy in order to invade

southern France, instead of pushing into the Balkans, was one of the outstanding political mistakes of the war. . . . Stalin knew exactly what he wanted in a political as well as military way: and the thing he wanted most was to keep us out of the Balkans. . . . It is easy to see, therefore, why Stalin favoured Anvil at Tehran. . . . I later came to understand, in Austria, the tremendous advantages that we had lost by our failure to press on into the Balkans. . . . Had we been there before the Red Army, not only would the collapse of Germany have come sooner, but the influence of Soviet Russia would have been drastically reduced.

Brooke in part felt that General Alexander had dropped the ball in Italy, having failed to smash the German forces south of the Apennines. Instead of breaking up the Germans on favourable ground he chose to fight them on their prepared Apennine defensive positions. Brooke's view was that there should have been a concentrated attack, instead of several small pushes all along the front, which could have swung right and left; instead the opportunity was lost and the Germans dug their heels in.

General Wilson recalled that Eisenhower's and Marshall's obsession with an invasion of the south of France and the seizure of Marseilles and Toulon seemed to 'imply a strategy aimed at defeating Germany during the first half of 1945 at the cost of an opportunity of defeating her before the end of 1944'. De Guingand was also of the view that Dragoon in fact weakened the push on the Rhine, observing:

If he [Eisenhower] had not taken the steps he did to link up at an early date with Anvil and had held back Patton, and had diverted the administrative resources so released to the north, I think it possible that we might have obtained a bridgehead over the Rhine before the winter – but not more.

In the Far East General Slim's amphibious operation to turn the Japanese flank, which had been sacrificed to Overlord and Dragoon, did not take place until 1 May 1945. In the event it proved to be a wasted show of force. Operation Dracula witnessed an airborne assault on the mouth of the Rangoon river, followed by amphibious landings on both banks. With British forces bearing down on them from the north, the

Japanese abandoned the Burmese capital and the two British forces linked up on the 6th.

Why did Roosevelt and the US Chiefs of Staff stick so doggedly to the implementation of Operation Anvil/Dragoon? Eisenhower was all for being flexible and adopting a policy of waiting to see how the strategic situation developed. Ultimately it was General Marshall who was the driving force; he spurned Eisenhower's opportunism. Marshall had already shown great strategic inflexibility; in 1942 his pushing for the seizure of the Cherbourg peninsula so delayed Operation Torch that the Allies lost their chance of defeating the Germans in Tunisia before the winter. Similarly the following year his opposition to the invasion of Italy meant the Allies lost their chance to exploit Mussolini's downfall. Building on the success in Italy did not fit his strategic concept. It has been said that Marshall's strengths were not as a strategist but as an administrator, a role in which he excelled. It was he who built the massive American Army from a standing start.

American war correspondent and military historian Chester Wilmot perhaps summed up the strategic failure of Dragoon most succinctly:

> The decision to switch the Mediterranean *Schwerpunkt* from Italy to southern France meant that from the start of July until the middle of August – during six irrecoverable weeks of summer campaigning, while the struggle in Normandy was at its height and while the Russian summer offensive was in full spate – the Allied assault along the whole southern flank of Europe was deliberately weakened and drastically curtailed. Hitler was spared the necessity of having to reinforce his southern front at the critical juncture when he was hard pressed to the point of desperation in the west and the east.

To the Americans' credit, General Patch's US 7th Army and de Lattre's French 1st Army cleared south and central France in half the time expected, taking some 100,000 prisoners at the cost of about 13,000 casualties as of mid-September.

Likewise, from the supporting logistical supply standpoint Dragoon was a triumph. Despite German efforts to wreck the facilities at Marseilles and Toulon, both ports were open for business by 20 September 1944. By the end of the month over 300,000 Allied troops,

69,000 vehicles and nearly 18,000 badly needed tons of gasoline had poured into France via the Dragoon bridgehead. Ultimately some good had come of it. Churchill, though, always felt that a much bigger opportunity had been lost and the world became a much worse place for it.

Annexes

1. Allied Forces Committed to Operation Dragoon, 15 August 1944
Western Task Force Vice Admiral H. Kent Hewitt USN
8th Fleet Amphibious Force
Six flotillas of landing craft.
Fleet: 505 US ships, 252 British, 19 French, 6 Greek and 263 merchantmen; 370 large landing ships and 1,267 small landing craft; 5 battleships (HMS *Ramillies*, USS *Arkansas*, USS *Nevada*, USS *Texas* and the French *Lorraine*), 4 heavy cruisers, 18 light cruisers, 9 aircraft carriers and 85 destroyers. French vessels included a battleship (*Lorraine*), 5 cruisers (*Duguay-Trouin*, *Emile Bertin*, *Fantasque*, *Terrible* and *Mailin*) and 5 torpedo-boats. Escort Carrier Force

Task Force 88 (TF88)
Rear-Admiral T.H. Troubridge RN
Rear-Admiral Calvin T. Durgin USN

Task Group 88.1
Carriers:
HMS *Attacker* (879 Naval Air Squadron equipped with Seafires)
HMS *Emperor* (800 Naval Air Squadron equipped with F6F Hellcats)
HMS *Khedive* (899 Naval Air Squadron equipped with Seafires)
HMS *Pursuer* (881 Naval Air Squadron equipped with F4F Wildcats)
HMS *Searcher* (882 Naval Air Squadron equipped with F4F Wildcats)
Light cruisers: HMS *Delhi* and HMS *Royalist* (flagship)
Also 5 British destroyers and a Greek destroyer
Task Group 88.2
Carriers:
HMS *Hunter* (807 Naval Air Squadron equipped with Seafires)
HMS *Stalker* (809 Naval Air Squadron equipped with Seafires)
USS *Kasaan Bay* (VF-74 equipped with F6F Hellcats)

USS *Tulagi* (VOF-01 equipped with F6F Hellcats)
Light cruisers: HMS *Colombo* and HMS *Caledon*
Also 6 US destroyers.

Assault Task Forces

Task Force 84 Alpha Force
1 Coastguard cutter and 1 fighter control ship
Bombardment Group: 1 battleship, 1 cruiser, 5 light cruisers, 6 destroyers
Minesweeper Group: 30 minesweepers, 6 submarine chasers, 2 Landing Craft Command
Assault Force: US 3rd Infantry Division
Assault Group: 2 attack transport ships, 3 attack cargo ships, three freighters, 25 LST, 55 LCI, 60 LCT, 20 LCM, 8 minesweepers, 9 patrol craft, 12 fire support craft, 10 LCC

Task Force 85 Delta Force
1 seaplane tender, 1 destroyer, 1 fighter direction tender
Bombardment Group: 2 battleships, 6 light cruisers, 8 destroyers
Minesweeper Group: 10 minesweepers
Assault Force: US 45th Infantry Division
Assault Group: 6 attack transport ships, 2 freighters, 1 LSI, 23 LST, 49 LCI, 48 LCT, 8 LCM, 8 fire support craft, 5 LCC, 6 submarine chasers
Salvage & Firefighting Group: 6 tugs

Task Force 86 Sitka Force
Bombardment Group: 1 battleship, 1 cruiser, 3 light cruisers, 4 destroyers
Assault Force: French 1st Special Service Force
Assault Group: 5 destroyer transports, 5 LSI, 17 patrol torpedo boats, 5 minesweepers

Task Force 87 Camel Force
1 attack cargo ship
Bombardment Group: 1 battleship, 1 cruiser, 5 light cruisers, 11 destroyers
Minesweeper Group: 31 minesweepers
Assault Force: US 36th Infantry Division

Assault Group: 3 attack transport ships, 2 attack cargo ships, 3 freighters, 21 LST, 1 LSI, 29 LCI, 45 LCT, 4 LCM, 7 fire support craft, 7 LCC, 17 submarine chasers, 16 patrol craft
Salvage & Firefighting Group: 6 tugs, 3 LCI, 1 LCT, 4 LCM

Airborne
1st Airborne Task Force, Brigadier-General Robert T. Frederick
550th Glider Infantry Battalion, plus a platoon of the 887th Engineer Company
509th Parachute Infantry Battalion, plus the 463rd Parachute Field Artillery Battalion
551st Parachute Infantry Battalion, plus a platoon of the 887th Engineer Company
517th Parachute Regimental Combat Team, plus a 460th Parachute Field Artillery Battalion, a 596th Parachute Engineer Company, an anti-tank platoon from the 442nd Infantry Regiment and Company D from the 83rd Chemical Mortar Battalion
British 2nd Independent Parachute Brigade, Brigadier C.H.V. Pritchard

US 7th Army
General Alexander M. Patch

US VI Corps
Major General Lucian Truscott
3rd Infantry Division
36th Infantry Division
45th Infantry Division

Armoured support
Duplex Drive (DD) amphibious tank units
191st, 753rd and 756th Tank Battalions
Combat Command Sudre from 1re Division *Blindée* (armoured division), also known as 1st Combat Command
Task Force Butler
French Armee B (French 1st Army), General de Lattre de Tassigny

French II Corps
General Goislard de Monsabert

1re Division *Blindée* (armoured division) 1re Division *Française Libre* (motorised infantry Division) 3e Division *d'infanterie algérienne* (infantry division) 9e Division *d'infanterie coloniale* (infantry division)

French I Corps
General Emile Béthouart
2e Division *d'infanterie marocaine* (infantry division), 4e Division *marocaine de montagne* (mountain infantry division), 5e Division *Blindée* (armoured division)

Allied Air Forces
Mediterranean Allied Air Force, General Ira C. Eaker, USAAF:
   Mediterranean Tactical Air Force (MATAF)
   USAAF 12th Air Force
   XII Tactical Air Command, Brigadier-General Gordon P. Saville
Provisional Troop Carrier Division:
   435th Troop Carrier Group (Horsa gliders)
   436th Troop Carrier Group (Waco Gliders)
   Plus detachments from the 79th, 80th, 81st and 82nd Troop Carrier Squadrons, with 526 C-47 transport aircraft and 452 Horsa and Waco gliders
Bomber Forces:
   42nd Bomb Wing (Medium)
   17th Bomb Group (including the 34th, 37th, 95th and 432nd Bomb Squadrons)
The French Air Force supplied 6 P-47 fighter-bomber groups, 4 B-26 bomber groups and a P-38 reconnaissance group

2. Allied Order of Battle, 1945
US 6th Army Group (became active 15 September 1944)

US 7th Army:
   36th Infantry Division
   44th Infantry Division
   103rd Infantry Division (arrived at Marseilles late October 1944)
VI Corps:
   10th Armored Division (assigned mid-March 1945)
   63rd Infantry Division (assigned mid-March 1945)
   100th Infantry Division (arrived at Marseilles late October 1944)

XV Corps (reassigned from US 3rd Army end of September 1944):
   3rd Infantry Division
   14th Armored Division (arrived at Marseilles late October 1944)
   45th Infantry Division
XXI Corps (assigned from reserve early January 1945 – initially 28th
and 75th Infantry and 12th Armored Divisions):
   4th Infantry Division
   12th Armored Division
   42nd Infantry Division (assigned mid-March 1945)
French 1st Army:
   with three additional divisions

3. German Forces in the South of France
3.1. Order of Battle, 15 August 1944
   Army Group G, General Johannes Blaskowitz

1st Army, General Kurt von der Chevallerie:
   LXXX (80th) Corps
   158th Reserve Infantry Division
   LXXXVI (86th) Corps
   159th Reserve Infantry Division

19th Army, General Friedrich Wiese:
   11th Panzer Division
   189th Reserve Infantry Division
   LXII (62nd) Reserve Corps
   157th Reserve Infantry Division
   242nd Infantry Division
   LXXXV (85th) Corps
   244th Infantry Division

3.2 Order of Battle, 31 August 1944

19th Army
   11th Panzer-Division
   IV Luftwaffe Field Corps
   189th Reserve Infantry Division
   716th Infantry Division
   LXXXV Corps
   198th Infantry Division

338th Infantry Division

3.3. Order of Battle, 16 September 1944

19th Army:
  LXVI Corps
  15th Panzergrenadier Division
  16th Infantry Division
  21st Panzer Division (elements)
  LXIV Corps
  189th Reserve Infantry-Division (remnants)
  716th Infantry Division
  IV Luftwaffe Field Corps
  159th Reserve Infantry Division
  198th Infantry Division
  338th Infantry Division
  LXXXV Corps
  11th Panzer Division

3.4. Order of Battle, 20 January 1945

19th Army, General der Infanterie Siegfried Rasp:
  2nd Mountain Division
  106th Panzer Brigade
LXIII Corps, Generalleutnant Erich Abraham:
  159th Infantry Division
  338th Infantry Division
  716th Infantry Division
LXIV Corps, Generalleutnant Max Grimmeiss:
  189th Infantry Division
  198th Infantry Division
  16th Volksgrenadier Division
  708th Volksgrenadier Divisions

4. Units lost by Army Group G to the Battle for Normandy

In total, Army Group G saw a total of thirteen divisions redeployed before Operation Dragoon commenced; these included elements of six infantry divisions, six panzer divisions and one panzergrenadier division.

1st Army:
    LXXX (80th) Corps
    708th Infantry Division (by 30 July)
    LXXXVI (86th) Corps
    276th Infantry Division (mid-June)
19th Army:
    IV Luftwaffe Field Corps
    271st Infantry Division (mid-July)
    272nd Infantry Division (mid-July)
    277th Infantry Division (29 June)
    LXXXV (85th) Corps
    338th Infantry Division (mid-August)
    XLVII (47th) Panzer Corps plus LXVI (66th) Reserve Corps
    2nd Panzer Division (mid-June)
    19th Panzer Division (returned to the Eastern Front in July)
    21st Panzer Division (went into action 6 June)
    116th Panzer Division *Windhund* (24 July)
    LVIII (58th) Reserve Panzer Corps
    2nd SS-Panzer Division *Das Reich* (mid-June)
    9th Panzer Division (6 August)
    I SS Panzer Corps
    17th SS Panzergrenadier Division *Götz von Berlichingen* (8 June)

5. French Unit Histories

1st Armoured Division

The French 1st Division *Blindée* was raised in May 1943, based on Colonel Vigier's Brigade *Legere Mecanique* which had served in the Vichy French garrison of North Africa and fought against the Axis forces in the Tunisian campaign. As part of French Army B (later redesignated the French 1st Army), the division sailed to southern France and landed in the follow-up of Operation Anvil/Dragoon.

1st Free French Division (Motorised Infantry)

The 1st Française Libre came into being at the beginning of February 1943 under General Koenig, drawing on Free French units that had seen action during the Libyan campaign. The division fought in Tunisia in April 1943 and was deployed to Syria in June 1943. It was subsequently redesignated the 1st Motorised Infantry Division or *Motorisée d'Infanterie* serving in Italy, France and Germany.

5th Armoured Division

The French 2nd Armoured Division, formed on 1 May 1943, was redesignated the 5th Armoured Division on 16 July 1943 (thus allowing the 2nd Free French Division to convert to the 2nd Armoured) in North Africa. Originally comprising a tank brigade and a support brigade, the 5th Armoured Division was re-equipped and reorganised to American standards with three combat commands that were commonly detached to support French infantry divisions.

2nd Moroccan Division

The French 2nd Moroccan Division was formed in Morocco in May 1943 from elements of the Meknes Division of the garrison of French North Africa. It moved to Italy in November 1943, campaigned as far north as Florence with the French Expeditionary Corps and then moved to southern France shortly after the Operation Anvil/Dragoon landings. It fought with the French 1st Army from Provence to the Rhine and the Danube.

3rd Algerian Division

The French 3rd Algerian Infantry Division was created in Algeria on 1 May 1943 from elements of the Constantine Division of the garrison of French North Africa. It moved to Italy in December 1943 and campaigned as far north as Siena as part of the French Expeditionary Corps, before withdrawing to prepare for the landings in southern France.

4th Moroccan Division

The French 4th Division *Marocaine de Montagne* was created at Casablanca in June 1943 from the redesignated 3rd Moroccan Infantry Division. Originally formed with three regiments of Moroccans, the 2nd *Régiment de Tirailleurs Marocains* was replaced by the 1st *Régiment de Tirailleurs Algériens* on 15 August 1944. The 27th Infantry Regiment joined the division in March 1945 and the 1st RTA was detached in April of that year.

The 4th DMM served with the French Expeditionary Corps in Italy in 1944, with two of its regiments temporarily assigned to the French Corps de Montagne. Following its arrival in southern France in September 1944, the division was separated into several tactical groups. Divisional Headquarters, the 1st RTM and other divisional assets moved to stabilise the situation in the Alps on the Franco-Italian border. The 6th RTM was detached to the Belfort-Vosges sector. Meanwhile, some elements of the 1st RTA garrisoned Marseilles while other elements of the regiment remained in Italy. The division was not reunited until December, after which time it continued to campaign in France and Germany.

9th Colonial Division

The 9th Colonial Division was officially activated on 16 July 1943 in Algeria, by which time some of its components had already suffered casualties: approximately 500 troops of the 4th RTS were lost on 20 April 1943 when their transport was torpedoed by *U-565* while en route to French North Africa, and 35 troops of the 13th RTS were killed in a Luftwaffe air raid on Algiers on the night of 4/5 June 1943. The 9th Colonial Division assembled in October at Mostaganem, with lead elements departing from Oran for Corsica in April 1944 to assist in liberating the island. By May the entire division garrisoned the island. In June the 4th and 13th *Régiments de Tirailleurs Sénégalais* made the assault landing on Elba and then returned to Corsica; in their wake the 6th RTS moved to Elba for garrison duty. By mid-July the division was reassembled on Corsica. The 9th Colonial Division also served with French Armee B/1st Army in France and Germany.

References

Chapter One: Pleasing Stalin – the Balkans or Southern France

p. 1 'one of the longest . . .' Dwight D. Eisenhower, *Crusade in Europe* (London, 1948), pp. 308–9

p. 2 'It developed that General . . .' Dwight D. Eisenhower, *At Ease: Stories I Tell to Friends* (London, 1968), p. 263

p. 4 'I emphasised that I . . .' Winston S. Churchill, *The Second World War. Volume V: Closing the Ring* (London, 1954), pp. 75–7

p. 6 'Our Chiefs of Staff . . .' Elliot Roosevelt, *As he saw it* (New York, 1946), p. 185

p. 9 'Stalin thought it . . .' Churchill, *Closing the Ring*, p. 313

p. 9 'The best course would be . . .' Ibid, pp. 313–14

p. 10 'that we should continue . . .' War Cabinet and Combined Chiefs of Staffs Papers, 88-3 Combined Chiefs of Staff, 132nd Meeting, cited in George Bruce, *Second Front Now! The Road To D-Day* (London, 1979), p. 148

p. 10 'he would like to . . .' Eureka conference, Minutes of Plenary Session, between the USA, Great Britain and the USSR, 30 November 1943, p. 559

p. 11 'took note that Operation . . .' The Tehran Conference, Declaration of the Three Powers, 1 December 1943

p. 11 '[Stalin] approved of Roosevelt's . . .' Arthur Bryant, A., *Triumph in the West 1943–1946. Based on the Diaries and Autobiographical Notes of Field Marshal The Viscount Alanbrooke* (London, 1960), p. 77

p. 12 'In order to give . . .' Churchill, *Closing the Ring*, p. 362

p. 13 'I had not long . . .' Field Marshal Sir William Slim, *Defeat into Victory* (London, 1956), p. 213

p. 13 'Reverting to the Riviera . . .' Ibid, p. 363

p. 14 'I had got the date of . . .' Bryant, *Triumph in the West*, p. 91

p. 15 'Within three days of . . .' Address of the President broadcast from Hyde Park, New York, 24 December 1943

p. 16 'I may say that . . .' Ibid

Chapter Two: De Gaulle – 'he is a very dangerous threat to us'

p. 17 'The future French government . . .' Franklin D. Roosevelt's statement on North African Policy, 17 November 1942

p. 19 'I am absolutely convinced . . .' David Irving, *The War between the Generals* (London, 1981), p. 134

p. 19 'I am perfectly willing . . .' Roosevelt's Memorandum for General Marshall, 2 June 1944

p. 21 'Scotland Yard was waiting . . .' Giles Whittell, *Spitfire Women of World*

War II (London, 2008), p. 121

p. 21 'Now is the time . . .' Winston Churchill, letter to Franklin D. Roosevelt, 16 December 1941

p. 21 'Churchill had made for . . .' Charles de Gaulle, *The Call to Honour* (London, 1955), p. 145

p. 22 'In the region now . . .' Eisenhower, *Crusade*, p. 102

p. 23 'However, there was nothing . . .' Ibid, p. 90

p. 25 'While there are men like. . .,' Graham Stewart, *His Finest Hours: The War Speeches of Winston Churchill* (Quercus, n.d.), p. 139

p. 27 'Ike had played a . . .' Captain Harry C. Butcher, *Three Years with Eisenhower: The Personal Diary of Captain Harry C. Butcher, USNR Naval Aide to General Eisenhower, 1942 to 1945* (London, 1946), p. 403

p. 27 'Today, General Giraud, through . . .' Eisenhower's Address at the French Rearmament Ceremony, Algiers, 8 May 1943

p. 27 'French valour and French patriotism . . .' Ibid

Chapter Three: Churchill and Monty take on Ike

p. 33 'My Chief was very . . .' Major General Sir Francis de Guingand, *Operation Victory* (London, 1947), p. 337

p. 33 'Our course allowed us . . .' Ibid, pp. 338–9

p. 34 'It is most undesirable . . .' Public Records Office (CAB Series 120/420), cited by Carlo D'Este, *Decision in Normandy: The Unwritten Story of Montgomery and the Allied Campaign* (London, 1984), p. 57

p. 34 'Today, 1 January 1944 . . .' Field Marshal Bernard Law Montgomery, *The Memoirs of Field Marshal The Viscount Montgomery of Alamein* (London, 1958), p. 211

p. 34 He said he had . . .' Ibid, p. 212

p. 34 'I asked for my . . .' Ibid

p. 35 'decided, off the cuff, . . .' Eisenhower letter to Ismay, 3 December 1960

p. 35 'he had only a . . .' , Montgomery, *Memoirs*, p. 210

p. 35 'It had been arranged . . .' de Guingand, *Operation Victory*, pp. 340–1

p. 36 'This can be done . . .' Secret, Urgent Incoming Message, Montgomery to Marshall/Eisenhower, 10 January 1944, p. 1

p. 36 'Having recently returned from . . .' Churchill, *Closing the Ring*, p. 517

p. 37 'We must remember that . . .' Nigel Hamilton, *Monty. Master of the Battlefield 1942–1944* (London, 1983), p. 517

p. 37 'Furthermore, there are certain . . .' Irving, *War between the Generals*, p. 32

p. 38 'The news from the . . .' Top Secret, Incoming Message, Marshall to Eisenhower, 16 January 1944, p. 1

p. 38 'It is my intention . . .' Ibid, p. 2

p. 40 'I regard Anvil as . . .' US Secret, Urgent Outgoing Message, Eisenhower to Marshal, 23 January 1944, p. 3, also cited 'Overlord and Anvil must be . . . Churchill, *Closing the Ring*, p. 451

p. 40 'On this telegram I . . .' Ibid, p. 452

p. 41 'They questioned the wisdom . . .' Ibid

p. 41 'Had a long Chiefs of Staff meeting . . .,' Bryant, *Triumph in the West*,

p. 114
p. 42 'This campaign will provide . . .' War Cabinet Military Planning Papers, WO 106-4150, COS(44) 35th Meeting, cited Bruce, *Second Front Now!*, p. 158
p. 42 'I had hoped that . . .' Churchill, *Closing the Ring*, p. 432
p. 43 'I think we have ridden . . .' Bryant, *Triumph in the West*, p. 118
p. 43 'During my absence on . . .' Hamilton, *Monty*, p. 523
p. 43 'From an Army point . . .' Ibid, p. 524
p. 44 'Luckily I had discovered . . .' Bryant, *Triumph in the West*, pp. 121–2
p. 44 'I had a little difficulty . . .' Ibid, p. 122
p. 44 'Ike, representing the US . . .' Butcher, *Three Years with Eisenhower*, p. 422
p. 45 'Monty thinks Anvil should . . .' Ibid
p. 45 'I am told by the . . .' Hamilton, *Monty*, pp. 524–5
p. 45 'Under these circumstances, I . . .' Ibid
p. 45 'As a result of what . . .' Ibid
p. 47 'Following Ike's representations to. . .' Butcher, *Three Years with Eisenhower*, pp. 425–6
p. 48 'This is, at last . . .' Hamilton, *Monty,* p. 541
p. 49 'A draft directive to the . . .' SCAEF 10th Meeting, Top Secret, Minutes of Meeting Held in Conference Room (C4 –Room 8) Widewing, 1100, 20 March 1944, p. 1
p. 49 'I will be asked . . .' Top Secret, Urgent Outgoing Message, Eisenhower to Marshall, 21 March 1944, p. 1
p. 50 'The fact has been . . .' Ibid
p. 50 'Although convinced that Anvil . . .' Ibid, p. 2
p. 51 'The Supreme Commander accordingly . . .' Ibid
p. 51 'would contribute substantially to . . .' SCAEF 12th Meeting, Top Secret, Lt Commander J.E. Reid, Minutes of Meeting Held in Conference Room, Widewing, 1430, 27 March 1944, p. 4
p. 51 'If we accept the . . .' Ibid, p. 3
p. 52 'was not prepared . . .' Ibid, p. 1
p. 52 'Sir Alan Brooke then . . .' Ibid, p. 2
p. 53 'Sir Andrew Cunningham inquired . . .' Ibid, p. 4
p. 54 'carefully worded answer to . . .' Ibid
p. 54 'We cannot accept a . . .' Top Secret, Incoming Message, from Marshal to Eisenhower, 31 March 1944, p. 1
p. 54 'Our view is that there . . .' Ibid
p. 54 '17 April. Arrived back early in . . .' Bryant, *Triumph in the West*, p. 147
p. 55 'to give the greatest possible . . .' Ibid, p. 148
p. 55 '19 April. At last all our troubles . . .' Ibid

Chapter Four: Ike says 'No' to Churchill

p. 57 'Today we did nothing . . .' Raleigh Trevelyan, R., *Rome '44. The Battle for the Eternal City* (London, 1981), p. 314
p. 57 'It is also significant. . .' Address of the President on the Fall of Rome, 5

June 1944

p. 58 'No great effort like . . .' Ibid

p. 58 'The Boche is defeated . . .' General Mark Clark, *Calculated Risk* (New York/London, 1951), p. 358

p. 59 'I have also to announce . . .,' Stewart, *His Finest Hours*, p. 169

p. 61 'the need for an . . .' General Wilson's Report to the Combined Chiefs of Staff on the Italian Campaign, p. 34

p. 64 'I attach such importance . . .' Hamilton, *Monty*, p. 703

p. 64 'Want to make it . . .' Ibid, p. 704

p. 64 'COS met at 10.30am . . .' Bryant, *Triumph in the West*, p. 181

p. 64 'Although in the planning . . .' Eisenhower, *Crusade*, p. 312

p. 65 'It quickly became obvious. . .' Eisenhower, *At Ease*, p. 273

p. 65 'He said that he could . . .' Bryant, *Triumph in the West*, p. 150

p. 66 'We had a long evening . . .' Ibid, p. 223

p. 66 'France is the decisive theatre. . . .' Clive Ponting, *Churchill* (London, 1994), p. 626

p. 66 'Let's not wreck one . . .' cited Carlo D'Este, *Eisenhower Allied Supreme Commander* (London, 2003), p. 551

p. 67 'You emphasised to me . . .' cited Martin Gilbert, *Churchill. A Life* (London, 2000), p. 781

p. 67 'What can I do, Mr President . . .' Ibid

p. 68 'strategically most attractive . . .' Slim, *Defeat into Victory*, pp. 374–5

p. 68 'This obviously cannot continue, . . .' cited Ponting, *Churchill*, p. 626

p. 69 'This argument, beginning almost . . .' Eisenhower, *Crusade*, p. 309

p. 69 'It was a great pity . . .' Bryant, *Triumph in the West*, p. 204

p. 70 'the maintenance and administrative . . .' Chester Wilmot, *The Struggle for Europe* (London, 1952), p. 456

p. 70 'The Prime Minister had . . .' Butcher, *Three Years with Eisenhower*, p. 545

p. 71 'Ike said no, continued . . .' Ibid, p. 546

p. 71 'Thus the PM also . . .' Ibid

p. 71 'The PM was still . . .' Ibid, p. 548

p. 72 'Ike has been increasingly . . .' Ibid, p. 549

p. 72 'To say that I . . .' Carlo D'Este, *Eisenhower*, p. 566

p. 73 'a cantankerous yet adorable . . .' Ibid

Chapter Five: The Second Front – Blaskowitz's Lost Divisions

p. 76 'One recognises the perplexity . . .' MS B-516 (Sodenstern, R.G. 338, N.A., also cited Richard Giziowski, *The Enigma of General Blaskowitz* (Barnsley, 1997), p. 276

p. 83 'there was no military . . .' MS 882 (Wilutzky), R.G. 338, N.A., also cited Giziowski, *General Blaskowitz*, p. 284

p. 83 'release of men and . . .' Giziowski, *General Blaskowitz*, p. 285 and A.F. Wilt, *The French Riviera Campaign of August 1944* (Southern Illinois University, 1981), p. 45

p. 84 'It's time to abandon . . .' Giziowski, *General Blaskowitz*, p. 294

Chapter Six: Dragoon Hots Up

p. 87 'An estimate is required . . .' cited John Frayn Turner and Robert Jackson, *Destination Berchtesgaden, The Story of the US 7th Army in World War II* (London, 1975), p. 28

p. 100 'systematic, especially heavy air attacks . . .' Wilt, *French Riviera Campaign*, p. 75

p. 101 'After all, he is a . . .' Gilbert, *Churchill*, p. 787

p. 102 'They did not know . . .' Ibid

Chapter Seven: Dragoon – 'irrelevant and unrelated'

p. 106 'Life has a quiet . . .' Bryant, *Triumph in the West*, p. 200

p. 107 'One of my reasons . . .' Winston S. Churchill to Clementine Churchill, 17 August 1944, cited Carlo D'Este, *Eisenhower*, p. 567

p. 107 'Here we saw long rows of . . .' Winston S. Churchill, *The Second World War. Volume VI: Triumph and Tragedy* (London, 1955), p. 95

p. 107 'we found ourselves in . . .' Gilbert, *Churchill*, p. 788

p. 107 'Your majesty knows my . . .' Ibid

p. 107 'To-day is D-Day for . . .' Butcher, *Three Years with Eisenhower*, p. 554

p. 108 'As usual the Prime . . .' Eisenhower, *Crusade*, p. 312

p. 108 'The Prime Minister has . . .' Butcher, *Three Years with Eisenhower*, p. 555

p. 108 'We have just heard . . .' Ibid, p. 554

p. 112 'The invasion fleet is . . .' cited Giziowski, *General Blaskowitz*, p. 309

p. 116 'The landing near Toulon . . .' Bryant, *Triumph in the West*, p. 201

p. 117 'could have broken into . . .' Gilbert, *Churchill*, p. 789

Chapter Eight: The 'Champagne Campaign'

p. 119 'I would like to express . . .' http://www.b26.com

p. 120 'Mission was guns at . . .' Sergeant Delbert F. Kretschmar, 95th Bomb Squadron, 17th Bomb Group, *Mission Report and Diary*, 16 August 1944

p. 125 'Mission was gun positions . . .' Ibid, 26 August 1944

p. 126 'What a farce . . .' cited Julian Jackson, *Charles de Gaulle* (London, 1990), p. 26

p. 126 'Can't you sew?' Ibid

p. 128 We fired our guns . . .' Eric Ethier, 'Riviera D-Day,' *America in WWII* (August 2006), p. 8

p. 131 'I'm expecting a hell . . .' Private First Class John A. Hyman, 'From the Riviera to the Rhine,' *T-Patch*, 36th Infantry Division Newspaper (1945), p. 3

p. 132 Under the 36th Division command . . .' Ibid

p. 135 They called it the . . .' Robert H. Adleman & Colonel George Walton, *The Champagne Campaign* (Boston, 1969), p. 209

Chapter Nine: De Gaulle Stakes his Claim – the Liberation of Paris

p. 137 'must not fall into . . .' Steven Zaloga, *Liberation of Paris 1944* (Oxford, 2008), p. 67

p. 139 'Perhaps. But it's my . . .' Willis Thorton, *The Liberation of Paris* (London, 1963), p. 161

p. 139 'His arguments, which he . . .' Irving, *War between the Generals*, p. 253

p. 140 'Paris since Sunday noon . . .' Ibid, p. 254

p. 141 'Throughout France the Free . . .' Eisenhower, *Crusade*, pp. 323–5

p. 142 'I hope you've no idea . . .' Thorton, *Liberation of Paris*, p. 193

p. 143 'Who in the devil is . . .' Irving, *War between the Generals*, p. 254

p. 144 'The Republic has never . . .' Thorton, *Liberation of Paris*, p. 199

p. 144 'From this battle front . . .' Eisenhower, 'Remarks for Broadcast on the Army Hour', 3 September 1944

p. 145 'I address my words . . .' Eisenhower, 'Remarks in Paris', 8 September 1944

Chapter Ten: The Battle of the Belfort Gap

p. 150 'It was an enigma . . .' MS B-787 (Weise), Record Group 338, Records of US Army Commands, 1942–, National Archives, Washington DC, cited Giziowski, *General Blaskowitz*, p. 356

Chapter Eleven: Lorraine and the Southern Push to the Rhine

p. 160 'The US 6th Army Group . . .' Hans von Luck, *Panzer Commander: The Memoirs of Colonel Hans von Luck* (New York, 1989), pp. 168–9

p. 163 'Our Panthers were superior . . .' Major-General F.W. von Mellenthin, *Panzer Battles* (London, 1984), pp. 377–8

p. 164 'On 20 September 1944 . . .' Ibid, p. 271

Chapter Twelve: Churchill and Monty were Right

p. 171 'As we had intended . . .' Ethier, *Riviera D-day*, p. 8

p. 171 'What a transformation now . . .' Stewart, *His Finest Hours*, p. 174

p. 171 'While this great operation . . .' Ibid, pp. 174–5

p. 172 'When I had the opportunity . . .' Ibid

p. 172 'We have, I regret . . .' Ibid

p. 172 'The aim of this operation . . .' Philip Warner, *World War Two: The Untold Story* (London, 2002), p. 239

p. 176 'The troops involved could . . .' Ethier, *Riviera D-day*, p. 9

p. 177 'I personally had always . . .' Montgomery, *Memoirs*, p. 221

p. 177 'It was a relief . . .,' Bryant, *Triumph in the West*, p. 200

p. 178 'The three frankly discussed . . .' William J. Donovan Papers, *OSS Reports to the White House*, Intelligence Cables covering the capitulation of the Nazi armies in northern Italy. Memoranda for the President: Sunrise, 26 February 1945

p. 179 'The weakening of the . . .' Clark, *Calculated Risk*, pp. 348–51

p. 179 'imply a strategy aimed at . . .' General Wilson's Report to the Combined Chiefs of Staff on the Italian Campaign, p. 34

p. 179 'If he [Eisenhower] had . . .' De Guingand, *Operation Victory*, p. 413

p. 180 'The decision to switch . . .' Wilmot, *Struggle for Europe*, p. 455

Bibliography

A Note on Sources

On the whole there is a curious disregard for Operation Dragoon among military historians; perhaps this is understandable in light of the momentous events in Normandy and on the Eastern Front in August 1944. Yet it is a glaring omission when one considers the attention paid over the years to all the other amphibious assaults in the Mediterranean, most notably Operations Torch and Husky and the landings at Anzio. The political storm over the diverting of resources from Italy to the south of France remains the main preoccupation of historians. But this omission presents a challenge to any military historian trying to research Operation Dragoon and assess its wider ramifications. The fact that there was no bloody Omaha on the beaches, no bitter slogging match for any of the major cities and no dramatic break-out does not nullify the fact that American and French lives were expended in expelling Army Group G from southern France.

Specific titles dealing with the liberation of southern France remain scarce in comparison to those available on Operation Overlord and the subsequent liberation of northern France and Paris. There are only two readily accessible studies, *The Champagne Campaign* by Robert Adleman and Colonel Walton, dealing with the airborne part of the operation, and William Breuer's *Operation Dragoon*, which again focuses on the airborne assault, but also covers the landings.

Other volumes worthy of note are *Eisenhower's Lieutenants: The Campaigns of France and Germany 1944–1945* by Russell F. Weigley, which provides one of the most comprehensive surveys of American military operations in Europe. Robert A. Miller's *August 1944: The Campaign for France* gives one of the best day-by-day overviews of operations in both the north and the south. Similarly *Destination Berchtesgaden, The Story of the US 7th Army in World War II* by John Frayn Turner and Robert Jackson provides an excellent account of the 7th Army's activities in Europe.

The best biography on General Blaskowitz, the commander of Army Group G, is easily that by Richard Giziowski, which covers his entire career in commendable detail, including Dragoon and the subsequent fighting in Lorraine. Nick Beale generously permitted me to draw on his detailed research on Luftwaffe operations during Dragoon.

The following list is far from a complete bibliography, but indicates the principal works and documents consulted.

Primary Sources

Dwight D Eisenhower Presidential Library, Overlord/Anvil Papers, December 1943–April 1944:
Secret, Urgent Incoming Message, Montgomery to Marshall/Eisenhower, 10 January 1944
Top Secret, Incoming Message, Marshall to Eisenhower, 16 January 1944
US Secret, Urgent Outgoing Message, Eisenhower to Marshall, 23 January 1944
Operation Policy Memoranda, 29 January 1944
SCAEF 10th Meeting, Top Secret, Minutes of Meeting Held in Conference Room (C4 –Room 8) Widewing, 1100, 20 March 1944
Top Secret, Urgent Outgoing Message, Eisenhower to Marshall, 21 March 1944
SCAEF 12th Meeting, Top Secret, Lt Commander J.E. Reid, Minutes of Meeting Held in Conference Room, Widewing, 1430, 27 March 1944
Top Secret, Incoming Message, Marshall to Eisenhower, 31 March 1944

Papers and Minutes of Meetings, Sextant and Eureka Conferences, November/December 1943:
Combined Chiefs of Staff, Amphibious Operation Against the South of France, Note by the Secretaries, 5 December 1943
Eureka Conference, Minutes of Plenary Session, Between the USA, Great Britain and the USSR, 30 November 1943

Papers and Minutes of Meetings, Quadrant Conference, August 1943:
Combined Chiefs of Staff, Operation Overlord – Outline Plan, 10 August 1943

Papers and Minutes of Meetings, Trident Conference, May 1943:
Combined Chiefs of Staff, Trident Minutes, 1st Meeting, The White House, 12 May 1943

Dwight D. Eisenhower Memorial Commission
Churchill, W.S., letter to Franklin D. Roosevelt, 16 December 1941
Eisenhower, Dwight D., 'Remarks in Paris', 8 September 1944
Eisenhower, Dwight D., 'Remarks for Broadcast on the Army Hour', 3 September 1944
Eisenhower, Dwight D., 'Address at French Rearmament Ceremony', Algiers, 8 May 1943
Roosevelt, F.D., Statement on North African Policy, 17 November 1942
The Tehran Conference, Declaration of the Three Powers, 1 December 1943
US Chiefs of Staff, Proposals on Mediterranean Operations

Franklin D. Roosevelt Presidential Library
Fire Side Chats File:
Address of the President broadcast from Hyde Park, New York, 24 December 1943
Address of the President on the Fall of Rome, 5 June 1944
The Safe Files:
Box 4: Roosevelt Memoranda for General Marshall, 2 June 1944
William J. Donovan Papers
OSS Reports to the White House
Intelligence Cables covering the capitulation of the Nazi armies in northern Italy
Memoranda for the President: Sunrise, 26 February 1945

US National Archives
Record Group 338. Records of the US Army Commands, 1942-44
MS A-875 (Richter)
MS B-888 (Kniess)
MS B-880 (Wietersheim)
MS B-800 (Blaskowitz)
MS B-787 (Wiese)
MS B-696 (Botsch)
MS B-488 (Gyldenfeldt)
US State Department, Foreign Relations of the United States
The Conferences at Washington and Casablanca 1942-43 (Washington DC, 1967)
The Conferences at Washington and Quebec 1943 (Washington DC, 1970)
The Conferences at Cairo and Tehran 1943 (Washington DC, 1961)

Other Published Primary Sources
Blaskowitz, Johannes von, *German reaction to the invasion of Southern France*, Historical Division, HQ US Army, Europe (Foreign Military Studies Branch, 1945)
Blaskowitz, Johannes von, *Army Group G (10 May–22 September 1944)*, Historical Division, HQ US Army, Europe (Foreign Military Studies Branch, 1947)
Blaskowitz, Johannes von, *German (OB South-west) estimate of situation prior to Allied invasion of Southern France*, Historical Division, HQ US Army, Europe (Foreign Military Studies Branch, 1954)
Bryant, A., *Triumph in the West 1943–1946. Based on the Diaries and Autobiographical Notes of Field Marshal The Viscount Alanbrooke* (London, 1960)
Butcher, Captain H.C., *Three Years with Eisenhower: The Personal Diary of Captain Harry C. Butcher, USNR Naval Aide to General Eisenhower, 1942 to 1945* (London, 1946)
Chandler, A.D. (ed.), *The Papers of Dwight David Eisenhower* (Baltimore, 1970)

Churchill, W.S., *The Second World War, Volume V: Closing the Ring* (London, 1954)

Churchill, W.S., *The Second World War, Volume VI: Triumph and Tragedy* (London, 1955)

Clark, General Mark., *Calculated Risk* (New York/London, 1951)

De Gaulle, General Charles, *The Call to Honour: 1940–2* (London, 1955)

De Gaulle, General Charles, *Unity: 1942–4* (London, 1959)

De Gaulle, General Charles, *Salvation: 1944–6* (London, 1960)

De Guingand, Major-General Sir Francis, *Operation Victory* (London, 1947)

De Lattre de Tassigny, General Jean, *The History of the French First Army* (London, 1952)

Eisenhower Dwight, D., *Crusade in Europe* (London, 1948)

Eisenhower, Dwight, D., *At Ease: Stories I Tell to Friends* (London, 1968)

Keitel, W., *The Memoirs of Field Marshal Keitel* (New York, 1965)

Kesselring, A., *A Soldier's Record* (New York, 1954)

Luck, Hans von, *Panzer Commander: The Memoirs of Colonel Hans von Luck* (New York, 1989)

Mellenthin, Major-General F.W. von, *Panzer Battles* (London, 1984)

Montgomery, Field Marshal Bernard Law, *The Memoirs of Field Marshal The Viscount Montgomery of Alamein* (London, 1958)

Patton, General G., *War as I Knew It* (Boston, 1947)

Roosevelt, E., *As he saw it* (New York, 1946)

Sodenstern, Georg von, *Southern France preparations for invasion*, Historical Division, HQ US Army, Europe (Foreign Military Studies Branch, 1945)

Truscott, General L.K., *Command Missions* (New York, 1954)

Warlimont, General W., *Inside Hitler's Headquarters: 1939–1945* (New York, 1964)

Westphal, General S., *The German Army in the West* (London, 1951)

Journals

Ashmore, W.C., 'Supply Planning for Beachhead Operations,' *Quartermaster Review* (January/February 1945)

Bigelow, M.E., 'General Truscott and the Campaign in Southern France,' *Military Review* (August 1944)

Budd, H.A., 'Air Force Beach Party,' *Military Review* (February 1947)

Coffin, R.E., and Scott, D., 'Operation Dragoon: A Forging of Allies,' *US Army Journal* (August 1944)

Devers, J.L., 'Operation Dragoon: The Invasion of Southern France,' *Military Affairs* (Summer 1946)

Gregory, S.S., 'Anti-Aircraft Artillery Planning for the invasion of Southern France,' *Coast Artillery* (September/October 1945)

Hyman, J.A., 'From the Riviera to the Rhine,' *T-Patch*, 36th Infantry Division Newspaper (1945)

Jenkins, R.E., 'Operation Dragoon – Planning and Landing Phase,' *Military Review* (August 1946)

Jenkins, R.E., 'Operation Dragoon – The Breakthrough,' *Military Review* (September 1946)

Kretschmar, D.F., 95th Bomb Squadron, 17th Bomb Group, *Mission Report and Diary* (9 June 1944–21 March 1945)

Lanza, C.H., 'The War in the South of France,' *Field Artillery Journal* (October 1944)

Lehman, M., 'Supplying the Seventh Army,' *Infantry Journal* (February 1945)

Walton, M., 37th Bomb Squadron, 17th Bomb Group, *Toulon, France* (Account of Sergeant Jesse A. Ward winning the Purple Heart and Distinguished Flying Cross, 16 August 1944)

Secondary Sources

Anvil/Dragoon

Adleman, R.H., and Walton, Colonel G., *The Champagne Campaign* (Boston, 1969)

Beale, N., *Operation Dragoon: Luftwaffe Operations 15–23 August 1944* (September 1995–March 2008, www.ghostbombers.com)

Bennett, R., *Ultra and Mediterranean Strategy 1941–45* (London, 1989)

Boddie, J.W., *Ammunition Support for Operation Dragoon, the invasion of Southern France: could we do it today?* (USAWC Military Studies Program Paper, 1987)

Breuer, W.B., *Operation Dragoon: The Allied Invasion of the South of France* (Shrewsbury, 1988)

Clarke, J.J., *Southern France*, The US Army Campaigns of World War II

Danby, J., *Day of the Panzer: A Story of American Heroism and Sacrifice in Southern France* (2007)

Funk, A.L., *Hidden Ally: The French Resistance, Special Operations and the Landings in Southern France 1944* (New York, 1992)

Gaujac, P. , *Dragoon. The Other Invasion of France* (Paris, 2004)

Howard, M., *The Mediterranean Strategy in the Second World War* (London, 1968)

Jacques, R., *The Second D-Day* (New York, 1969)

Leslie, P. , *The Liberation of the Riviera* (1980)

Miller, R.A., *August 1944 The Campaign for France* (Novato, California, 1996)

Morin, C.R., *Anvil Revisited: The Impact of ULTRA on the decision to invade Southern France* (USAWC Military Studies Program Paper, 1984)

Wilt, A.F., *The French Riviera Campaign of August 1944* (Southern Illinois University, 1981)

Biography

Ambrose, S., *Eisenhower* (New York, 1983)

Barnett, C., *Hitler's Generals* (New York, 1989)

Burns, J.M., *Roosevelt: The Soldier of Freedom* (New York, 1979)

Clark, Brigadier Stanley, *The Man who is France* (London, 1960)

Clayton, A., *Three Marshals of France* (London, 1992)

Cook, D., *Charles De Gaulle* (New York, 1983)

Crawley, A., *De Gaulle* (London, 1969)

Crozier, B., *De Gaulle the Warrior* (London, 1973)

D'Este, C., *Eisenhower Allied Supreme Commander* (London, 2003)

Gilbert, M., *Churchill. A Life* (London, 2000)

Giziowski, R., *The Enigma of General Blaskowitz* (Barnsley, 1997)

Griffiths, R., *Marshal Pétain* (London, 1994)

Hamilton, N., *Monty. Master of the Battlefield 1942–1944* (London, 1983)

Hough, R., *Winston and Clementine* (London, 1991)

Humble, R., *Hitler's Generals* (St Albans, 1976)

Jackson, J., *Charles de Gaulle* (London, 1990)

Jenkins, R., *Churchill A Biography* (New York, 2001)

Kersaudy, F., *Churchill and De Gaulle* (London, 1981)

Ledwidge, B., *De Gaulle* (London, 1982)

Mitcham Jr, S.W., *Hitler's Field Marshals and Their Battles* (London, 1988)

Paterson, M., *Winston Churchill. His military life 1895–1945* (Newton Abbot, 2005)

Pitt, B., *Churchill and the Generals* (London, 1981)

Ponting, C., *Churchill* (London, 1994)

Slim, Field Marshal Sir William, *Defeat into Victory* (London, 1956)

Summersby, K., *Eisenhower Was My Boss* (New York, 1948)

Tompkins, P., *The Murder of Admiral Darlan* (New York, 1965)

Trez, Michel de, *First Airborne Task Force: Pictorial History of the Allied Paratroops in the invasion of Southern France* (1998)

Other Published Secondary Sources

Aron, R. (translated by Humphrey Hare), *De Gaulle Before Paris: The Liberation of France June–August 1944* (London, 1962)

Atkin, N., *The Forgotten French: Exiles in the British Isles 1940–44* (Manchester, 2003)

Atkinson, R., *An Army at Dawn. The War in North Africa, 1942–1943* (London, 2003)

Badsey, S., *Normandy 1944: Allied landings and breakout* (Oxford, 2004)

Bekker, C., *The Luftwaffe War Diaries* (London, 1972)

Berton, S., *Allies At War* (London, 2001)

Blackwell, I., *Anzio* (Barnsley, 2006)

Bonn, K., *When the Odds Were Even: The Vosges Mountains Campaign, October 1944–January 1945* (2006)

Bourne, M.J., *Naval Warfare Outside The Pacific: Operation 'Menace' The Assault on Dakar* (Barrow-in-Furness, 1997)

Breuer, W.B., *Operation Torch: The Allied Gamble to Invade North Africa* (New York, 1985)

Bruce, G., *Second Front Now! The Road To D-Day* (London, 1979)

Clark, L., *Anzio, The Friction of War. Italy and the Battle for Rome, 1944* (London, 2006)

Cole, H.M., *The Lorraine Campaign* (US Army, 1981)

Colley, D.P., *Decision at Strasbourg: Ike's Strategic Mistake to Halt the Sixth Army Group at the Rhine in 1944* (2008)

Corrigan, D., *Blood, Sweat and Arrogance and the Myths of Churchill's War* (London, 2006)

Dallek, R., *Franklin D. Roosevelt and American Foreign Policy* (New York, 1979)

Doherty, R., *Eighth Army in Italy 1943–45, The Long Hard Slog* (Barnsley, 2007)

Ellis, J., *Cassino. The Hollow Victory: the Battle for Rome January–June 1944* (London, 1984)

D'Este, C., *Fatal Decision: Anzio and the Battle for Rome* (New York, 1991)

D'Este, C., *Bitter Victory: The Battle for Sicily July–August 1943* (London, 1988)

D'Este, C., *Decision in Normandy: The Unwritten Story of Montgomery and the Allied Campaign* (London, 1984)

Fletcher, D., *Swimming Shermans* (Oxford, 2006)

Footit, H., *War and Liberation: Living with the Liberators* (Basingstoke, 2004)

Ford, K., *Falaise 1944. Death of an army* (Oxford, 2005)

Forty, G., *Fifth Army at War* (Shepperton, 1980)

Forty, G., *United States Tanks of World War II in Action* (Poole, 1983)

Gabel, Dr C.R., *The Lorraine Campaign: An Overview, September–December 1944*, Combat Studies Institute (Fort Leavenworth, Kansas, 1985)

Gaunson, A., *The Anglo-French Clash in Lebanon and Syria 1940–45* (London, 1987)

Gregory, B., and Batchelor, J., *Airborne Warfare 1941–1945* (London, 1979)

Griess, T.E., *The Second World War Europe and the Mediterranean* (West Point Military History Series, 2002)

Harman, N., *Dunkirk The Necessary Myth* (London, 1990)

Hastings, M., *Das Reich* (London, 1981)

Irving, D., *The Rise and Fall of the Luftwaffe: The Life of Luftwaffe Marshal Erhard Milch* (London, 1973)

Irving, D., *The War Between The Generals* (London, 1981)

Jackson, R., *Dunkirk* (London, 1979)

Katcher, P., *The US Army 1941–45* (London, 1977)

Katcher, P., *The US Army 1941–45* (London, 1993)

Kershaw, A., and Close, I. (eds), *The Desert War* (Avon, 1975)

Kingseed, C.C., *Old Glory Stories, American Combat Leadership in World War II* (Annapolis MD, 2006)

Liddell Hart, B.H., *History of the Second World War* (London, 1979)

Linklater, E., *The Campaign in Italy* (London, 1951)

Lucas, J., *Hitler's Enforcers: Leaders of the German War Machine 1933-1945* (London, 1999)

MacDonald, C.B., *The Mighty Endeavour: American Armed Forces In the European Theater In World War II* (New York, 1969)

Macksey, Major K.J., *Afrika Korps* (London, 1972)

Mitcham Jr, S.W., *Hitler's Legion's: The German Army Order of Battle, World War II* (New York, 1988)

Moore, Major B.V., *The Secret Air War Over France: USAAF Special Operations Units in the French Campaign of 1944* (School of Advanced Air Power Studies, Alabama, 1992)

Moorhead, A., *The End in Africa* (London, 1943)

Morison, S.E., *The Invasion of France and Germany 1944–1945* (Boston, 1968)

Pack, Captain S.W.C, *Operation 'Husky'. The Allied Invasion of Sicily* (New York, 1977)

Picknett, L., Prince, C., and Pricer, S., *Friendly Fire, The Secret War Between the Allies* (Edinburgh, 2005)

Pogue, F., *The Supreme Command: The European Theatre of Operations* (Washington DC, 1954)

Province, C.M., *Patton's Third Army* (New York, 1992)

Rees, L., *World War Two Behind Closed Doors* (London, 2008)

Roberts, A., *Masters and Commanders: How Roosevelt, Churchill, Marshall and Alanbrooke Won the War in the West 1941–45* (London, 2008)

Rottman, G.L., *US World War II Amphibious Tactics Mediterranean & European Theaters* (Oxford, 2006)

Seaton, A., *The Fall of Fortress Europe 1943–1945* (London, 1981)

Stewart, G., *His Finest Hours: The War Speeches of Winston Churchill* (Quercus, no date)

Strawson, J., *The Battle for North Africa* (London, 1969)

Sumner, I., & Vauvillier, F., *The French Army 1939–45 (2): Free French, Fighting French & The Army of Liberation* (London 1998)

Thomas, R., *Britain and Vichy: The Dilemma of Anglo-French Relations 1941–42* (London, 1979)

Thompson, R.S., *Pledge To Destiny* (New York, 1974)

Thorton, W., *The Liberation of Paris* (London, 1963)

Trevelyan, R., *Rome '44. The Battle for the Eternal City* (London, 1981)

Tucker-Jones, A., *Hitler's Great Panzer Heist: Germany's Foreign Armour in Action 1939–45* (Barnsley, 2007)

Tucker-Jones, A., *Falaise, the Flawed Victory: The Destruction of Panzergruppe West, August 1944* (Barnsley, 2008)

Tucker-Jones, A., *Stalin's Revenge: Operation Bagration & the Annihilation of Army Group Centre* (Barnsley, 2009)

Turner, J.F., and Jackson R., *Destination Berchtesgaden, The Story of the US 7th Army in World War II* (London, 1975)

Tute, W., *The Deadly Stroke* (London, 1973)

Tute, W., *The North African War* (London, 1976)

Tute, W., *The Reluctant Enemies* (London, 1990)

Vader, J., *The Fleet Without A Friend* (London, 1973)

Vickers, P., *Das Reich* (Barnsley, 2000)

Warner, P., *World War Two: The Untold Story* (London, 2002)

Weigley, R.F., *Eisenhower's Lieutenants, The Campaigns of France and Germany, 1944–1945* (London, 1981)
White, D.S., *Seeds of Discord: De Gaulle, Free France and the Allies* (New York, 1964)
Whiting, C., *West Wall: The Battle for Hitler's Siegfried Line* (London, 2002)
Whiting, C., *Siegfried: The Nazis' Last Stand* (London, 2003)
Whittell, G., *Spitfire Women of World War II* (London, 2008)
Williamson, M., *Strategy For Defeat: The Luftwaffe, 1933–1945* (New York, 1986)
Wilmot, C., *The Struggle For Europe* (London, 1952)
Wilson, P., *Dunkirk From Disaster to Deliverance* (Barnsley, 1999)
Wragg, D., *Sink the French: The French Navy after the Fall of France* (Barnsley, 2007)
Zaloga, S., *Lorraine 1944: Patton vs Manteuffel* (Oxford, 2005)
Zaloga, S., *Liberation of Paris 1944* (Oxford, 2008)

Journals
Baxter, C.F., 'Winston Churchill: Military Strategist?' *Military Affairs* (February 1983)
Ethier, E., 'Riviera D-Day,' *America in WWII* (August 2006)
Ganz, A, H., 'The 11th Panzers in the Defense, 1944,' *Armor Magazine* (March–April 1994)
Pallud, J.P., 'The Riviera Landings,' *After the Battle* (No. 110)
Randall, W.S., 'The Other D-Day,' *Military History Quarterly* (Spring 1994)
Stanton, W.I., 'Could WW2 Have Ended in 1944: Was Anvil a Big Mistake?' *Army Quarterly* (July 1992)
Tucker-Jones, A., 'Who Liberated Paris?,' *Military Illustrated* (October 2006)
Tucker-Jones, A., 'When Britain and America fought Vichy France,' *Military Illustrated* (November 2006)
Tucker-Jones, A., 'Kesselring's Coup,' *Military Illustrated* (February 2007)
Tucker-Jones, A., 'Churchill vs Eisenhower,' *Military Illustrated* (May 2008)
Tucker-Jones, A., 'Churchill's Dieppe Disaster,' *Military Illustrated* (September 2008)
Tucker-Jones, A., 'Stalin's D-Day,' *Military Illustrated* (January 2009)

Websites
http://www.b26.com
http://www.cia.govlibrary/center-for-the-study-of-intelligence/kent
http://www.eisenhower.archives.gov
http://www.eisenhowermemorial.org
http://www.fdrlibrary
http://www.ghostbombers.com/dragoon/odnav.html
http://www.texasmilitaryforcesmuseum.org/museum.htm
http://www.yale.edu/lawweb/avalon/avalon.htm

Index